Zhao-hui Wu
Hua-jun Chen

# Semantic Grid: Model, Methodology, and Applications

With 64 figures

## AUTHORS:

**Prof. Zhao-hui Wu**,
College of Computer Science,
Zhejiang University,
310027, Hangzhou, China
E-mail: wzh@cs.zju.edu.cn

**Dr. Hua-jun Chen**,
College of Computer Science,
Zhejiang University,
310027, Hangzhou, China
E-mail: huajunsir@gmail.com

ISBN 978-7-308-05830-8 **Zhejiang University Press, Hangzhou**
ISBN 978-3-540-79453-0 **Springer Berlin Heidelberg New York**
e-ISBN 978-3-540-79454-7 **Springer Berlin Heidelberg New York**

Series ISSN 1995-6819 Advanced topics in science and technology in China
Series e-ISSN 1995-6827 Advanced topics in science and technology in China

Library of Congress Control Number: 2008925537

This work is subject to copyright. All rights are reserved, whether the whole or part of the material is concerned, specifically the rights of translation, reprinting, reuse of illustrations, recitation, broadcasting, reproduction on microfilm or in any other way, and storage in data banks. Duplication of this publication or parts thereof is permitted only under the provisions of the German Copyright Law of September 9, 1965, in its current version, and permission for use must always be obtained from Springer-Verlag. Violations are liable to prosecution under the German Copyright Law.

©2008 Zhejiang University Press, Hangzhou and Springer-Verlag GmbH Berlin Heidelberg
**Co-published by Zhejiang University Press, Hangzhou and Springer-Verlag GmbH Berlin Heidelberg**

**Springer is a part of Springer Science+Business Media**
springer.com

The use of general descriptive names, registered names, trademarks, etc. in this publication does not imply, even in the absence of a specific statement, that such names are exempt from the relevant protective laws and regulations and therefore free for general use.

Cover design: Joe Piliero, Springer Science + Business Media LLC, New York
Printed on acid-free paper

ADVANCED TOPICS
IN SCIENCE AND TECHNOLOGY IN CHINA

# ADVANCED TOPICS
# IN SCIENCE AND TECHNOLOGY IN CHINA

Zhejiang University is one of the leading universities in China. In Advanced Topics in Science and Technology in China, Zhejiang University Press and Springer jointly publish monographs by Chinese scholars and professors, as well as invited authors and editors from abroad who are outstanding experts and scholars in their fields. This series will be of interest to researchers, lecturers, and graduate students alike.

Advanced Topics in Science and Technology in China aims to present the latest and most cutting-edge theories, techniques, and methodologies in various research areas in China. It covers all disciplines in the fields of natural science and technology, including but not limited to, computer science, materials science, life sciences, engineering, environmental sciences, mathematics, and physics.

# Preface

The Internet has been an indispensable means of communication in our daily life. We rely upon it to communicate with others, search information to procure a solution to a knotty problem, book tickets to arrange our trips, look for business opportunities, entertain ourselves, and so forth. Without the Internet our life would have been a largely different one. However, has the Internet reached its full potential? Can it change our life more than we have seen? What will the Internet and the Web look like 20 years later?

A plurality of researchers from different areas have been working on these issues for a long time. At the fore, two distinguished and influential ones are Grid Computing and the Semantic Web.

The term the Grid was first used around 1990 as a metaphor for making the use of computer power as easy as the electric power Grid. It was originally coined as a new paradigm for solving computation-intensive problems by taking advantage of the computation power of idling computers, which could be a super computer or just a desktop computer. Grids were then described as well-organized virtual systems that may span across many organizational boundaries. Grid applications feature in the capability of the dynamic formation of cross-institutional Virtual Organizations in an *ad hoc* way to enable coordinated resource sharing and problem-solving across multiple administrative domains on the Internet.

The term Semantic Web was coined around 1998 by the web inventor Tim Berners Lee. It aims at leading the Web to its full potential by making its content machine-understandable. It draws on the standardization effort of a formal representation framework and advanced web languages such as RDF/OWL that can be used to enrich web resources with semantic descriptions and describe complex semantic relations among them. The semantic theory underlying this formal representation framework provides a formal account of meaning in which the logical relationship of web resources, which can be a webpage, a database record, a program, a web service, and so forth, can be explicitly described and specified without loss of the original meaning. This makes the web smarter and more intelligent, thereby enabling more sensible searches, far more accurate information retrieval, and seamless information integration.

Basically, Grids are concerned with the design and development of the architecture of the future Internet. Their ultimate goal is to provide a flexible, adaptive, manageable, service-oriented architecture for future Internet-based applications. Meanwhile, the Semantic Web looks at the semantic heterogeneity issue that has hindered almost all integration systems in the perspective of information representation. Although these two technologies offer different solutions, they actually complement each other. The concept of the Semantic Grid was then brought up by many researchers with the intention of combining them together to address many difficult problems that cannot be resolved by only one of them.

Commonly, the *Semantic Grid* refers to a branch subject under the umbrella of *Grid Computing* in which computing resources and services are described in a meaningful way that can be discovered, aggregated, joined up more readily and automatically. The description typically draws upon the technology of the Semantic Web, such as the Resource Description Framework (RDF) and Web Ontology Language (OWL). It is stated that the semantic grid, as a combination of the technologies from both grid computing and the semantic web, would provide a promising alternative for developing a future interconnection environment, particularly geared to enable highly selective resource sharing, very sensible knowledge discovery and collective intelligence.

As a synthesis of many different technologies, the Semantic Grid has a broad spectrum of topics. The book attempts to give a comprehensive introduction of these topics, including knowledge representation and semantic description for semantic grid applications, semantic-based data integration, grid service management and process orchestration, trust management in grids, ontology management for problem solving in the semantic grid, and integrative knowledge discovery based on the integration capability of the semantic grid.

**How to use this book.** This book can be a reference book for researchers in Internet-related technologies. Generally, the topics in Chapters 2-4 are introduced in a fundamental way, while the ones in Chapters 5-8 are presented from an applied perspective. Moreover, Chapters 9,10 are devoted to the experience of applying specific semantic grid technology to two typical application domains: the life science domain and an intelligent transportation system. Specifically, this book is organized in the following structure:

- Chapter 2 describes the relationship between knowledge representation and the semantic grid. The semantic web languages largely draw upon the fruits of the long-standing research on knowledge representation in the area of artificial intelligence. A good information representational framework is vital for a smarter and more intelligent grid system. For example,

grid resource discovery relies upon a better description of the resources and the relationships between them. Rules are useful for specifying mappings, coordination policy, security settings, transaction configurations, and trust dependencies for grid applications.
- Chapter 3 describes typical issues such as sub-ontology management for a problem solving in the Semantic Grid. With the Semantic Grid as the problem solving environment, we will face many unexpected problems as in traditional problem solving. The problems to be solved are often complex and refer to large-scale domain knowledge from crossover disciplines. This chapter focuses on how to manage and reuse ontology that embodies domain knowledge based on the infrastructure of the Semantic Grid.
- Chapter 4 mentions an important issue: trust management in the Semantic Grid. Enabling trust to ensure more effective and efficient interaction is at the heart of the Semantic Grid vision. This chapter presents an integrated computational trust model based on statistical decision theory and Bayesian sequential analysis. The model helps users to select an appropriate service provider within the Semantic Grid environment.
- Chapter 5 introduces specific technology that can be used for semantic data integration in the Semantic Grid, with particular emphasis on integrating relational databases with semantic web ontologies. Integrating legacy relational databases is important for both Grid and Semantic Web applications. However, experience in building such applications has revealed a gap between semantic web languages and the relational data model. This chapter presents an intelligent framework with a formal mapping system to bridge the gap, and studies the problem of reasoning and query answering using the semantic view of the mapping system.
- Chapter 6 provides a comprehensive introduction to service management in the Semantic Grid including service description, service orchestration, service discovery, service composition, and so on. How to collaborate, cooperate and co-experiment conveniently and efficiently in the grid environment has become a hot topic in the research and application of the grid, and service flow management will be the key technology in solving the problem.
- Chapter 7 proposes the general ideas and the preliminary implementation of knowledge discovery in the Semantic Grid, with the emphasis on mining based semantic integration. The Semantic Grid provides a new computational environment, and also a new architecture for data mining. The dynamic extension of the algorithm, the transparent integration of data, and the circular refinement of knowledge, are main characteristics of knowledge discovery using such architecture, as high-level services of the Semantic Grid, data mining and knowledge discovery greatly enhance the effectiveness of the Semantic Grid.
- Chapter 8 presents a semantic grid platform called DartGrid. The Semantic Grid combines many technologies coming from the Grids, the Web

Service and the Semantic Web. Organic integration of these technologies that are actually complement each other can result in competent implementation for both Grid and Semantic Web applications. This chapter presents a semantic grid implementation, called DartGrid, which is made up of several components that are intended to support data integration and service management in Grids.
- Chapter 9 introduces the application of the specific technology of the Semantic Grid in building an e-Science environment for the Traditional Chinese Medicine community from the perspectives of knowledge engineering, data integration, and knowledge discovery.
- Chapter 10 introduces the attempted application in an intelligent transportation system, the goal of which is to build an integrated intelligent transportation information and service platform, to integrate traffic data resources and cooperate with existing ITS subsystems and services.

The book is the result of several years of study, research and development of the faculties, PhD candidates and many others affiliated to the CCNT Lab of Zhejiang University. We would like to give particular thanks to Yuxin Mao, Xiaoqing Zheng, Shuiguang Deng, Yi Feng, Yu Zhang, Chunyin Zhou, Tong Yu, Wei Shi, Guozhou Zheng, Jian Wu who have devoted their energy and enthusiasm to the book and relevant projects.

In addition, the work in this book was mainly sponsored by the China 973 project of the Semantic Grid initiative (NO. 2003CB317006), the National Science Fund for Distinguished Young Scholars of China NSF Program (NO. NSFC60533040), the Program for New Century Excellent Talents in University of the Ministry of Education of China (NO. NCET-04-0545). The work was also partially supported by the National Program for Modern Service Industry (2006BAH02401), the Program for Changjiang Scholar(IRT0652) and the NSFC Program under Grant NO. NSFC60503018 and NSFC60603025.

The Semantic Grid is still an undergoing area of rapid development. Although this book cannot give a complete account of all issues and topics, we hope it can shed some light on the most important aspects relevant to the future Internet and can be valuable for those who are interested in the future development of the amazing Internet technology.

*Zhaohui Wu*
Zhejiang University
October 2007

# Contents

**1 Introduction** .......... 1
  1.1 Background .......... 1
    1.1.1 Grid Computing .......... 1
    1.1.2 Semantic Web .......... 4
  1.2 Semantic Grid .......... 7
    1.2.1 Basic Concepts .......... 7
    1.2.2 Brief History .......... 8
  1.3 Basic Issues .......... 9
    1.3.1 Knowledge Representation for the Semantic Grid .......... 9
    1.3.2 Semantic Data Integration .......... 9
    1.3.3 Semantic Service Composition and Process Coordination .......... 10
    1.3.4 Semantic Mining and Knowledge Discovery in the Semantic Grid .......... 10
    1.3.5 Trust and Security .......... 10
  1.4 Case Studies .......... 11
    1.4.1 myGrid .......... 11
    1.4.2 CombeChem .......... 11
    1.4.3 CoAKTinG .......... 12
    1.4.4 K-WF Grid .......... 12
    1.4.5 Semantic Grid Research and Development in China .......... 12
  1.5 Summary and Conclusion .......... 13
  References .......... 14

**2 Knowledge Representation for the Semantic Grid** .......... 15
  2.1 Introduction .......... 15
  2.2 Knowledge Representation .......... 17
    2.2.1 Mathematical Logic .......... 17
    2.2.2 Semantic Network .......... 18
    2.2.3 Frames .......... 20

|  | 2.2.4 | Ontology | 21 |
|---|---|---|---|
| 2.3 | | Description Logic | 23 |
| 2.4 | | Knowledge Representation Framework for the Semantic Grid. | 26 |
| | 2.4.1 | XML and XML Schema | 27 |
| | 2.4.2 | RDF and RDF Schema | 28 |
| | 2.4.3 | Web Ontology Language | 29 |
| 2.5 | | Ontology Development and Application for TCM | 32 |
| | 2.5.1 | Ontology Design and Development for UTCMLS | 32 |
| | 2.5.2 | TCM Ontology | 37 |
| 2.6 | | Summary and Conclusion | 45 |
| References | | | 46 |

## 3 Dynamic Problem Solving in the Semantic Grid ......... 48

| 3.1 | | Introduction | 48 |
|---|---|---|---|
| | 3.1.1 | Problem Solving | 48 |
| | 3.1.2 | Cooperative Distributed Problem Solving | 49 |
| | 3.1.3 | Multi-Agent System | 50 |
| 3.2 | | Grid-based Problem Solving | 51 |
| | 3.2.1 | Grid and Problem Solving | 51 |
| | 3.2.2 | Problem Solving in the Semantic Grid | 53 |
| 3.3 | | Ontology Management for Grid-based Problem Solving | 54 |
| | 3.3.1 | Grid-based Ontology Management | 55 |
| | 3.3.2 | Ontology Grid Node | 56 |
| | 3.3.3 | Semantic View | 59 |
| 3.4 | | Ontology Reuse for Grid-based Problem Solving | 61 |
| | 3.4.1 | Dynamic Memory Model | 61 |
| | 3.4.2 | Case-based Ontology Repository | 63 |
| 3.5 | | Dynamic Problem Solving Based on SubO Evolution | 66 |
| | 3.5.1 | Sub-Ontology Manipulations | 67 |
| | 3.5.2 | Terminology | 69 |
| | 3.5.3 | Problem-Solving Environment | 69 |
| | 3.5.4 | Sub-Ontology Based Problem Solving | 71 |
| 3.6 | | The Relationship between Problem Solving and the Semantic Grid | 73 |
| 3.7 | | Related Works | 75 |
| 3.8 | | Summary and Conclusion | 76 |
| References | | | 76 |

## 4 Trust Computing in the Semantic Grid ................. 79

| 4.1 | | Introduction | 79 |
|---|---|---|---|
| 4.2 | | Trust for the Semantic Grid | 80 |
| | 4.2.1 | Characteristic Features of Trust | 81 |
| | 4.2.2 | Cost and Utility | 82 |
| | 4.2.3 | Distributed vs. Centralized | 83 |
| | 4.2.4 | Semantics of Information | 83 |

|     |       |                                                              |     |
| --- | ----- | ------------------------------------------------------------ | --- |
|     | 4.3   | Closed Trust Model                                           | 86  |
|     | 4.4   | Open Trust Model                                             | 91  |
|     | 4.5   | Experiments                                                  | 93  |
|     | 4.6   | Related Work                                                 | 98  |
|     | 4.7   | Summary and Conclusion                                       | 101 |
|     | References                                                           | 102 |
| 5   | **Data Integration in the Semantic Grid**                            | 103 |
|     | 5.1   | Introduction                                                 | 103 |
|     |       | 5.1.1 Related Work                                           | 104 |
|     |       | 5.1.2 Preliminaries                                          | 106 |
|     | 5.2   | Semantic Mapping in the Semantic Grid                        | 108 |
|     |       | 5.2.1 The Mapping Issue                                      | 108 |
|     |       | 5.2.2 Basic Mapping System                                   | 110 |
|     |       | 5.2.3 Constraint Mapping                                     | 110 |
|     | 5.3   | Semantic Query Processing in the Semantic Grid               | 112 |
|     |       | 5.3.1 Answering Queries Using $\mathcal{SHIQ}\text{-}\mathcal{RDM}$ Views | 112 |
|     |       | 5.3.2 Rewriting SPARQL Queries Using $\mathcal{SHIQ}\text{-}\mathcal{RDM}$ Views | 116 |
|     | 5.4   | Summary and Conclusion                                       | 122 |
|     | References                                                           | 123 |
| 6   | **Service Flow Management in the Semantic Grid**                     | 126 |
|     | 6.1   | Introduction                                                 | 126 |
|     | 6.2   | Research Framework of Service Flow Management                | 127 |
|     |       | 6.2.1 Service Matchmaking and Discovery                      | 128 |
|     |       | 6.2.2 Service Composition                                    | 129 |
|     |       | 6.2.3 Service Composition Verification                       | 130 |
|     | 6.3   | Service Matchmaking in DartFlow                              | 131 |
|     |       | 6.3.1 An Extended Service Model                              | 131 |
|     |       | 6.3.2 Service Matchmaking                                    | 134 |
|     |       | 6.3.3 Performance Evaluation                                 | 139 |
|     | 6.4   | Service Composition in DartFlow                              | 141 |
|     |       | 6.4.1 Service Composition Framework                          | 142 |
|     |       | 6.4.2 Rules Types and Definitions                            | 144 |
|     |       | 6.4.3 Automatic Service Composition Based on Rules           | 147 |
|     | 6.5   | Service Flow Verification in DartFlow                        | 148 |
|     |       | 6.5.1 Overview of $\pi$-Calculus                             | 148 |
|     |       | 6.5.2 Modeling Service Behavior Using $\pi$-Calculus         | 150 |
|     |       | 6.5.3 Verification of Service Compatibility                  | 152 |
|     | 6.6   | Summary and Conclusion                                       | 155 |
|     | References                                                           | 155 |

## 7  Data Mining and Knowledge Discovery in the Semantic Grid ... 157
- 7.1 Introduction ... 157
- 7.2 Development of KDD System Architecture ... 159
  - 7.2.1 Single-computer-based Architecture ... 159
  - 7.2.2 Parallelized Architecture ... 160
  - 7.2.3 Distributed Architecture ... 161
  - 7.2.4 Grid-based Architecture ... 161
  - 7.2.5 A Summary of the Development of KDD System Architecture ... 165
- 7.3 Knowledge Discovery Based on the Semantic Grid ... 165
  - 7.3.1 Virtual Organizations of Knowledge Discovery in the Semantic Grid ... 165
  - 7.3.2 Architecture and Components of Knowledge Discovery in the Semantic Grid ... 167
  - 7.3.3 Characteristics of Knowledge Discovery in the Semantic Grid ... 169
- 7.4 Drug Community Discovery Utilizing TCM Semantic Grid ... 171
  - 7.4.1 Semantic Graph Mining Methodology ... 172
  - 7.4.2 Use Case: TCM Formulae Interpretation and Herb-Drug Interaction Analysis ... 174
- 7.5 Summary and Conclusion ... 176
- References ... 176

## 8  DartGrid: A Semantic Grid Implementation ... 179
- 8.1 Introduction ... 179
- 8.2 DartD3–A Semantic Data Integration Toolkit ... 180
  - 8.2.1 Overview ... 180
  - 8.2.2 System Features ... 181
  - 8.2.3 System Architecture ... 182
  - 8.2.4 Mapping from Relational Data to Semantic Web Ontology ... 183
  - 8.2.5 Semantic Browser and Query Tool ... 184
  - 8.2.6 Semantic Search Engine ... 185
- 8.3 DartFlow–A Service Flow Management Prototype ... 188
  - 8.3.1 Overview ... 188
  - 8.3.2 System Architecture ... 188
  - 8.3.3 Main Functions ... 190
- 8.4 Summary and Conclusion ... 194

## 9  Semantic Grid Applications for Traditional Chinese Medicine ... 195
- 9.1 Background, Status, and Problems of TCM Informatics ... 195
  - 9.1.1 Background of TCM Informatics ... 196
  - 9.1.2 Status of TCM Informatics ... 196

|  | 9.1.3 Problems of TCM Informatics ..................... 197 |
|---|---|
| 9.2 | The Architecture of TCM e-Science Semantic Grid ......... 199 |
|  | 9.2.1 Overview ........................................ 199 |
|  | 9.2.2 Three Layers of TCM e-Science Environment ........ 200 |
|  | 9.2.3 Application Platforms in TCM e-Science Environment 200 |
| 9.3 | Collaborative TCM Ontology Engineering ................. 202 |
| 9.4 | Creating a Semantic Grid of TCM Databases .............. 204 |
| 9.5 | A Semantic Grid Environment for Database Construction ... 206 |
| 9.6 | TCM Knowledge Discovery Platform ..................... 207 |
| 9.7 | Summary ............................................. 209 |
|  | References ................................................ 209 |

**10 Semantic Grid Applications in Intelligent Transportation Systems** .................................................. 210
    10.1 Introduction ............................................ 210
        10.1.1 ITS System and Grid Computing ................... 211
        10.1.2 ITS System and Ontology ......................... 213
    10.2 Layered Architecture for ITS-Grid ....................... 214
    10.3 ITS Semantic Grid ...................................... 215
        10.3.1 The Development of an ITS Ontology .............. 215
        10.3.2 ITS-Grid Applications ............................ 217
    10.4 Case Study ............................................. 222
    10.5 Summary and Conclusion ............................... 224
    References ................................................ 225

**Index** ...................................................... 227

# 1
# Introduction

**Abstract:** The Semantic Grid commonly refers to a branch subject under the umbrella of Grid Computing. In a typical semantic grid application, the network resources and services are described in a meaningful way so that the resources can be discovered, aggregated, joined up more readily and automatically. The description typically draws upon the technology from the Semantic Web, such as the Resource Description Framework (RDF) and Web Ontology Language (OWL). In this chapter an overview to the background of the Semantic Grid is given.

## 1.1 Background

The concept of the Semantic Grid was derived from Grid Computing and the Semantic Web. This section offers the background introduction on the basic concepts and histories of these two technologies.

### 1.1.1 Grid Computing

Grid computing (Foster I, 2002a) was originally coined as a new paradigm for solving computation-intensive problems by taking advantage of the computation power of idling computers, which can be a super computer or just a desktop computer. The Grids were then described as a well-organized virtual cluster that may span many organizational boundaries. Grid applications feature in the capability for the dynamic formation of cross-institutional *Virtual Organizations* (VO) in an *ad hoc* way to enable coordinated resource sharing and problem-solving across multiple administrative domains. The features make themselves distinguishable from traditional computer clusters or distributed computing that are often confined to a local domain and within only one organization.

**1.1.1.1 Basic Concepts**

In the beginning, the Grids were particularly advocated as a brand-new solution for solving those "big-science" problems such as those in life science, physics, climate modeling, financial computing and others. At the present time, as the concept of the Grid grows broader, Grids are also considered as a means of offering information as a utility service such as a computational center or a data center for commercial purposes, with those clients paying as they use it, just like other traditional utilities (electricity, water, etc.).

As Grids have kept gaining considerable momentum since their emergence, a wide variety of definitions about Grid Computing are proposed by different communities. The rather authoritative definition is from Ian Foster, who identifies the real and specific problem that underlies the Grid concept as coordinated resource sharing and problem solving in dynamic, multi-institutional virtual organizations, and defined the concept of Grid in his article "What Is the Grid? A Three Point Checklist"(Foster I, 2002b). The three points of this checklist are: a) Computing resources are not administered centrally, b) Open standards are used, c) Non-trivial quality of service is achieved.

Another popular definition for the Grid concept comes from IBM who defines Grid Computing as "the ability, using a set of open standards and protocols, to gain access to applications and data, processing power, storage capacity and a vast array of other computing resources over the Internet. A Grid is a type of parallel and distributed system that enables the sharing, selection, and aggregation of resources distributed across 'multiple' administrative domains based on their (resources) availability, capacity, performance, cost and users' quality-of-service requirements." [1]

From a general perspective, Grid computing involves sharing and managing heterogeneous resources with different hardware architecture, software platforms, and network protocols across geographical locations and administrative domains over a network, and emphasizing an open-standard-based approach. Functionally, Grids can be classified into several types:

- **Computational Grid** that focuses primarily on the sharing of computational power such as a CPU cycle with computationally-intensive operations.
- **Data Grid** emphasizing the controlled sharing and management of large amounts of distributed data, usually at a tera-scale.
- **Device Grid** that offers the service of controlling the equipment such as a telescope remotely and analyzing the data produced.

Additionally, more Grid-inspired concepts have been proposed, such as the Access Grid intended to support group-to-group video-based interactions across the Grid, the Semantic Grid as a synthesis of grid technology and the Semantic Web technology.

---

[1] http://www-306.ibm.com/software/globalization/terminology/gh.jsp

**1.1.1.2 Brief History**

The term Grid Computing sprang up in the early 1990s as a metaphor for making the utilization of computer power as easy as that of an electric power grid. The basic ideas and concepts were firstly brought together and further formalized by Ian Foster, Carl Kesselman and Steve Tuecke (Foster I, Kesselman C, Tuecke S, 2001).

The early Grid development was mostly propelled by the massive computational requirements of scientific applications. During that time the most prominent development was the Globus Toolkit (Foster I, 2006)[2], led by Ian Foster. As the concept of the Grid evolves, the open source Globus Toolkit has included software services and libraries for not only CPU cycle sharing and disk storage management, but also many other non-high-performance-computational-oriented components, such as those for data integration, resource monitoring, security provisioning, agreement negotiation, notification mechanisms, and dynamic service aggregation. It provides a wide variety of choices of the basic building blocks for developing various grid application developments and a real-time running environment. Similar toolkits and development endeavors such as the Unicore[3], CGSP [4] emerged quickly and world-wide.

With the rapid swelling of the Grid community and because of the well-recognized fact that the success of Grid technology heavily relies upon well-defined standards, the Global Grid Forum (GGF) was established in 2001 as a standing global organization to standardize Grid specifications and solutions. Since then the GGF has produced numerous standards, specification documents and best practices. The first fruitful outcome of the GGF is the Open Grid Service Architecture and Open Grid Service Infrastructure (OGSA/OGSI)(Foster I, Kesselman C, Tuecke S, 2002). The goal of OGSA is to standardize all of the most basic services that one can find in typical grid applications, such as those for job management, resource management, security services, etc., while the OGSI gives more concrete specifications with respect to how Grid Services can be implemented and function coordinately as a virtual organization.

Another important event that happened in grid history was the convergence of core grid standards and web service standards. WSRF (the Web Service Resource Framework) (Humphrey M, Wasson G, et al, 2005), as a successor of OGSI, was first announced in 2004 by many key players from both the grid computing community and the web service community. WSRF, as a result of the merging of the Grid and Web Services, provides the standards and a set of operations that make web services stateful and supports the fine-grained control and management of the resource status, which was

---

[2]Globus Toolkit: http://www.globus.org/
[3]Unicore: http://www.unicore.org/
[4]China Grid Supporting Platform: http://www.chinagrid.edu.cn/cgsp/

absent in web service specification before, but crucial for status monitoring and resource scheduling for almost all grid applications.

Year 2004 also saw the phenomenal involvement of enterprise players and the promotion of the commercial adoption and usage of Grid technology. Particularly, several IT enterprises formed the Enterprise Grid Alliance (EGA) in early 2004. In comparison with the goal of GGF, the EGA was focused exclusively on accelerating grid adoption in enterprise and e-business applications, particularly for data center applications which provide data storage and information services. The alliance published the enterprise grid reference model and use cases, a security requirements document and data/ storage provisioning document, to accommodate the specific needs of e-commerce enterprise.

In order to promote the application and deployment of the Grid technology, a new organization called Open Grid Forum (OGF)[5] was created in 2006, which is a merger of the Global Grid Forum (GGF) and the Enterprise Grid Alliance (EGA). Currently the OGF community consists of thousands of individuals from both industry and academic communities, involving over 400 organizations in more than 50 countries.

### 1.1.2 Semantic Web

The semantic web (Tim BL, Hendler J, Lassila O, 2001; Shadbolt N, Tim BL, Hall W, 2006; Hendler J, Tim BL, Miller E, 2002) is an evolving extension of the World Wide Web in which web resources are annotated, identified, and interlinked in a meaningful way, thus permitting software agents to find, share and integrate information more easily and readily.

#### 1.1.2.1 Basic Concepts

The concept derives from W3C director Tim Berners-Lee's vision of the Web as a universal medium for data, information, and knowledge exchange. The official website of W3C's Semantic Web Activity[6] gives a more definitive description:

> *The Semantic Web is about two things. It is about common formats for integration and combination of data drawn from diverse sources, where on the original Web mainly concentrated on the interchange of documents. It is also about language for recording how the data relates to real world objects. That allows a person, or a machine, to start off in one database, and then move through an unending set of databases which are connected not by wires but by being about the same thing.*

---

[5] Open Grid Forum: http://www.ogf.org
[6] W3C Semantic Web Activity: http://www.w3.org/2001/sw/

1.1 Background 5

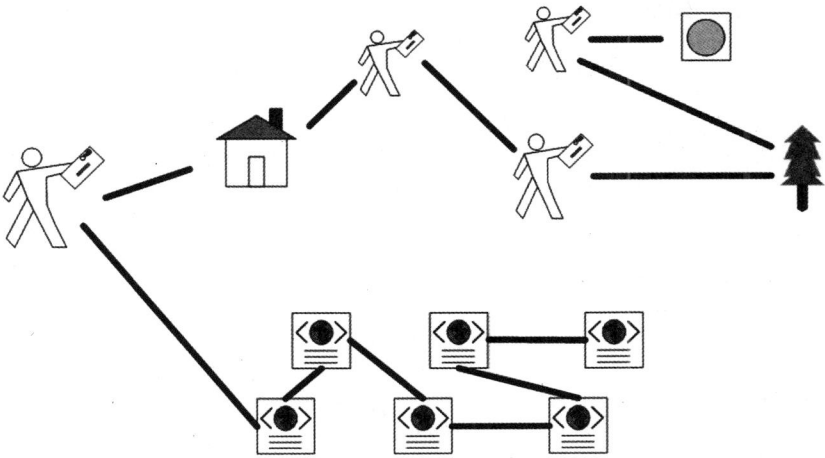

**Fig. 1.1.** The discrepancy between the linked documents and the linked objects in the real world

The definitive concept of the semantic web was formally articulated in the original Scientific American article that appeared in 2001 (Tim BL, Hendler J, Lassila O, 2001). It envisions the future evolution of the current Web composed of linked documents for human browsing to the future one that includes semantically linked data and information for computers to manipulate intelligently. This is not a new vision. Tim Berners-Lee articulated it at the very first World Wide Web Conference in 1994.

> *This is a pity, as in fact documents on the web describe real objects and imaginary concepts, and give particular relationships between them but we could not process them at all...*
> *Tim Berners-Lee, WWW Conference, 1994*

The Semantic Web draws on the standardization effort of a formal representation framework for describing the semantics of web resources. The semantic theory underlying this formal representation framework provides a formal account of "meaning" in which the logical relationship of web resources, which can be a webpage, a database record, a program, a web service, and so forth, can be explicitly described and specified without loss of the original meaning. Functionally speaking, it would enable us to aggregate and recombine the right data we want seamlessly and instantly, for example, automatically scheduling meetings across the calendars of different people, arranging travel based on the profiles of both providers and requestors, facilitating integrative knowledge discovery from an unbound set of data repositories, etc.

### 1.1.2.2 Brief History

The concept of the Semantic Web was first formally elucidated by the inventor of the web, Tim Berners-Lee, in his roadmap document about the future web in 1998 [7]. In this roadmap he proposed the concept of an "understandable web" in which information is well-defined and organized in order to be understandable to computers, and proposed a basic assertion model for representing web semantics as the foundation for achieving this goal.

As the crucial factors in realizing the vision are well-defined resource description model and web languages for sharing meaning, the standard organizations like the Internet Engineering Task Force and the World Wide Web Consortium (W3C), have devoted and directed major efforts at specifying, developing, and deploying the semantic web languages.

In 1999, the W3C released the first semantic web standard, the Resource Description Framework (RDF) specification, as a W3C recommendation. RDF provides a simple but powerful triple-based representation language for describing web resources and the relationship between them. The simplicity consists in the triple statement model, which actually cannot be simpler for describing something in the world. This simplicity guarantees extensibility and adaptability for future development.

The RDF Schema, as a basic vocabulary language, became a recommendation in February 2004. RDFS takes the basic RDF specification and extends it to support the expression of structured vocabularies such as classes and properties. It provides the basic constructs to develop ontology but lacks the necessary expressiveness for many advanced applications.

For those who require greater expressiveness in their objects and relation descriptions, the OWL[8] (the Web Ontology Language) is the choice. OWL has more advanced facilities and representing constructs such as those for describing property restrictions, concept cardinality, making it a full-fledged knowledge representation language capable of describing knowledge from simple meta-data such as tags to complex conceptual models such as a biological ontology. Chapter 2 gives a comprehensive introduction to RDF and OWL.

As the semantic languages have gained concrete ground and mature commercial RDF/OWL reasoners and stores have also been ready at customers' disposal, the need arises for reliable and standardized access to the RDF data they hold. The SPARQL language[9], which has become a W3C recommendation in 2007, was designed to meet this requirement. SPARQL can be viewed as the standardized ontology query language for retrieving and querying the RDF repository.

Further, other significant progress includes the GRDDL (Gleaning Resource Descriptions from Dialects of Languages[10], which provides a means of

---

[7] http://www.w3.org/DesignIssues/Semantic.html
[8] http://www.w3.org/TR/2004/REC-owl-features20040210
[9] http://www.w3.org/TR/rdf-sparql-query
[10] http://www.w3.org/2004/01/rdxh/spec

extracting RDF from XML and XHTML documents using transformations expressed in XSLT (Extensible Stylesheet Language), and the Rule Interchange Format[11], an attempt to support and interoperate across a variety of rule-based formats, by which a more advanced rule-based reasoning capability can be achieved.

Most recently more advanced efforts have been made on top of these standards and technologies. For example, the suggested Named Graph[12] allows users to attach contextual information such as a digital signature, trust policies, time stamps, provenance information, etc., onto a group of RDF assertions. The extension of RDF to Named Graphs provides a formally defined framework to be a foundation for the Semantic Web trust layer.

Along with busy production line standardization efforts are the phenomenal endeavors in industry-level tool development and commercialization such as Jena [13], Racer [14]. The past few years have seen the involvement of many major IT players including HP, Nokia, IBM, Oracle, and many new starters such as NetworkInference, Racer, Semagix, Andua.

## 1.2 Semantic Grid

The Semantic Grid can be viewed as a combination of Grid technology and Semantic Web technology. It refers to an approach to Grid computing in which Grid resources and services are described or annotated by explicit semantics so that the information resources can be more easily aggregated and consumed by others. The descriptions constitute metadata or ontologies, and are typically represented using the technology of the Semantic Web, such as the RDF (Resource Description Framework) and OWL (Web Ontology Language).

### 1.2.1 Basic Concepts

As the Grid originated from the requirements of big science applications, the concept of the Semantic Grid was also firstly proposed to meet the requirements coming from e-Science applications. However, the Semantic Grid emphasizes more the issue of semantic heterogeneity. For example, it aims at enabling the type of scientific research that requires the combination of scientific data with proprietary forms and formats, closing the gap between heterogeneous scientific application interfaces, organizing resources based on ontology description, and so on.

---

[11] http://www.w3.org/2005/rules
[12] http://www.w3.org/2004/03/trix/
[13] http://jena.sourceforge.net/
[14] http://www.racer-systems.com/products/racerpro/index.phtml

### 1.2.2 Brief History

The concept of the Semantic Grid (Roure DD, 2005; Roure DD, Hendler J, 2004; Roure DD, 2003; Zhuge H, 2005a) was first elucidated in the context of e-Science. John Taylor, the then director general of UK Research Councils, defined e-Science as being "about global collaboration in key areas of science and the next generation of infrastructure that will enable it." Grid computing was widely considered as being capable of providing the necessary informatics infrastructure during that time.

With the growing momentum in the development of the Semantic Web technology, more and more researchers agreed that these two then-prevalent technologies have actually complementary features and roles in supporting the improvement of a future interconnected environment (Globle C, 2005; Zhuge H, 2005b). Meanwhile, researchers from Grid communities were increasingly conscious of the incompetence of the then-practiced Grid technologies in many e-Science applications, particularly for those ones demanding harmonizing heterogeneous resources.

Early in 2001, a report by David De Roure, Nick Jennings and Nigel Shadbolt [15] was released, presenting a new research agenda for an e-Science infrastructure concerned with an organic synthesis of Grid computing, Web Services, and knowledge technologies. Thereafter a series of events were held to bring together researchers from the two communities to discuss the critical issues related to the integration of grid and semantic web technologies. For instance, a special panel session was held at the international World Wide Web Conference in May 2002, featuring the involvement of Ian Foster, Jim Hendler, Eric Miller and Carole Goble. GGF-5 saw the first Semantic Grid BoF session in 2002. After a second successful BoF at GGF-6 in October 2002 in Chicago, the Semantic Grid Research Group was created in November 2002. The group was then chaired by David De Roure, Carole Goble and Geoffrey Fox.

There followed a fast increase in semantic grid development as numerous Semantic Grid projects reached maturity across the globe. Typical semantic grid projects include the myGrid[16], IntelligGrid[17], K-WF Grid[18], OntoGrid[19], etc.

It is worth noting that China has also been actively engaged in this field since the beginning (Zhuge H, 2005a; Zhuge H, 2005b; Chen HJ, Wu ZH, 2006; Wu ZH, 2005; Wu ZH, Chen HJ, Xu JF, 2003). In 2003 China funded a national initiative for advanced research in the Semantic Grid, for which a

---

[15] http://www.semanticgrid.org/documents/semgrid-journal/semgrid-journal.pdf
[16] myGrid: http://www.mygrid.org.uk/
[17] IntelligGrid: http://www.inteligrid.com/
[18] K-WF Grid http://www.kwfgrid.net/
[19] OntoGrid: http://www.ontogrid.net/

national research team was then formed. Featured researchers include Professor Zhuge Hai from China Academy of Science who defined the semantic grid as "an Internet-centered interconnection environment that can effectively organize, share, cluster, fuse, and manage globally distributed versatile intelligent applications by meaningfully interconnecting resources in semantic spaces where machines and humans can understand each other."(Zhuge H, 2005a)

Most recently a special working group has been created at the Open Grid Forum in 2007. The so-called Semantic Grid Research Group (SEM-RG) is to realize the added value of emerging Web technologies and approaches, in particular Semantic Web and Web 2.0, for Grid users and developers. We believe that more convergence of these emerging new Internet technologies with the Semantic Grid research will happen in the foreseeable future.

## 1.3 Basic Issues

Proposed on the top of both the Semantic Web and the Grid technologies, semantic grid calls for more innovative approaches to solving problems challenging modern scientific research and enterprise information systems, particularly those related to semantic heterogeneity among decentralized resources. Herein below we identify a set of basic issues concerned with the semantic grid, around which the whole book is organized from varied perspectives and specificity.

### 1.3.1 Knowledge Representation for the Semantic Grid

The Grid is characterized by a significantly huge amount of heterogeneous resources spanning computational resources, storage resources, softwares, databases, instrumental devices, and so forth. The diversity and heterogeneous nature of grid resources calls for more advanced, formal, explicit, flexible, scalable approaches to describe them, so as to enable more intelligent resource coordination, automated resource discovery, and accurate resource matching. Ontology plays an important role in alleviating the problem, and is crucial for information exchange among the elements of a VO. Rules are useful for specifying mappings, coordination policy, security settings, transaction configurations, trust dependencies, etc. Deep investigation is required to specify a representation framework catering specifically to meet the requirements of the Grid.

### 1.3.2 Semantic Data Integration

Data are presently the dominant resources on the Internet. The Semantic Grid is required to provide a common framework that allows data to be shared and reused across the boundaries of application, enterprise, and community boundaries. A typical example comes from the life science domain. Advances in biotechnology and computing technology have made the information growth in biomedicine phenomenal. Researchers working on one aspect of analysis may need to look for and explore results from other institutions, from other subfields within his or her discipline, or even from completely different biomedical disciplines. For example, the research on neuron-related diseases such as Parkinson, Alzheimer, Huntington, requires the researcher to combine knowledge from different research institutions and spans the disciplines of neuroscience, psychiatry, biochemistry, molecular biology, computer science, and so forth. To make data readily available for unanticipated applications, and to enable meaningful queries over heterogeneous data repositories on the Grids, it requires a standard means of sharing, mapping, mediating, aggregating, organizing data stemming from different domains and organizations.

### 1.3.3 Semantic Service Composition and Process Coordination

The Grid system constitutes varying sizes of resources that, typically, present themselves as grid services. Service description, discovery, registration and composition are common requirements of all grid systems. Semantically-enriched services possess a more advanced capability of communicating with each other, forming VOs to coordinately solve problems that go beyond the ability of singular resource. Besides, different systems may draw on different process models although they are created for fulfilling identical missions. To orchestrate such a grid system it is crucial to provide unified ways to represent the process semantics and bridge the discrepancies and mismatches among different process models.

### 1.3.4 Semantic Mining and Knowledge Discovery in the Semantic Grid

On the one hand, most of the data semantics are presently hidden in various forms such as articles, web documents, news, and so forth. Semantic mining is a process for discovering the hidden semantics to make them explicitly available for other applications. On the other hand, well-formed semantic information and semantically linked data even enable a more advanced knowledge discovery capability. Data mining based on semantic relations or semantic link analysis has been gaining more attention recently, and the semantic integration capability of the semantic grid allows for logic-based reasoning and high-level semantic association discovery from a possibly unlimited web of data repositories.

### 1.3.5 Trust and Security

One defining characteristic of a VO is the need for trust and security. In such an open grid environment with multiple organizations involved, trust management and related security issues such as authentication, encryption and privacy are even more protrusive and tricky. In such a setting, a grid system requires all of these to be handled with as minimal as possible human intervention. The relevant issue here is how to represent and describe the trust dependencies and security policies, so that the semantics of access control can be uniformly communicated with consistent interpretation. Besides, high-level reasoning processes may be involved in coordinating the access control across multiple domain ownerships.

## 1.4 Case Studies

A number of Semantic Grid projects are now in progress and these activities have been reported at many semantic grid events. In this section we illustrate the typical ones as case studies.

### 1.4.1 myGrid

The myGrid [20] is a UK e-Science project led by Carole Goble. In general it is composed of a group of loosely coupled components and services aimed at supporting an in-silico life science research cycle. Life science researchers traditionally need to routinely download data, manually translate it into a required format amenable to specific analytical tools. The myGrid project draws on several semantic web and web service technologies to provide a service-based workflow engine for automating the entire in-silico experimental processes and alleviating the burdensome data and program integration.

In the core architecture of myGrid is the myGrid semantic bus, upon which a number of myGrid services are implemented, including the data service, identity service, provenance service, publication service, and discovery service. Domain ontology, workflow ontology, and many others are utilized to describe the services, through which improving the discovery, matching, tracing of the services are done. In a convenient way, life science researchers can weave and describe complex but meaningful workflows. The enriched semantics therefore enables the automatic execution of these integrated workflows. The myGrid has been used for building discovery workflows for investigations into Williams-Beuren Syndrome and Grave's Disease by collaborating with life scientists.

### 1.4.2 CombeChem

CombeChem [21] is also an e-Science project focused on the field of combinatorial chemistry that requires the synthesis of new chemical compounds by

---

[20] myGrid: http://www.mygrid.org.uk/
[21] http://www.combechem.org/

mixing large numbers of different compounds. Because of the sheer number of possible combinations, the synthesis processes produce large volumes of new chemical knowledge, and demand the integration and corporation of many relevant research institutes.

A key concept of this project is "publication at the source", which draws mainly on making the generated knowledge explicit and machine understandable through the use of the Semantic Web technology. Through publication at source, all the data is made available for subsequent reuse in support of other scientific research processes. The entire system was developed upon a service-based grid computing infrastructure with consideration for provenance management and experimental automation.

### 1.4.3 CoAKTinG

The CoAKTinG [22] (Collaborative Advanced Knowledge Technologies in the Grid) project is funded by the UK e-Science Programme. Its main objective is "to advance in a collaborative e-Science working environment through the application of advanced knowledge technologies." The typical role of the knowledge technologies in this project includes using ontologies to describe the information structure to enhance multi-modal and multi-media group discussions, and knowledge-based planning and task support to enhance issue-based process/activity discussions. Besides, the project aims to support e-Science collaboration by integrating and demonstrating the utility of tools and techniques developed in Grid communities such as the Access Grid.

### 1.4.4 K-WF Grid

K-WF Grid[23] stands for "Knowledge-based Workflow for Grid". It is also one of the European grid projects with the objective of addressing the need for a knowledge-based workflow infrastructure for the future Grid environment. Basically, it assists its users in composing powerful Grid workflows by means of a rule-based expert system, and enables the configuration of a complex semantic-based Grid execution environment. The emphasized applications are coordinated traffic management, enterprise resource planning, and a flood forecasting simulation cascade.

### 1.4.5 Semantic Grid Research and Development in China

China has been very active in semantic grid research since the birth of the Semantic Grid. Noticeably, a national research team was formed in 2003. The five-year semantic grid initiative [24] funded by China Ministry of Science and Technology, about $3.1M in total, constitutes eight subjects:

---

[22] http://www.aktors.org/coakting
[23] http://www.kwfgrid.eu
[24] China Semantic Grid initiative: http://www.semgrid.net/eng_pro_int.htm

- Theory, model, method, and tools for web resource space model.
- Process semantics, verification theory and service integration on the Semantic Grid.
- Semantic-Grid-based semantic association model and management and communication platform.
- Resource description model, formalization theory and support technology on the Semantic Grid and its application in bioinformatics.
- Semantic-Grid-based knowledge supply theory and technology for cooperative and creative product design.
- Application of the Semantic Grid in Chinese traditional medicine.
- Semantic-based information retrieval, integration and its application in travel.
- Application of the Semantic Grid in meteorological resource sharing and services.

Typical semantic grid tool development includes the DartGrid system [25] that will be introduced in detail in Chapter 8, and the Falcon system [26] that is a semantic search engine developed for many advanced semantic technologies.

## 1.5 Summary and Conclusion

Basically, Grids involve the design and development of the architecture of the future Internet. The ultimate goal is to provide a flexible, adaptive, manageable, service-oriented architecture for future Internet-based applications, while the Semantic Web looks at the semantic heterogeneity issue that has hindered almost all integration systems in the perspective of information representation. Although these two technologies offer different solutions, they actually complement each other. The concept of the Semantic Grid was then brought up by many researchers with the intention of combining them to address many difficult problems that cannot be resolved by only one of them.

The Semantic Grid poses many challenging issues including data integration, service management, knowledge discovery, trust computing, distributed problem-solving, which are the main subjects of this book and will be introduced in much detail in the following chapters. It is stated that the semantic grid, as a combination of the technologies from both grid computing and the semantic web, would provide a promising alternative for developing a future interconnected environment, particularly geared to enabling highly selective resource sharing, sensible knowledge discovery and collective intelligence.

---

[25] http://ccnt.zju.edu.cn/projects/dartgrid
[26] http://xobjects.seu.edu.cn/project/falcon/

## References

Berners Lee T, Hendler J, Lassila O (2001) The Semantic Web. Scientific American, May: 29-31

Chen HJ, Wu ZH (2006) DartGrid: A Semantic Infrastructure for Building Database Grid Application. Journal of Concurrency and Computation: Practice and Experience. v18(11):1811-1828

Foster I (2002a) The Grid: A New Infrastructure for 21st Century Science. Physics Today, v55(2):42-47

Foster I (2002b) What is the Grid? A Three Point Checklist. GRIDToday, July 20

Foster I (2005) Service-Oriented Science. Science, May 6, v308:814-817

Foster I (2006) Globus Toolkit Version 4: Software for Service-Oriented Systems. IFIP International Conference on Network and Parallel Computing, v3779:2-13

Foster I, Kesselman C, Tuecke S (2001) The Anatomy of the Grid: Enabling Scalable Virtual Organizations. Lecture Notes in Computer Science, v2150:1-26

Foster I, Kesselman C, Tuecke S (2002) Grid Services for Distributed System Integration. Computer, v35(6):37-46

Goble C (2005) Using the Semantic Web for e-Science: inspiration, incubation, irritation. In Proceedings of 4th International Semantic Web Conference, 1-3

Hendler J, Tim BL, Miller E (2002) Integrating Applications on the Semantic Web, Journal of the Institute of Electrical Engineers of Japan, v122(10): 676-680

Humphrey M, Wasson G, et al (2005) State and Events for Web Services: A Comparison of Five WS-Resource Framework and WS-Notification Implementations. 4th IEEE International Symposium on High Performance Distributed Computing (HPDC-14):24-27

Roure DD (2003) On Self-Organization and the Semantic Grid. in IEEE Intelligent Systems, v18:77-79

Roure DD (2005) The Semantic Grid: Past, Present, and Future. The Proceedings of IEEE. v93(3):669-680

Roure DD, Hendler J (2004) e-Science: The Grid and the Semantic Web. IEEE Intelligent System. January/February, v19(1):65-71

Shadbolt N, Tim BL, Hall W (2006) The Semantic Web Revisited, IEEE Intelligent Systems 21(3): 96-101

Wu ZH (2005) DartGrid II: A Semantic Grid Platform for ITS, IEEE Intelligent Systems, v20(3):12-15

Wu ZH, Chen HJ, Xu JF (2003) Knowledge Base Grid: A Generic Grid Architecture for Semantic Web, Journal of Computer Science and Technology. v18(4):462-473

Zhuge H (2005a) Semantic Grid: Scientific Issues, Infrastructure, and Methodology. Communication of ACM. v48(4): 117-120

Zhuge H (2005b) The Future Interconnection Environment. IEEE Computer. April, v38(4):27-33

# 2

# Knowledge Representation for the Semantic Grid

**Abstract**: Representation, acquirement and application of knowledge are three main research topics in artificial intelligence. Knowledge representation serves as a starting point or basis of the latter two. In this chapter we briefly review some basic methods of knowledge representation. After that the major layers of the Semantic Web blueprint and their relationship to the Semantic Grid are discussed. We then present a semantic language system, the Unified Traditional Chinese Medical Language System. We introduce the methodology, design and development of ontology, as well as the case-based knowledge representation and sharing for semantic web applications. Finally, this chapter also presents some trends in the development of knowledge representation: hybrid or combination, methodology of Ontology, Object-Oriented and Web-Oriented.

## 2.1 Introduction

The Web has changed the way people communicate with each other and the way business is conducted. It lies at the heart of a revolution that is currently transforming the developed world towards a knowledge economy and, more broadly speaking, to a knowledge society. This development has also changed the way we think of computers. Originally they were used for numerical calculations. Currently their predominant use is for information processing, for using databases, for text processing, and for games. At present there is a transition in focus towards the view of computers as entry points to the information highways (Antoniou G, Harmelen FV, 2004).

Most of today's Web content is suitable for human consumption. Typical uses of the Web today involve people's seeking and making use of information, searching for and getting in touch with other people, reviewing catalogs of online stores and ordering products by filling out forms. These activities are not particularly well supported by software tools. Apart from the existence of links that establish connections between documents, the main valuable tools are search engines. Keyword-based search engines, such as AltaVista, Yahoo, and Google, are the main tools for using today's Web. It is clear that the Web would not have been a huge success, were it not for search engines. However, there are serious problems associated with their use (Antoniou G, Harmelen FV, 2004):

- High recall, low precision. Even if the most relevant pages are retrieved, they are of little use if another 28,758 mildly relevant or irrelevant documents were also retrieved. Too much can easily become as bad as too little.
- Low or no recall. Often it happens that we don't get any answer to our request, or that important and relevant pages are not retrieved. Although low recall is a less frequent problem with current search engines, it does occur.
- Results are highly sensitive to vocabulary. Our initial keywords do not often lead to the results we want; in these cases the relevant documents use different terminology from the original query. This is unsatisfactory because semantically similar queries should return similar results.
- Results are single Web pages. If we need information that is spread over various documents, we must initiate several queries to collect the relevant documents, and then we must manually extract parts of the information and put them together.

Following (Antoniou G, Harmelen FV, 2004), the main obstacle to providing better support to Web users is that, at present, the meaning of Web content is not machine-accessible. One solution is to use the content as it is represented today and to develop increasingly sophisticated techniques based on artificial intelligence and computational linguistics. This approach has been followed for some time now, but despite some advances the task still appears too tough. An alternative approach is to represent Web content in a form that is more easily machine-processable and to use intelligent techniques to take advantage of these representations. This plan of revolutionizing the Web is normally referred as the Semantic Web initiative.

The value of applying Semantic Web technology to the information and knowledge in Grid application is apparent. It enables user, agent and program to maximally reuse software, services, information and knowledge. Semantics and ontologies in the Grid can offer high-level support for managing Grid resources and for designing complex application. "The Semantic Grid vision is to achieve a high degree of easy-to-use and seamless automation to facilitate flexible collaborations and computations on a global scale, by means of machine-processable knowledge both on and in Grid" (Roure DD, Jennings NR, Shadbolt NR, 2005). Thus, OWL and RDF form a foundation of knowledge representation for the Semantic Grid.

The remainder of this chapter is organized as follows. In Section 2.2, a brief overview of research on knowledge representation is presented. Section 2.3 discusses Tim Berners-Lee's "layer cake" of the Semantic Web, which describes the main layers of the Semantic Web design and vision. Then, in Sections 2.4 and 2.5, we present methodology, design and development of ontology for the Unified Traditional Chinese Medical Language System (UTCMLS). The conclusions and future work are summarized in Section 2.6.

## 2.2 Knowledge Representation

Knowledge representation was developed as a branch of artificial intelligence, the science of designing computer systems to perform tasks that would normally require human intelligence. But today advanced systems everywhere are performing tasks that used to require human intelligence: information retrieval, stock-market trading, recourse allocation, circuit design, virtual reality, speech recognition, and machine translation. As a result the AI design techniques have converged with techniques from other fields, especially database and object-oriented systems. In that sense knowledge representation is a multidisciplinary subject that applies theories and techniques from three other fields (Sowa JF, 2003):

- Logic provides the formal structure and rules of inference.
- Ontology defines the kinds of things that exist in the application domain.
- Computation supports the applications that distinguish knowledge representation from pure philosophy.

Without logic a knowledge representation is vague, with no criteria for determining whether statements are redundant or contradictory. Without ontology the terms and symbols are ill-defined and confusing. And without computable models the logic and ontology cannot be implemented in computer programs. Knowledge representation is the application of logic and ontology to the task of constructing computable models for some domain.

### 2.2.1 Mathematical Logic

Logic-based formalisms play a prominent role in modern Artificial Intelligence (AI) research. The numerous logical systems employed in various applications can roughly be divided into three categories (Kutz O, Lutz C, Wolter F, Zakharyaschev M, 2004):

- Very expressive but undecidable logics, typically variants of first- or higher-order logics;
- Quantifier-free formalisms of low computational complexity (typically P- or NP complete), such as (fragments of) classical propositional logic and its non-monotonic variants;
- Decidable logics with restricted quantification located 'between' propositional and first-order logics; typical examples are modal, description and propositional temporal logics.

The use of formalisms of the third kind is motivated by the fact that logics of the second category are often not sufficiently expressive, e.g., for terminological, spatial, and temporal reasoning, while logics of the first kind are usually too complex to be used for efficient reasoning in realistic application domains.

Thus the trade-off between expressiveness and effectiveness is the main design problem in the third approach, with decidability being an important indicator that the computational complexity of the language devised might be sufficiently low for successful applications. Over the last few years enormous progress has been made in the design and implementation of special purpose languages in this area – witness surprisingly fast representation and reasoning systems of description and temporal logics (Hustadt U, Konev B, 2002; Schwendimann S, 1998). In contrast to first-order and propositional logics, however, these systems are useful only for very specific tasks, say, pure temporal, spatial, or terminological reasoning.

Since realistic application domains comprise usually various aspects of the world, the next challenge within the third approach is the design of suitable combinations of formalisms to model each of these aspects. The underlying idea is to devise useful languages that are a compromise between expressiveness and effectiveness. The problem is then to find combination methodologies which are sufficiently robust in the sense that the computational behavior of the resulting hybrids should not be much worse than that of the combined components. The need for such methodologies has been clearly recognized by the AI community and various approaches for combining logics have been proposed, e.g., description logics with concrete domains (Lutz C, 2003), multi-dimensional spatio-temporal logics (Wolter F, Zakharyaschev M, 2000), independent fusions and fibring (Baader F, Lutz C, Sturm H, Wolter F, 2002; Fine K, Schurz G, 1996; Gabbay D, 1999), temporalized logics (Finger M, Gabbay D, 1992), temporal epistemic logic (Fagin R, Halpern J, Moses Y, Vardi M, 1995), or more general logics of rational agency (Hoek W, Wooldridge M, 2003). Kutz, et al. in (Kutz O, Lutz C, Wolter F, Zakharyaschev M, 2004) proposes a new combination method which is computationally robust in the sense that the combination of decidable formalisms is again decidable, and which, nonetheless, allows non-trivial interactions between the combined components. The method, called $\varepsilon$-connection, is defined in terms of abstract description systems (ADSs), a common generalization of description logics, many logics of time and space, as well as modal and epistemic logics. The basic idea of $\varepsilon$-connections is that the interpretation domains of $n$ combined systems are disjointed, and that these domains are connected by means of $n$-ary "link relations".

### 2.2.2 Semantic Network

A semantic network or net is a graphic notation for representing knowledge in patterns of interconnected nodes and arcs. Computer implementations of semantic networks were first developed for artificial intelligence and machine translation. Earlier versions have long been used in philosophy, psychology, and linguistics.

What is common to all semantic networks is a declarative graphic representation that can be used either to represent knowledge or to support automated systems for reasoning about knowledge. Some versions are highly informal. But other versions are formally defined systems of logic. The following are six of the most common kinds of semantic networks (Sowa JF, 1992).

- Definitional networks emphasize the subtype or "is-a" relation between a concept type and a newly defined subtype. The resulting network, also called a generalization or subsumption hierarchy, supports the rule of inheritance for copying properties defined for a supertype to all of its subtypes. Since definitions are true by definition, the information in these networks is often assumed to be necessarily true.
- Assertional networks are designed to assert propositions. Unlike definitional networks, the information in an assertional network is assumed to be contingently true, unless it is explicitly marked with a modal operator. Some assertional networks have been proposed as models of the conceptual structures underlying natural language semantics.
- Implicational networks use implication as the primary relation for connecting nodes. They may be used to represent patterns of beliefs, causality, or inferences.
- Executable networks include some mechanisms, such as marker passing or attached procedures, which can perform inferences, pass messages, or search for patterns and associations.
- Learning networks build or extend their representations by acquiring knowledge from examples. The new knowledge may change the old network by adding and deleting nodes and arcs or by modifying numerical values, called weights, associated with the nodes and arcs.
- Hybrid networks combine two or more of the previous techniques, either in a single network or in separate, but closely interacting networks.

Some of the networks have been explicitly designed to implement hypotheses about human cognitive mechanisms, while others have been designed primarily for computer efficiency. Sometimes computational reasoning may lead to the same conclusion as psychological evidence. The distinction between definitional and assertional networks, for example, has a similarity to Tulving's distinction (Tulving E, 1972) between semantic memory and episodic memory.

Network notations and linear notations are both capable of expressing equivalent information, but certain representational mechanisms are better suited to one form or the other. Since the boundary lines are vague, it is impossible to give necessary and sufficient conditions that include all semantic networks while excluding other systems that are not usually called semantic networks.

### 2.2.3 Frames

In his famous paper on frames, Marvin Minsky (Minsky M, 1975) cited Bartlett as a source of inspiration. Meanwhile he defined frames in more implementable terms (Sowa JF, 2003):

A frame is a data-structure for representing a stereotyped situation, like being in a certain kind of living room, or going to a child's birthday party. Attached to each frame are several kinds of information. Some of this information is about how to use the frame. Some is about what one can expect to happen next. Other information is about what to do if these expectations are not confirmed.

We can think of a frame as a network of nodes and relations. The "top levels" of a frame are fixed, and represent things that are always true of the supposed situation. The lower levels have many terminals, "slots" that must be filled by specific instances or data. Each terminal can specify conditions that its assignments must meet. (The assignments themselves are usually smaller "sub-frames".) Simple conditions are specified by markers that might require a terminal assignment to be a person, an object of sufficient value, or a pointer to a sub-frame of a certain type. More complex conditions can specify relations among the things assigned to several terminals.

From a formal point of view it was unsatisfying that the semantics of frames and inheritance were specified only operationally. So, subsequent research in the area of knowledge representation addressed these problems. In the area of defeasible inheritance, principles based on non-monotonic logics together with preferences derived from the topology of the inheritance network were applied in order to derive a formal semantics (Touretzky DS, 1986; Selman B, Levesque HJ, 1993). The task of assigning declarative semantics to frames was addressed by applying methods based on first order logic.

(Hayes PJ, 1979) argued that "most of 'frames' is just a new syntax for first-order logic." Although this means that frames do not offer anything new in expressiveness, there are two important advantages that frame-based systems may have over systems using first-order logic. Firstly, they offer a concise way to express knowledge in an object-oriented way. Secondly, by using only a fragment of first order logic, frame-based systems may offer a more efficient means for reasoning. These two points are addressed by the so-called description logics (also called terminological logics, concept languages, and attributive description languages), which formalize the declarative part of frame-based systems and grow out of the development of the frame-based system KL-ONE (Brachman RJ, Schmolze JG, 1985).

### 2.2.4 Ontology

In logic, the existential quantifier is a notation for asserting that something exists. But logic itself has no vocabulary for describing the things that exist. Ontology fills that gap: it is the study of existence, of all the kinds of entities – abstract and concrete – that make up the world. It supplies the predicates of predicate calculus and the labels that fill the boxes and circles of conceptual graphs. The two sources of ontological categories are observation and reasoning. Observation provides knowledge of the physical world, and reasoning makes sense of observation by generating a framework of abstractions called metaphysics (Sowa JF, 2003).

In the context of knowledge sharing, ontology is a specification of a conceptualization. That is, ontology is a description (like a formal specification of a program) of the concepts and relationships that can exist for an agent or a community of agents. This definition is consistent with the usage of ontology as set-of-concept-definitions, but more general. And it is certainly a different sense of the word than its use in philosophy.

For AI systems, what "exists" is that which can be represented. When the knowledge of a domain is represented in a declarative formalism, the set of objects that can be represented is called the universe of discourse. This set of objects, and the describable relationships among them, are reflected in the representational vocabulary with which a knowledge-based program represents knowledge. Thus, in the context of AI, we can describe the ontology of a program by defining a set of representational terms. In such ontology, definitions associate the names of entities in the universe of discourse (e.g., classes, relations, functions, or other objects) with human-readable text describing what the names mean, and formal axioms that constrain the interpretation and well-formed use of these terms. Formally, ontology is the statement of a logical theory.

Ontology defines a common vocabulary for researchers who need to share information in a domain. It includes machine-interpretable definitions of basic concepts in the domain and relations among them. Some reasons for developing ontology are (Noy NF, Musen MA, 1999):

- *Sharing common understanding of the structure of information among people or software agents is one of the most common goals in developing ontologies.* For example, suppose several different Web sites contain medical information or provide medical e-commerce services. If these Web sites share and publish the same underlying ontology of the terms they use, then computer agents can extract and aggregate information from these different sites. The agents can use this aggregated information to answer user queries or as input data for other applications.
- *Enabling reuse of domain knowledge is one of the driving forces behind the recent surge in ontology research.* For example, models for many different domains need to represent the notion of time. This representation includes

the notions of time intervals, points in time, relative measures of time, and so on. If one group of researchers develops such ontology in detail, others can simply reuse it for their domains.
- *Making explicit domain assumptions underlying an implementation makes it possible to change these assumptions easily if our knowledge about the domain changes.* Hard-coding assumptions about the world in programming language code make these assumptions not only hard to find and understand but also hard to change, especially for someone without programming expertise. In addition, explicit specifications of domain knowledge are useful for new users who only need to learn what terms in the domain mean.
- *Separating the domain knowledge from the operational knowledge is another common use of ontologies.* We can describe the task of configuring a product from its components according to a required specification and implement a program that does this configuration independently of the products and components themselves.
- *Analyzing domain knowledge is possible once a declarative specification of the terms is available.* Formal analysis of terms is extremely valuable when both attempting to reuse existing ontologies and extend them.
- *Often ontology of the domain is not a goal in itself.* Developing ontology is akin to defining a set of data and their structure for other programs to use. Problem-solving methods, domain-independent applications, and software agents use ontologies and knowledge bases built from ontologies as data.

According to (Ding Y, Foo S, 2002), in general they observe the following salient points and features in ontology generation to date:

- Source data are more or less semi-structured and some seed-words are provided by the domain experts for not only searching the source data but also as the backbone for ontology generation. Learning ontology from free-text or heterogeneous data sources is still within the research lab and far removed from real applications.
- For concept extraction, there already exist some quite-mature techniques (such as POS, word sense disambiguation, tokenizer, pattern matching, etc.) that have been employed in the field of information extraction, machine learning, text mining and natural language processing. The results of these individual techniques are promising as basic entities and should prove very useful in the formation of concepts in ontology building.
- Relation extraction is a very complex and difficult problem to solve. It has turned out to be the main impediment to ontology learning and applicability. Future research is encouraged to find appropriate and efficient ways to detect or identify the relations either semi-automatically or automatically.
- Ontologies are highly reused and reusable. Based on a basic ontology, other forms of ontologies may be lifted to cater to specific application

domains. This is important due to the cost of generation, abstraction and reusability.
- Ontologies can be represented as graph (conceptual graph), logic (description logic), web standards (XML), or a simple hierarchy (conceptual hierarchy). Currently there is a standard ontology representation language called OWL which combines the merits of description logic, formal logic and web standards.
- A number of tools have been created to facilitate ontology generation in a semi-automatic or manual way. For instance, University of Karlsruhe (Germany) developed and commercialized a semi-automatic ontology editor called OntoEdit (now owned by the Spin-off Company called Ontoprice). Stanford University exploited and provided an ontology-editing environment called Protégé with massive users. University of Manchester owns OilEd, an ontology editor for supporting DAML+OIL.

## 2.3 Description Logic

DL (Description Logic) is one of the logical foundations for RDF and OWL (Web Ontology Language), so we only give a simplified introduction to DL here. Description Logics are considered as the most important knowledge representation formalism unifying and giving a logical basis to the well-known traditions of Frame-based systems, Semantic Networks, Object-Oriented representations, semantic data models, and type systems. Description Logic is the most recent name for a family of knowledge representation formalisms that represent the knowledge of an application domain (the "world") by first defining the relevant concepts of the domain (its terminology), and then using these concepts to specify properties of objects and individuals occurring in the domain (the world description). One of the characteristics of these languages is that, unlike some of their predecessors, they are equipped with a formal, logic-based semantics. Firstly, we give a short introduction to the history of DL.

Research in the field of knowledge representation and reasoning is usually focused on methods for providing high-level descriptions of the world that can be effectively used to build intelligent applications. Approaches to knowledge representation developed in the 1970's are sometimes divided roughly into two categories: logic-based formalism, which evolved out of the intuition that predicate calculus could be used unambiguously to capture facts about the world; and the other, non-logic-based representations. The latter were often developed by building on more cognitive notions, for example, network structures and rule-based representations derived from experiments on recall from human memory and human execution of tasks like mathematical puzzle solving. Even though such approaches were often developed for specific representational chores, the resulting formalisms were usually expected to serve in general use.

One important advance in this direction was the recognition that frames (at least their core features) could carry semantics in the form of first-order logic (Hayes PJ, 1979). The basic elements of the representation are characterized as unary predicates, denoting sets of individuals, and binary predicates, denoting relationships between individuals. However, such a characterization does not capture the constraints of semantic networks and frames with respect to logic. Indeed, although logic is the natural basis for specifying a meaning for these structures, it turns out that frames and semantic networks (for the most part) do not require all the machinery of first-order logic, instead they could be regarded as fragments of it. As a result of this realization, research in the area of Description Logics began under the label terminological systems, to emphasize that the representation language was used to establish the basic terminology adopted in the modeled domain. Later the emphasis was on the set of concept-forming constructs admitted in the language, giving rise to the name concept languages. In more recent years, after attention was further moved towards the properties of the underlying logical systems, the term Description Logics became popular. Within a knowledge

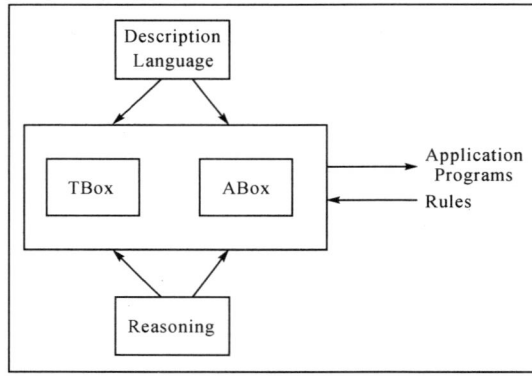

**Fig. 2.1.** Architecture of a knowledge representation system based on Description Logic

base one can see a clear distinction between *intensional knowledge*, which is general knowledge about the problem domain, and *extensional knowledge*, which is specific to a particular problem. A KR system based on Description Logic provides facilities to set up knowledge bases, to reason about their content, and to manipulate them. Fig. 2.1 sketches the architecture of such a system (Baader F, Lutz C, Sturm H, Wolter F, 2002). A DL knowledge base is analogously typically comprised of two components, a "TBox" and an "ABox". The TBox contains intensional knowledge in the form of a terminology (hence the term "TBox", but "taxonomy" could be used as well) and is built through declarations that describe general properties of concepts.

Because of the nature of the subsumption relationships among the concepts that constitute the terminology, TBoxes are usually thought of as having a lattice-like structure; this mathematical structure is entailed by the subsumption relationship, and it has nothing to do with any implementation. The ABox contains extensional knowledge – also called assertional knowledge (hence the term "ABox"), knowledge that is specific to the individuals of the domain of discourse. Intensional knowledge is usually thought not to change –to be "timeless", in a way – and extensional knowledge is usually thought to be contingent, or dependent on a single set of circumstances, and therefore subject to occasional or even constant change.

The vocabulary consists of concepts, which denote sets of individuals, and roles, which denote binary relationships between individuals. In addition to atomic concepts and roles (concept and role names), all DL systems allow their users to build complex descriptions of concepts and roles. The language for building descriptions is a characteristic of each DL system, and different systems are distinguished by their description languages. The description language has a model-theoretic semantics. Thus, statements in the TBox and in the ABox can be identified with formulae in first-order logic or in some cases, a minor extension of it.

A DL system not only stores terminologies and assertions, but also offers services that reason about them. Typical reasoning tasks for a terminology are determining whether a description is satisfiable (i.e., non-contradictory), or whether one description is more general than another one, that is, whether the first subsumes the second. Important problems for an ABox are to find out whether its set of assertions is consistent, that is, whether it has a model, and whether the assertions in the ABox imply that a particular individual is an instance of a given concept description. Satisfiability checking of descriptions and consistency checking of sets of assertions are useful to determine whether a knowledge base is meaningful at all. With subsumption tests, one can organize the concepts of a terminology into a hierarchy according to their generality. A concept description can also be conceived as a query, describing a set of objects which one is interested in. Thus, with instance tests, one can retrieve the individuals that satisfy the query.

In real applications, a KR system is embedded into a larger environment. Other components interact with the KR component by querying the knowledge base and by modifying it, that is, adding and retracting concepts, roles, and assertions. A restricted mechanism to add assertions is a rule. Rules are an extension of the logical core formalism, which can still be interpreted logically. However, many systems, in addition to an application programming interface that consists of functions with a well-defined logical semantics, provide an escape hatch by which application programs can operate on the KB in arbitrary ways.

## 2.4 Knowledge Representation Framework for the Semantic Grid

As the Internet is shifting its focus from information and communication to a knowledge delivery infrastructure, we see the Grid moving from computation and data management to a pervasive, worldwide knowledge management infrastructure. (Cannataro M, Talia D, 2004) foresaw an evolution of computational grids to what they called the next-generation grid, with a particular focus on the use of semantics and knowledge discovery techniques and services. As such, OWL and RDF are also the foundation of knowledge representation for the Semantic Grid, therefore we will discuss the main layers of the Semantic Web design and vision.

Fig. 2.2 (cited from Tim Berners-Lee's talk at XML 2000) shows the "layer cake" of the Semantic Web (attribute to Tim Berners-Lee) (Antoniou G, Harmelen FV, 2004). At the bottom of the "layer cake" is XML, a language that allows writing structured Web documents with a user-defined vocabulary. XML is particularly suitable for sending documents across the Web.

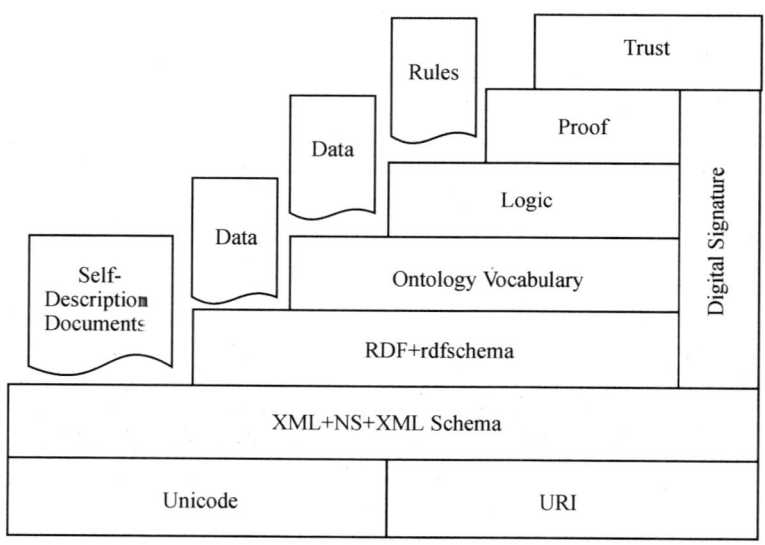

**Fig. 2.2.** Layered approach to the Semantic Web

*RDF* is a basic data model, like the entity-relationship model, for writing simple statements about Web objects (resources). The RDF data model does not rely on XML, but RDF has an XML-based syntax. Therefore, in Fig. 2.2, it is located on top of the XML layer.

## 2.4 Knowledge Representation Framework for the Semantic Grid    27

*RDF Schema* provides modeling primitives for organizing Web objects into hierarchies. Key primitives are class and property, subclass and subproperty relationship, and domain and range restrictions. RDF Schema is built on top of RDF. RDF Schema can be viewed as a primitive language for writing ontologies. But there is a need for more powerful ontology languages beyond RDF Schema and to allow the representation of more complex relationships between Web objects.

The *Logic* layer is used to further the ontology language and to allow the writing of application-specific declarative knowledge.

The *Proof* layer involves the actual deductive process as well as the representation of proofs in Web languages (from lower levels) and proof validation.

Finally, the *Trust* layer will emerge through the use of digital signatures and other kinds of knowledge, based on recommendations by trusted agents or on rating and certification agencies and consumer bodies. Sometimes "Web of Trust" is used to indicate that trust will be organized in the same distributed and chaotic way as the World Wide Web itself.

### 2.4.1 XML and XML Schema

Extensible Markup Language (XML) is a simple, flexible text format derived from SGML (ISO 8879). Originally designed to meet the challenges of large-scale electronic publishing, XML is also playing an increasingly important role in the exchange of a wide variety of data on the Web and elsewhere. XML Schemas express shared vocabularies and allow machines to carry out rules made by people. They provide a means for defining the structure, content and semantics of XML documents.

The tags used to mark up HTML documents and the structure of HTML documents are predefined. The author of HTML documents can only use tags that are defined in the HTML standard (like <p>, <h1>, etc.). XML allows the author to define his own tags and his own document structure. It is important to understand that XML is not a replacement for HTML. In future Web development it is most likely that XML will be used to describe the data, while HTML will be used to format and display the same data. The best description of XML may be: XML is a cross-platform, software and hardware independent tool for transmitting information. It has been amazing to see how quickly the XML standard has been developed and how quickly a large number of software vendors have adopted the standard. XML will be as important to the future of the Web as HTML has been to the foundation of the Web, and XML will be the most common tool for all data manipulation and data transmission.

An XML document is well-formed if it respects certain syntactic rules. However, those rules say nothing specific about the structure of the document. Now, imagine two applications try to communicate, and wish to use the same vocabulary. For this purpose it is necessary to define all the elements and attribute names that may be used. Moreover, the structure should also be defined: what values an attribute may take, which elements may or must occur within other elements, and so on.

In the presence of such structured information we have an enhanced possibility of document validation. We say that an XML document is valid if it is well-formed, uses structured information, and respects that structured information. There are two ways of defining the structure of XML documents: DTDs, the older and more restricted way, and XML Schema, which offers extended possibilities, mainly for the definition of data types.

### 2.4.2 RDF and RDF Schema

Although often called a "language", RDF (Resource Definition Framework) is essentially a data model. Its basic building block is a subject-predicate-object triple, called a statement. Of course, an abstract data model needs a concrete syntax in order to be represented and transmitted, and RDF defines its syntax in the form of XML. As a result, it inherits the benefits associated with XML. However, it is important to understand that other syntactic representations of RDF, not based on XML, are also possible; XML-based syntax is not a necessary component of the RDF model.

RDF is domain-independent in that no assumptions about a particular domain of use are made. It is up to users to define their own terminology in a schema language called RDF Schema (RDFS). The name RDF Schema is now widely regarded as an unfortunate choice. It suggests that RDF Schema has a similar relationship to RDF as XML Schema has to XML, but in fact this is not the case. XML Schema constrains the structure of XML documents, whereas RDF Schema defines the vocabulary used in RDF data models. In RDFS we can define the vocabulary, specify which properties apply to which kinds of objects and what values they can take, and describe the relationships between objects. For example, we can write

*Primates is a subclass of mammal.*

This sentence means that all primates are also mammal. It is important to understand that there is an intended meaning associated with "is a subclass of". It is not up to the application to interpret this term; its intended meaning must be respected by all RDF processing softwares. Through fixing the semantics of certain ingredients, RDF/RDFS enables us to model particular domains. This kind of information makes use of the semantic model of the particular domain, and cannot be represented in XML or in RDF but is typical of knowledge written in RDF Schema. Thus RDFS makes semantic information machine-accessible, in accordance with the Semantic Web vision.

The fundamental concepts of RDF are resources, properties and statements (Antoniou G, Harmelen FV, 2004).We can think of a resource as an object on a "thing" we want to talk about. Resources may be authors, books, publishers, places, people, hotels, rooms, search queries, and so on. Every resource has a Universal Resource Identifier (URI). A URI can be a URL (Unified Resource Locator, or Web address) or some other kind of unique

## 2.4 Knowledge Representation Framework for the Semantic Grid

identifier; note that an identifier does not necessarily enable access to a resource. A URI scheme has been defined not only for web-location but also for such diverse objects as telephone numbers, ISBN numbers and geographic locations. There has been a long discussion about the nature of URI, even touching on philosophical questions (for example, what is an appropriate unique identifier for a person?), but we will not go into details here. In general, we assume that a URI is the identifier of a Web resource.

Properties are special kinds of resources; they describe relations between resources, for example "written by", "age", "title", and so on. Properties in RDF are also identified by URIs (and in practice by URLs). This idea of using URIs to identify things and the relations in-between is quite important. This choice gives us, in one stroke, a global, worldwide, unique naming scheme. The use of such a scheme greatly reduces the homonym problem that has plagued distributed data representation to date.

Statements assert the properties of resources. A statement is a subject-predicate-object triple, consisting of a resource, a property, and a value. Values can either be resources or literals. Literals are atomic values (strings), the structure of which we will not discuss further. An example of a statement is (Antoniou G, Harmelen FV, 2004)

*David Billington is the owner of the Web page http://www.cit.gu.edu.au/~db. The simplest way of interpreting this statement is to use the definition and consider the triple ("David Billington", http://www.mydomain.org/site-owner, http://www.cit.gu.edu.au/~db).*

We can think of this triple $(x, P, y)$ as a logical formula $P(x, y)$, where the binary predicate $P$ relates the object $x$ to the object $y$. In fact, RDF offers only binary predicates (properties).

### 2.4.3 Web Ontology Language

RDF is limited to binary ground predicates, and RDF Schema is limited to a subclass hierarchy and a property hierarchy, with domain and range definitions of these properties. However, the Web Ontology Working Group of W3C identified a number of characteristic use cases for the Semantic Web that would require much more expressiveness than RDF and RDF Schema. This led to a joint initiative to define a richer language, called DAML+OIL. DAML+OIL in turn was taken as the starting point for the W3C Web Ontology Working Group in defining OWL, the language that is to be the standardized and broadly accepted ontology language of the Semantic Web. RDF and RDFS allow the representation of some ontological knowledge. The main modeling primitives of RDF/RDFS concern the organization of vocabularies in typed hierarchies: subclass and subproperty relationships, domain and range restrictions, and instances of classes. However, a number of other features are missing. Here we list a few (Antoniou G, Harmelen FV, 2004):

- *Local scope of properties.* In RDF Schema we cannot declare range restrictions that apply to some classes only. For example, we cannot say that cows eat only plants, while other animals may eat meat, too.
- *Disjointness of classes.* Sometimes we wish to say that classes are disjointed. For example, male and female are disjointed. But in RDF Schema we can only state subclass relationships, e.g., female is a subclass of person.
- *Boolean combinations of classes.* Sometimes we wish to build new classes by combining other classes using union, intersection, and complement. For example, we may wish to define the class person to be the disjointed union of the classes male and female. RDF Schema does not allow such definitions.
- *Cardinality restrictions.* Sometimes we wish to place restrictions on how many distinct values a property may or must take. For example, we would like to say that a person has exactly two parents, or that a course is taught by at least one lecturer. Again, such restrictions are impossible to be expressed in RDF Schema.
- *Special characteristics of properties.* Sometimes it is useful to say that a property is transitive (like "greater than"), unique (like "is mother of"), or the inverse of another property (like "eats" and "is eaten by").

However, ontology languages should allow users to write explicit, formal conceptualizations of domain models. The main requirements are:

- A well-defined syntax
- Efficient reasoning support
- A formal semantics
- Sufficient expressive power
- Convenience of expression

Thus we need an ontology language that is richer than RDF Schema, a language that offers these features and more. In designing such a language one should be aware of the trade-off between expressive power and efficient reasoning support. Generally speaking, the richer the language is, the more inefficient the reasoning support becomes, often crossing the border of non-computability. Thus we need a compromise that can be supported by reasonably efficient reasoners while being sufficiently expressive for large classes of ontologies and knowledge.

Ideally, OWL would be an extension of RDF Schema, in the sense that OWL would use the RDF meaning of classes and properties and would add language primitives to support the richer expressiveness required. Such an extension of RDF Schema would also be consistent with the layered architecture of the Semantic Web. Unfortunately, simply extending RDF Schema would work against obtaining expressive power and efficient reasoning. RDF Schema has some very powerful modeling primitives. Constructions such as

## 2.4 Knowledge Representation Framework for the Semantic Grid

rdfs:Class (the class of all classes) and rdf:Property (the class of all properties) are very expressive and lead to uncontrollable computational properties if the logic is extended with such expressive primitives.

The full set of requirements for an ontology language that seem unobtainable: efficient reasoning support and convenience of expression for a language as powerful as a combination of RDF Schema with a full logic. Indeed, these requirements have prompted W3's Web Ontology Working Group to define OWL as three different sub-languages, each of which fulfills different aspects of this full set of requirements.

- **OWL Full**
  The entire language is called OWL Full and uses all the OWL languages primitives. It also allows the combination of these primitives in arbitrary ways with RDF and RDF Schema. This includes the possibility (also present in RDF) of changing the meaning of the predefined (RDF or OWL) primitives by applying the language primitives to each other. For example, in OWL Full we could impose a cardinality constraint on the class of all classes, essentially limiting the number of classes that can be described in any ontology. The advantage of OWL Full is that it is fully upward-compatible with RDF, both syntactically and semantically: any legal RDF document is also a legal OWL Full document, and any valid RDF/RDF Schema conclusion is also a valid OWL Full conclusion. The disadvantage of OWL Full is that the language has become so powerful as to be undecidable, dashing any hope of complete (or efficient) reasoning support.
- **OWL DL**
  In order to retain computational efficiency, OWL DL (short for Description Logic) is proposed as a sub-language of OWL Full that restricts the way in which the constructors from OWL and RDF may be used, thus ensuring that the language corresponds to a well-studied description logic. The advantage of this is that it permits efficient reasoning support. The disadvantage is that we lose full compatibility with RDF: an RDF document will in general have to be extended in some ways and restricted in others before it becomes a legal OWL DL document. Every legal OWL DL document is a legal RDF document.
- **OWL Lite**
  An even further restriction limits OWL DL to a subset of the language constructors. For example, OWL Lite excludes enumerated classes, disjointness statements, and arbitrary cardinality. The advantage of this is a language that is both easier to grasp (for users) and easier to implement (for tool builders). The disadvantage is of course restricted expressivity.

## 2.5 Ontology Development and Application for TCM

Traditional Chinese Medicine (TCM) is a complete system of medicine based on a wide range of human experience. Thousands of scientific studies that support traditional Chinese medical treatments are published yearly in journals around the world. However, even patients who benefit from treatments such as acupuncture or Chinese herbal therapy may not understand all the components of the TCM system. That may be, in part, because TCM is based on a dynamic understanding of energy and flow that has more to do with Western physics than Western medicine. TCM embodies rich dialectical thoughts, such as the holistic connections and the unity of *yin* and *yang*.

With the development of information technology and wide use of the Internet, an immense amount of disparate isolated medical databases, Electronic Patient Record (EPR), Hospital Information Systems (HIS) and knowledge sources were developed. In 2000 we developed a unified Web accessible multi-databases query system of TCM bibliographic databases and specific medical databases to address the distributed, heterogeneous information sources retrieval in TCM. It has been available online for registered users for five years. As a complete system with complex disciplines and concepts, TCM has the main obstacle that a large amount of ambiguous and polysemous terminologies exist during the information processing procedure. We have initiated the UTCMLS project since 2001, which is funded by the China Ministry of Science and Technology to study the terminology standardization, knowledge acquisition and integration in TCM. We recognized that there are three main challenges in the UTCMLS project.

- Design a reusable and refinable ontology that integrates and accommodates all the complex TCM knowledge.
- Harness a broad collaboration of different domain experts in distributed sites in ontology development.
- Develop a knowledge infrastructure for the TCM Semantic Grid.

### 2.5.1 Ontology Design and Development for UTCMLS

The development of ontologies is a modeling activity that needs ontological engineers who have sufficient understanding of the domain of concern and are familiar with knowledge representation languages. Problems like ontology and conceptual modeling need to be studied in a highly interdisciplinary perspective. Ontology construction is a complex and labor-intensive activity. Several controlled vocabularies and many special terminology lexicons exist in TCM. But combining and synchronizing individual versions of existing medical terminology vocabularies into a unified terminological system is still a problem, because of the heterogeneity and indistinctness in the terminology used to describe the terminological systems. This has been made worse by the various and non-standard use of words in clinical practice.

## 2.5 Ontology Development and Application for TCM

The ontology development for UTCMLS is still in the preliminary stage. By the year 2005, only a small part of sub-ontologies (e.g. The Basic Theory of TCM, Formula of Herbal Medicine, Chinese Materia Medica and Acupuncture) had been developed. About 8,000 class concepts and 50,000 instance concepts are defined in the current TCM ontology, whereas we estimate the number of concepts of TCM will be as many as several hundreds of thousands, maybe even reaching several millions. Furthermore, because the terminology knowledge is mastered and used in practice by different groups of experts, there should be a broad co-operation in the knowledge acquisition procedure. A methodology of loosely coupled development and quality assurance is needed to build a formal final ontology. Although agreement on a high level schema is a prerequisite for effective co-operation between different groups of modelers, it is not practically possible to build a philosophically perfect model; we would rather aim to assure the ontology fits closely enough with most usage requirements, is refinable and reusable. We give a summary discussion of the methodology, knowledge acquisition, design and development of ontology in TCM in the successive sections.

### 2.5.1.1 Methodology of Ontology Development

The use and importance of ontologies is widespread. However, building ontologies is largely a black art. All the methodologies, such as TOVE (Uschold M, 1996), SENSUS (Spackman KA, Campbell KE, Cote RA, 1997), are task-specific. (Uschold M, Grninger M, 1996) emphasized that no unified methodology is suitable for all the jobs, but different approaches are required for different circumstances. (Jones D, 1998) had an overview of ontology methodologies and proposed guidelines for ontology development. It shows that ontological engineering is still a craft rather than a science at present. There are two main tasks involved in content development for TCM ontology: knowledge acquisition and conceptualization from disparate TCM information sources; and formalization and implementation of ontology schema. The building of TCM domain ontology conforms to several principles:

- Refinement is needed. The methodology, based on the prototype ontology, is preferred in TCM ontology building for the vast, complex and dynamic knowledge system in TCM.
- Development should be based on informal ontologies. There are many terminology lexicons and a number of controlled vocabularies. These knowledge sources can be viewed as the informal ontologies at the starting point.
- Evaluation is essential and important. Ambiguity and polysemia are the characteristic phenomena of TCM concepts. No standard has been agreed regarding the concept structure and relationship in the TCM discipline. The ontology development of TCM is a continuous procedure of evaluation and development.

- The methodology of distributed loosely-coupled development is required. The task of building TCM ontology is distributed across 17 sites in China and each site is responsible for the corresponding sub-domain terminology work of TCM.

(Rector AL, 2001) had the practice of distributed cooperative ontology development in the medical domain, in which an intermediate representation at the knowledge level has been used to control the quality of ontology development. We also adopt the intermediate representation mechanism based on tabular and graph notations. The knowledge acquisition, conceptualization, integration, implementation, evaluation and documentation activities are involved in ontology development. The evaluation mainly focuses on the quality control of the intermediate representation from the distributed domain experts. We also make guidelines and the criteria of (Gruber TR, 1995) for domain experts to control the process of knowledge acquisition and conceptualization. According to the above principles, we applied development criteria to both whole TCM ontology and individual sub-ontologies as shown in Fig. 2.3. Our current practice has shown that this criterion assures the quality control of ontology, interaction, communication between domain experts and central knowledge engineering team.

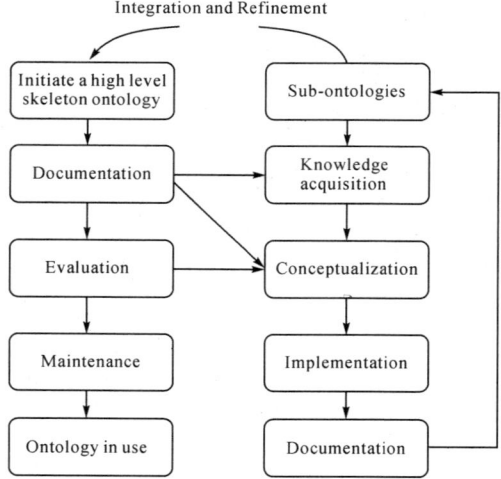

**Fig. 2.3.** Cooperative loosely-coupled development of TCM ontology

A core generic framework of TCM ontology is designed at the starting point of ontology development. About 14 sub-ontologies and 6 core top-level classes are defined as the initial skeleton ontology. The sub-ontologies are defined according to the disciplines of TCM based on the viewpoints of most domain experts as shown in Table 2.1.

## 2.5 Ontology Development and Application for TCM

**Table 2.1.** The 14 core sub-ontologies defined corresponding to the disciplines of Traditional Chinese Medicine

| Sub-ontologies | Characterization of content |
|---|---|
| Basic Theory of Traditional Chinese Medicine | Defines TCM basic theoretical notions, such as *yinyang*, five elements, symptoms, Etiology, Pathogenesis, Physiology and Psychology, etc. |
| The Doctrines of Traditional Chinese Medicine and Relevant Science | Defines basic notions about the doctrines of TCM, which are based on Chinese ancient philosophy and TCM clinical practice. The concept knowledge of TCM relevant science is also defined. |
| Chinese Materia Medica | Contains the natural medicinal materials used in TCM practice such as plants, animals and minerals. |
| Chemistry of Chinese Herbal Medicine | Contains basic notions of chemical ingredients such as rhein, Arteannuin and Ginsenoside Rb2, which are distilled, separated, identified from herbal medicine and their structures are also measured. |
| Formula of Herbal Medicine | Defines basic notions such as benzoin tincture compound, rhubarb compound and cinnabar compound, etc. |
| Acupuncture | Defines basic notions of the modern acupuncture discipline, on the basis of thoughts of ancient acupuncture and uses traditional and modern techniques to study the issues of meridians, point, rules of therapy and mechanism, etc. |
| Pharmaceutics, Agriculture | Defines basic concepts of medical techniques in the manufacture and process of medicinal materials and ontological categories of agriculture issues relevant to medicine planting. |
| Humanities | Defines basic notions about terminology interpretation and relevant knowledge of TCM ancient culture and TCM theories. |
| Informatics and Philology | Contains basic notions of TCM relevant informatics and philology. |
| Medicinal Plants and Other Resources | Defines the medicinal plants and other resources, which are used in health care and disease prevention/cure. |
| Other Natural Sciences | Defines basic notions of TCM relevant disciplines, which study the natural and physical phenomenon. |
| Prevention | Defines basic notions of the science of preventing the occurrence and development of disease. |
| Administration | Defines basic notions of medical research organizations and relevant administration. |
| Geography | Contains the basic notions (e.g. toponym, climate and soil) which are relevant to TCM. |

### 2.5.1.2 Knowledge Acquisition

In 2001, the China Academy of Traditional Chinese Medicine and College of Computer Science, Zhejiang University, initiated and organized the project of UTCMLS as the basis of all the TCM information related work. We aimed to implement a unified TCM language system, which stimulates knowledge and concept integration in TCM information processing.

The National Library of Medicine in the United States has assembled a large multi-disciplinary, multi-site team to work on the Unified Medical Language System (UMLS) (Lindberg D, Humphreys BL, McCray AT, 1993), aimed at reducing fundamental barriers to the application of computers to medicine. UMLS is a successful task in medical terminology research, which inspired our research of TCM knowledge and terminology problems. Many good experiences have been learned from UMLS. The structure of TCM ontology is heavily influenced by the semantic network of UMLS. However, the work of TCM as a complete discipline system and complex giant system is much more complicated. Some principles should be followed during the knowledge acquisition procedure:

- Deep analysis of specialized lexicons as the knowledge source: The scientific control of the conceptual glossary of a discipline is the most important issue in natural and artificial language processing. We combine the pre-controlled vocabulary and post-controlled vocabulary and have a multi-level description of the conceptual glossary such as morphologic, lexics, semantics and pragmatics, etc.
- A good construction of the TCM-oriented concept framework: TCM involves the complete discipline system including medicine, nature, agriculture and humanities, etc. The knowledge system of TCM has complex semantic concept structures, types and relationships, which refer to multi-disciplinary content. Therefore, comprehensive analysis and research of the terminology of TCM is needed before the ontology design. A TCM-oriented concept framework should be constructed to address all the knowledge engineering problems of related disciplines.
- Efficient combination of controlled vocabularies and specialized lexicons: As TCM has various concept taxonomical frameworks, a unified concept infrastructure should be established on the basis of controlled vocabularies and specialized lexicons. The controlled vocabulary can be viewed as an ontology, which has no instances. The specialized lexicon can be viewed as the instances of ontology. Both of them constitute a knowledge base.

From the perspective of TCM discipline, considering the medical concept and its relationship, we define the TCM knowledge system by two components: concept system, and semantic system. The concept system initially contains about 14 sub-ontologies according to the division of TCM discipline and 4 basic top-level classes to define each concept. The semantic system concerns the semantic type and semantic relationship of concept (see Fig. 2.4).

## 2.5 Ontology Development and Application for TCM

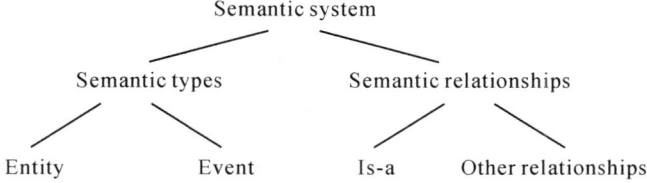

**Fig. 2.4.** Semantic system framework

### 2.5.1.3 Integrating and Merging of TCM Ontology

Information integration is a major application area for ontologies. Ontology integration is possible only if the intended models of the original conceptualizations that the two ontologies associated with overlap (Guarino N, 1998). In the procedure of TCM ontology development, we must let ontology be built by different experts in a distributed environment for the very complex knowledge acquisition work of TCM. We use the top-down approach to develop the 14 sub-ontologies and another 6 core top-level classes and distribute the 14 sub-ontologies to the domain experts of about 17 TCM research organizations in China. The bottom-up approach is used during the development of each sub-ontology. Therefore, ontology merging (information integration) is a must. We use IMPORT to merge the sub-ontologies from different sources into a unified TCM ontology. IMPORT is a plug-in of the Protégé 2000, which is the latest version of SMART (Noy NF, Musen MA, 1999). It is seen from TCM ontology practice that IMPORT is an effective tool for merging ontologies.

### 2.5.2 TCM Ontology

The development of UTCMLS is a process for building a systematized general knowledge oriented TCM terminological system through an ontology approach. We have a nomenclature committee consisting of seven TCM linguistic and terminological experts to evaluate the nomenclature standard and fix the final definitions with the other participating linguistic and domain experts. More than 30 experts in the fields of traditional Chinese medicine, medical informatics, knowledge engineering, and medical administration were consulted about the development of TCM ontology. The categories of the structure of TCM ontology are formed according to the structures of the controlled vocabularies and the standard textbooks. More than one hundred controlled terminologies have been chosen as the sources for TCM ontology, which are stored in a simple ontology named reference book ((8) in Fig. 2.5). *Chinese Traditional Medicine and Material Medical Subject Headings, Traditional Chinese Medical Subject Headings, Chinese Library Classification, National Standard and Pharmacopoeia of the People's Republic of China,* etc. are some of the reference books used as main knowledge sources.

38  2 Knowledge Representation for the Semantic Grid

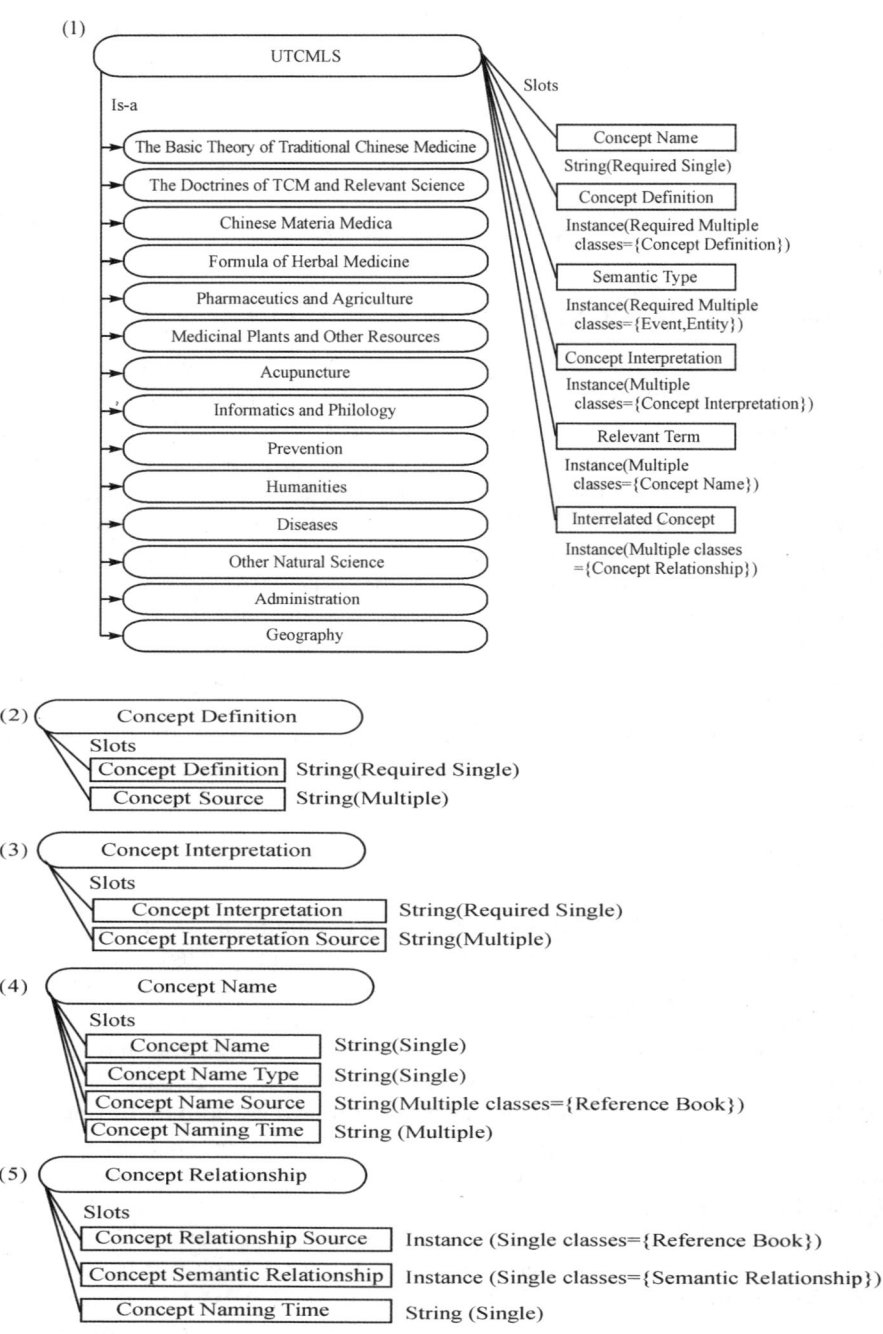

## 2.5 Ontology Development and Application for TCM

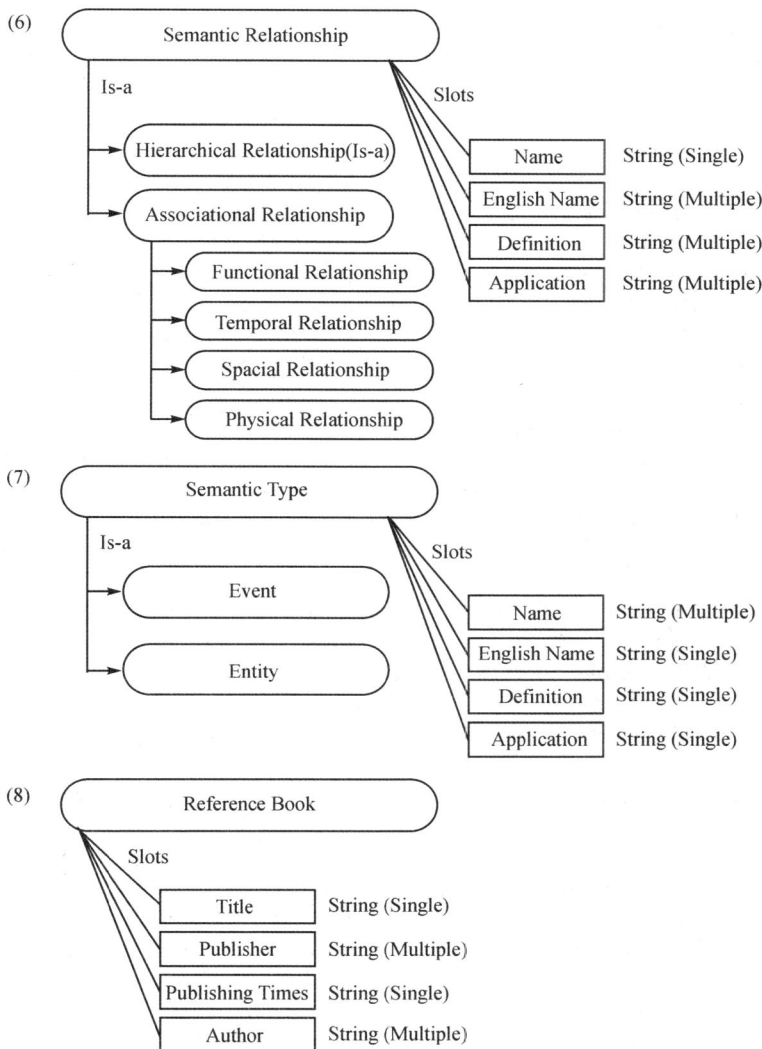

**Fig. 2.5.** Core top-level categories of TCM ontology. (1) is the highest-level ontology and has 6 basic slots and 14 sub-ontologies; (2)(3)(4)(5) constitute the concept system; (6)(7) form the semantic system and (8) is a simple ontology of a reference book

The approaches to concept definition and organization are manual knowledge distilling and organization of these existing controlled vocabularies. A basic principle we conform to is that the three controlled vocabularies namely *Chinese Traditional Medicine and Material Medical Subject Headings*, *Traditional Chinese Medical Subject Headings* and *Chinese Library Classifica-*

*tion* (4th Edition) are considered as the main knowledge sources of ontology, but we prefer to use National Standard and Clinical Diagnosis and Treatment Terms (e.g. Classification and codes of diseases and ZHENG of traditional Chinese medicine/ GB/T 15657-1995, Clinic terminology of traditional Chinese medical diagnosis and treatment—Diseases, Syndromes, Therapeutic methods/GB/T 16751.1-1997, GB/T 16751.2-1997, GB/T 16751.3-1997). When the terminology definitions of the above three controlled vocabularies conflict with those of the two terminological systems, the final definitions are defined by the participant domain experts and nomenclature committee. The translation from those sources to the TCM ontology is done by building the relations between terms. 17 medical information institutes or medical libraries joined the research group to establish the principles and rules for TCM ontology development, as well as to build the ontology. The translation from the sources to the TCM ontology was done according to the following principles. The relationships between terms were built based on the concepts. Different terms from various sources with the same concepts were connected in this way. The synonyms in different forms were translated by the system into the corresponding subject headings. All the terms with the same concepts were selected from the sources first, and then the relationships between terms were built. The nomenclature committee and experts defined the subclasses of each category in the TCM ontology. There were some intensive debates. For example, there were 12 subclasses in the category of the Basic Theory of Traditional Chinese Medicine in the first draft of the structure. Since some of experts did not agree to this classification, after the discussion a new structure with 6 subclasses was developed. The UTCMLS project is still in progress. The core top-level categories such as the concept relevant categories, semantic type and semantic relationship, and the first level subclass definitions of 14 essential sub-ontologies are currently finished. Furthermore, the complete ontology definitions and knowledge acquisition of some sub-ontologies (e.g. The Basic Theory of TCM, Acupuncture and Formula of Herbal Medicine) also have been completed. The rest of this section provides the current main results and experience of ontology development by introducing the whole framework of the skeleton top-level categories of TCM ontology and the Semantic Types. Fig. 2.5 shows the whole framework of the skeleton top-level class definitions of TCM ontology in Protégé 2000 (RDFS is the underlying knowledge representation language and storage format).

### 2.5.2.1 Core Top-level Categories

To unify and initiate the whole ontology development and knowledge acquisition, we have defined the core top-level categories of TCM ontology with essential instances (e.g. 104 TCM semantic types and 59 semantic relationships). We provide 6 core top-level categories, which are treated as the instances of the metaclass: STANDARD-CLASS in Protégé 2000, and on the basis of them define all the intentional and extensional content of concepts

## 2.5 Ontology Development and Application for TCM

in UTCMLS. Meanwhile, 14 sub-ontologies with first level sub-classes are defined. But the second or deeper level sub-class definitions are mainly determined by the corresponding groups of domain experts who take charge of the knowledge acquisition work, because the bottom-up method is used to facilitate the knowledge acquisition and to decrease the labor efforts. As is shown in Fig. 2.5, three basic components constitute the core top-level TCM ontology.

- Sub-ontologies and the Hierarchical Structure
  The sub-ontologies and their hierarchical structure reflect the organization and content of TCM knowledge. The initial 14 sub-ontologies as shown in Table 2.1 and the 6 basic slots have been defined ((1) of Fig. 2.5). The 6 basic slots are concept name, concept definition, concept interpretation, relevant term, interrelated concept and semantic type. The concept name slot gives the standard name of a concept, and the concept definition slot and interpretation slot give the descriptive content of the meaning of a concept. The relevant term slot defines the different terms of a concept used in the other relevant vocabulary sources, by which we can construct the relations between UTCMLS and other terminological sources. The interrelated concept slot identifies the concepts that have some kind of semantic relationship with a concept. The semantic type slot gives the semantic type definition of a concept. More slots can be defined for an individual sub-ontology, if necessary. The complete sub-ontologies with concept instances will become a medical language knowledge based system.
- Concept Structure
  Using Protégé 2000, we provide a knowledge representation method to define the concept in a unified mode. We consider that every TCM concept consists of three basic intentional attributes, namely definition, interpretation and name, hence three classes, namely concept definition, concept name and concept interpretation ((2), (3), (4) in Fig. 2.5) are defined to construct a terminological concept. The class of concept definition involves the definitions of essential meanings of a concept. The class of concept interpretation gives the explanation of a concept. The class of concept name defines the synonyms, abbreviations and lexical variants of a concept, i.e. the relevant terminological names of a concept from different controlled vocabularies. Together with the concept name slot of each sub-ontology, these three classes give knowledge of a concept at the lexicon level. However, the semantic structure aims at knowledge on the semantic level of a concept.
- Semantic Structure
  The semantic type and relationship classes ((6), (7) in Fig. 2.5) form the foundation of knowledge at the semantic level of a concept. The semantic types provide a consistent categorization of all concepts represented in UTCMLS, and the semantic relationships define the relations that may

hold between the semantic types. Classification and inference are supported by these definitions of semantic type and relationship of a concept. As Fig. 2.5 shows, we define a semantic relationship as a slot of concept relationship class and semantic type, an essential slot of TCM ontology in assigning the semantic content to concept. Each concept of UTCMLS is assigned at least one semantic type. In all cases the most specific semantic type available in the hierarchy is assigned to the concept. The semantic structure enables us to construct an abstract semantic network for all the concepts in UTCMLS, so it is vital to TCM ontology.

### 2.5.2.2 Semantic Types and Semantic Relationships

The semantic network of UMLS (Lindberg D, Humphreys BL, McCray AT, 1993) is a high-level representation of the biomedical domain based on Semantic Types under which all the Metathesaurus concepts are categorized. The semantic network makes UMLS a unified medical language system, which is different from other classification and terminological systems. We define the semantic structure in UTCMLS to construct the semantic level knowledge framework of the TCM concept from the idea of the semantic network of UMLS.

We define the semantic type and semantic relationship as one of the two top-level categories of TCM ontology. The structures of the semantic type and semantic relationship are defined as Fig. 2.5 shows. Most of the semantic relationships in TCM ontology are the same as UMLS. In addition there are five new semantic relationships in TCM ontology, namely being exterior-interiorly related, produced, transformed to, restricted, and cooperated with. Those are special ones used in the unique system of Traditional Chinese Medicine. For example, being exterior-interiorly related is the relationship between the concepts with *zang-fu* semantic type, which is a special semantic category in TCM. We have defined 104 semantic types (including 40 entity definitions and 64 event definitions) to describe the high-level concept categories in TCM. The 40 TCM oriented entity semantic types and the hierarchical structure are depicted in Fig. 2.6 and the 64 TCM event semantic types are listed in Fig. 2.7. All the definitions of the semantic system are finally fixed by intensive debates and rigorous evaluation. Incompleteness and imperfection are permitted in practice under a certain tolerable level. The detailed definitions of semantic types and relationships, and the rules of their applications to concepts are given in the technical report (Yin A, Zhang R, 2001) and also are contained in the core top-level ontology of TCM. The whole ontology will be published and shared on the Internet when finished, so this book does not give further descriptions of them.

## 2.5 Ontology Development and Application for TCM

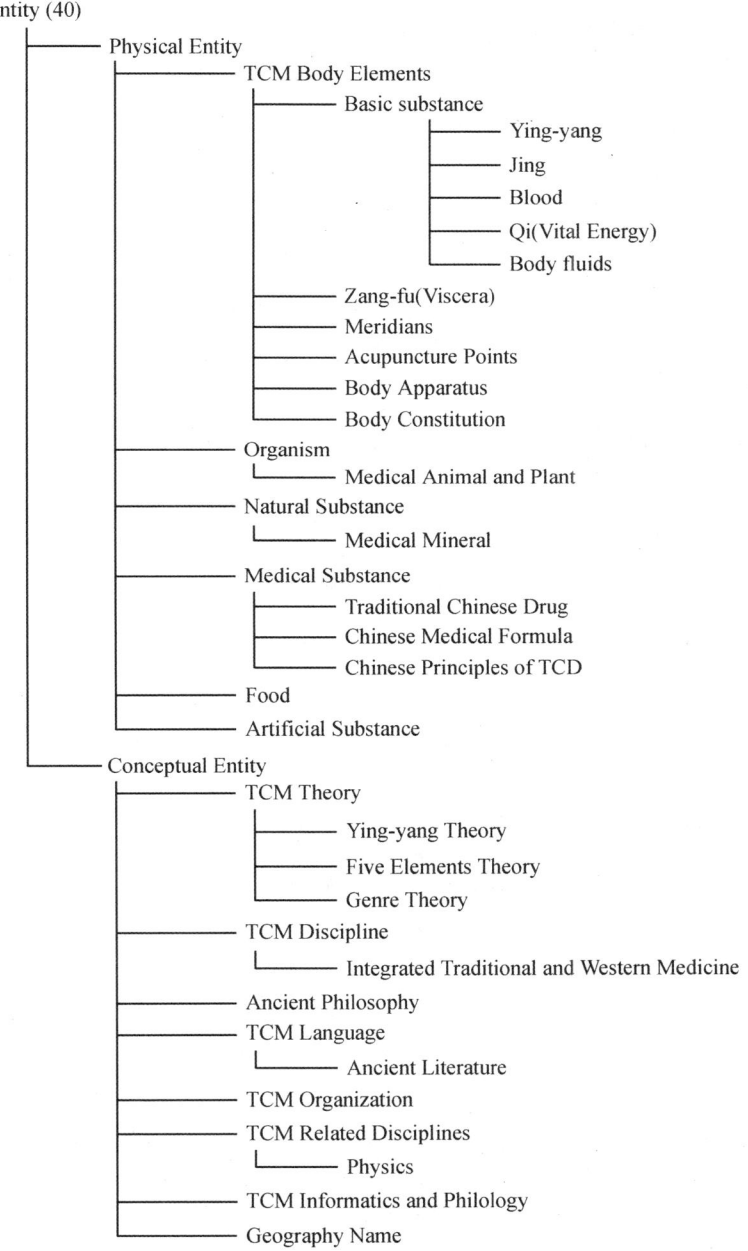

**Fig. 2.6.** Entity definitions of semantic type, which are different from UMLS

## 2 Knowledge Representation for the Semantic Grid

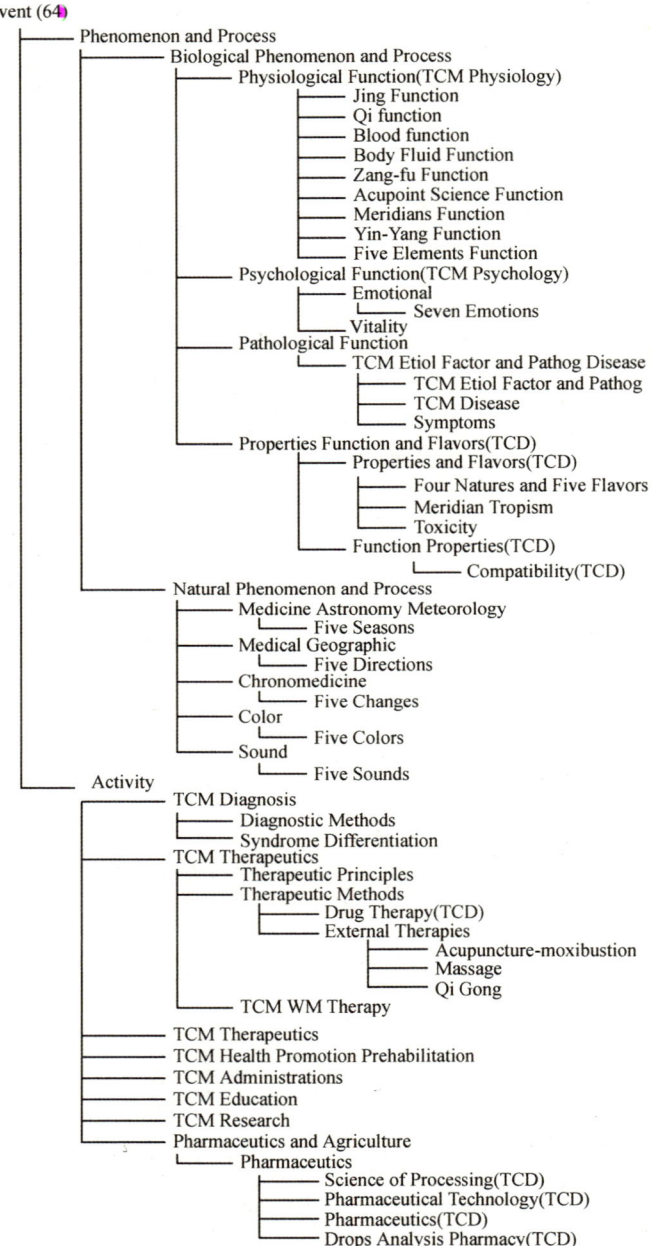

**Fig. 2.7.** 64 TCM special event definitions of semantic type

## 2.6 Summary and Conclusion

Since the early 1990s, developers have designed several intelligent techniques to mimic human decision-making processes and consolidated them with practical experiences. These designers used such representative techniques as logic programming, fuzzy theory, artificial neural networks, and evolutionary computations. Now designers are beginning to hybridize these intelligent techniques to enhance current expert system capability. Funabash and Madea classified hybrid architectures into four types: combination, fusion, integration, and association in (Funabash M, Maeda A, Morooka Y, Mori K, 1995).

- *Combination.* Current intelligent techniques mimic certain brain activities in a complementary way. As a result we can enhance a system's problem-solving capabilities by combining intelligent techniques. A typical hybrid architecture is the sequential combination of neural networks and rules or fuzzy system.
- *Integration.* Combination is basic hybrid architecture, but in some cases the integration of other intelligent elements helps determine the total system behavior. For example, the integrator selects the most appropriate elements to achieve a specific goal and then merges the selected elements' responses.
- *Fusion.* A distinctive feature of neural network technology and evolutionary algorithms is a strong mathematical optimization capability. This capability sometimes works as learning and adaptation. When other techniques incorporate this feature they should be able to increase their learning efficiency. From a topological view of hybrid architectures, this type of architecture is a fusion of intelligent techniques.
- *Association.* Flexible intelligent systems require a distributed architecture where each element works autonomously and cooperatively. This architecture will let developers create a wide variety of intelligent agents for different situations. At this point, due to a lack of experience, this architecture is still not reliable enough for industrial tasks.

As mentioned above, knowledge representation for the Semantic Grid is built on top of the Semantic Web. At present the Semantic Web consists of several hierarchical layers, where the Ontology layer, in form of the OWL Web Ontology Language (recommended by the W3C), is currently the highest layer of sufficient maturity. On top of the Ontology layer, the Rules, Logic, and Proof layers of the Semantic Web will be developed next, which should offer sophisticated representation and reasoning capabilities. Finally, we propose some trends in the development of KR: hybrid or combination, methodology of Ontology, Object-Oriented and Web-Oriented, in particular, representation languages that combine the expressive power of Horn rules and description logics with decidable inference algorithms and reasoning ability under uncertainty.

# References

Antoniou G, Harmelen FV (2004) A Semantic Web primer. The MIT Press, Cambridge, Massachusetts, MA, 238

Baader F, Calvanese D, McGuinness DL, et al (2002) Description logic handbook. Cambridge University Press, 494

Baader F, Lutz C, Sturm H, Wolter F (2002) Fusions of description logics and abstract description systems. Journal of Artificial Intelligence Research 16:1-58

Brachman RJ, Schmolze JG (1985) An overview of the KL-ONE knowledge representation system. Cognitive Science 9(2):171-216

Cannataro M, Talia D (2004) Semantic and knowledge Grids: building the next-generation Grid. IEEE Intelligent Systems 19(1):56-63.

Ding Y, Foo S (2002) Ontology research and development, Part 1: a review of ontology generation. Journal of Information Science 28(5):375-388

Fagin R, Halpern J, Moses Y, Vardi M (1995) Reasoning about knowledge. The MIT Press, Cambridge, MA, 491

Fine K, Schurz G (1996) (1996) Transfer theorems for stratified modal logics. Journal of Logic and Reality, Essays in Pure and Applied Logic 6:169-213

Finger M, Gabbay D (1992) Adding a temporal dimension to a logic system. Journal of Logic Language Inform 2:203-233

Funabash M, Maeda A, Morooka Y, Mori K (1995) Fuzzy and neural hybrid expert systems: synergetic AI. IEEE Expert 10(4):32-40

Gabbay D (1999) Fibring logics. Journal of Logic, Language and Information 9(4):511-513

Gruber TR (1995) Toward principles for the design of ontologies used for knowledge sharing. International Journal of Human and Computer Studies 43(5/6): 907-928

Guarino N (1998) Formal ontology and information systems. Int. FOIS 1:3-15

Hayes PJ (1979) The logic of frames. In D. Metzing (ed.), Frame Conceptions and Text Understanding. Berlin: deGruyter:46-61

Hoek W, Wooldridge M (2003) Towards a logic of rational agency. Journal of IGPL 11(2):133-157

Hustadt U, Konev B (2002) TRP++: A temporal resolution prover. 3rd Int. Workshop on the Implementation of Logics 1:65-79

Jones D (1998) Methodologies for ontology development. IT&KNOWS Conference, XV IFIP World Computer Congress 1:62-75

Kutz O, Lutz C Wolter F, Zakharyaschev M (2004) Connections of abstract description systems. Artificial Intelligence 156(1): 1-73

Lindberg D, Humphreys BL, McCray AT (1993) The unified medical language system. Meth Informa Medicine 32:81-91

Lutz C (2003) Description logics with concrete domains: A survey. Advances in Modal Logic, 4:265-296

Minsky M (1975) A framework for representing knowledge. The psychology of computer vision, P H Winston (ed.), McGraw-Hill, 163-189

Noy NF, McGuinness DL (2001) Ontology development 101: A guide to creating your first ontology. Available at: http://www.ksl.stanford.edu/people/dlm/papers/ontology101/ontology101-noy-mcguinness.html

Noy NF, Musen MA (1999) SMART: automated support for ontology merging and alignment. 12th Int. Workshop on Knowledge Acquisition, Modeling and Management (KAW'99), Available at: http://smi.stanford.edu/smi-web/reports/SMI-1999-0813.pdf

Rector AL (2001) Untangling taxonomies and relationships: personal and practical problems in loosely coupled development of large ontologies. Proceedings of the First International Conference on Knowledge Capture 1:139-146

Roure DD, Jennings NR, Shadbolt NR (2005) The Semantic Grid: past, present, and future. Proc. of the IEEE 93(3):669-681

Schwendimann S (1998) Aspects of computational logic. PhD Thesis, University of Bern, Switzerland, Available at: http://iamwww.unibe.ch/~lwb/publications/thesis_ss.ps.gz

Selman B, Levesque HJ (1993) The complexity of path-based defeasible inheritance. Artificial Intelligence 62:303-339

Sowa JF (1992) Encyclopedia of artificial intelligence (2nd edition). In S C Shapiro (ed.), Wiley, 897

Sowa JF (2003) Knowledge representation: logical. philosophical and computational foundations. China Machine Press, 594

Spackman KA, Campbell KE, Cote RA (1997) SNOMED RT: a reference terminology for health care. Int. AMIA Fall Symposium 1:540-644

Touretzky DS (1986) The mathematics of inheritance systems. Los Altos, CA: Morgan Kaufmann, 216

Tulving E (1972) Episodic and semantic memory. In E Tulving & W Donaldson (Eds.), Organization of memory. New York: Academic Press:381-403

Uschold M (1996) Building ontologies: towards a unified methodology. Proceedings of the second Australasian workshop on Advances in ontologies, 72:7-15

Uschold M, Grninger M (1996) Ontologies: principles, methods and applications. Knowledge Engineering Review 11(2):93-155

Wolter F, Zakharyaschev M (2000) Spatio-temporal representation and reasoning based on RCC-8. 7th Int. Principles of Knowledge Representation and Reasoning, Breckenridge 1:3-14

Yin A, Zhang R (2001) The blue print of a unified traditional Chinese medical language system. Technical Report (in Chinese)

# 3

# Dynamic Problem Solving in the Semantic Grid

**Abstract:** With the Semantic Grid as the problem solving environment, we will face many unexpected problems, as in traditional problem solving. The problems to be solved are often complex and refer to large-scale domain knowledge from crossover disciplines. The relationship between problem solving and the Semantic Grid is our topic in this chapter. And we will focus on how to manage and reuse ontology that embodies domain knowledge based on the infrastructure of the Semantic Grid. The major goal is to harness the Semantic Grid to support efficient and dynamic problem solving.

## 3.1 Introduction

*A problem exists if a living organism has a goal but does not know how this goal is to be reached (Karl Duncker).*

### 3.1.1 Problem Solving

Briefly, problem solving is to achieve a goal not currently in your grasp. Broadly, problem solving is required if you want something that is not immediately available, e.g. solving a puzzle, selecting a good chess move, getting *Apollo* 13 back to earth, cooking Chinese food, designing a house, writing a story. Whenever you have a goal which is blocked for any reason: lack of resources, information, knowledge, and so on, you have a problem. Whatever you do in order to achieve your goal is problem solving. To the field of computer science, problem solving is one of the fundamental areas in Artificial Intelligence (AI). As a science for exploring human intelligence activities, AI originates from problem solving. The aim of AI research in the long run is to explore the basic mechanisms of intelligence. According to the definition of (Nilsson N, 1971), in the broadest sense, problem solving encompasses all of computer science because any computational task can be regarded as a problem to be solved. In the narrow sense within AI research, problem solving can be defined as searching for a solution in a space of possible solutions.

There are two basic elements of problem solving: representation (to represent a problem in an economical way with smaller state space) and search (efficient or simple). A problem often consists of five elements:

- State: Specification of situation.
- Goal: The desired state.
- Operator: An action that changes one state into another.
- Solution: A sequence of operators that transforms the initial state into the goal state.
- Constraints: Restrictions on what can be done.

An agent's task is to get from the initial state to the goal state by means of a series of actions that change the state. The problem is solved if such a series of actions have been found, and the goal has been reached. In general, problem-solving is a component of goal-directed action or control.

Problem solving can be seen as a search through a problem space of possibilities. We start with a situation we want to transform into something new. Do so by applying the different options we have. If we could categorize the structure of problems, we could teach successful strategies for solving all kinds of problems. We could consider the processes and strategies adopted by problem solvers by studying transformation problems that involve moves transforming one situation into another. The most important aim of problem solving research is the development of a theory of problem solving that explains the interactions between a problem situation and the user. The use of formal logic and proof-finding methods in a problem solver could be told new information merely by adding axioms to its memory rather than reprogramming it to solve problems in a wide variety of domains.

### 3.1.2 Cooperative Distributed Problem Solving

Many complex problems are related to multi-disciplines and cannot be solved by a single computer simulation algorithm. Recently, distributed AI has become a new research issue with the emergent network techniques. Many traditional AI issues are extending to the distributed environment and traditional problem solving has evolved towards Cooperative Distributed Problem-Solving (CDPS) (Durfee EH, Lesser VR, Corkill DD, 1989). Here *Distributed* refers to the fact that problems and resources are decentralized, and *Cooperative* refers to the fact that multiple rational agents cooperate with each other to solve the problem. Emerging network techniques have the centralized problem-solving methods (e.g., problem reduction, constraints satisfaction) make use of distributed and dynamic resources to support complex problem solving. CDPS studies how a loosely-coupled network of problem solvers can work together to solve problems that are beyond their individual capabilities. Each problem-solving node in the network is capable of sophisticated problem solving and can work independently, but the problems faced by the nodes cannot be completed without cooperation.

Cooperation is necessary because no single node has sufficient expertise, resources and information to solve a problem, and different nodes might have expertise for solving different parts of the problem. There are several major reasons for cooperation:

First, different nodes may have their own problem-solving experiences. For example, several nodes are faced with a problem of designing a house. The first node has some problem-solving experience on the strength of structural materials. The second node has some experience on space requirements of various houses. The third node has some experience on setting pipelines. The fourth node has some experience on laying cables.

Second, different nodes may have different resources, e.g., high-performance computing ability, a high-speed network, and large-scale storage.

Finally, different nodes may have different viewpoints on the same problem. For example, when several nodes monitor the movement of an aircraft, they will collect different signals and obtain different sensor data. The system has to integrate the information in order to determine the movement situation of the aircraft.

When CDPS nodes solve a problem cooperatively, they often solve sub-problems with local experience, resources and information respectively, and then integrate the solutions of sub-problems together into a global solution to the problem. CDPS has become an important research issue in AI and plays an important role in solving complex domain-specific problems in many fields like medicine and commerce.

### 3.1.3 Multi-Agent System

Recently, distributed problem solving (DPS) has been receiving increasing attention. There are two major research issues for DAI: distributed problem solving (DPS) (Durfee EH, Lesser VR, Corkill DD, 1991) and a multi-agent system (MAS) (Ferber J, 1999). Generally speaking, an *agent* is a computer system that is capable of independent (autonomous) action on behalf of its user or owner (figuring out what needs to be done to satisfy design objectives, rather than constantly being told). A *multi-agent system* (MAS) is one that consists of a number of agents, which interact with one another (Wooldridge M, 2002). In the most general case, agents will be acting on behalf of users with different goals and motivations. To successfully interact, they will require the ability to cooperate, coordinate, and negotiate with each other, much the same way as people do. Some complex problems can be solved by the cooperation of multiple agents, which is so-called multi-agent problem solving (MAPS).

Although individual agents are far less powerful than traditional deliberative agents, distributed multi-agent systems based on such simple agents offer several advantages over traditional approaches: especially robustness, flexibility, and scalability. Simple agents are less likely to fail than more complex ones. If they do fail they can be pulled out entirely or replaced without significantly affecting the overall performance of the system. They are, therefore, tolerant of agent error and failure. They are also highly scalable — increasing the number of agents or task size does not require changes in the agent control programs nor compromise the performance of the system. In systems using deliberative agents, on the other hand, the high communications and computational costs required to coordinate group behavior limit the size of the system to, at most, a few dozen agents. Larger versions of such systems require division into subgroups with limited and simplified interactions between the groups. In many cases these interacting subgroups can, in turn, be viewed abstractly as agents following relatively simple protocols like, for example, in market-based approaches to multi-agent systems.

## 3.2 Grid-based Problem Solving

In this section we will mainly talk about Grid-based problem solving. The relationship between Grid and problem solving is discussed.

### 3.2.1 Grid and Problem Solving

The Grid (Foster I, Kesslman C, 1999; Foster I, Kesslman C, Tuecke S, 2001) theory is very close to problem solving. According to the definition of Ian Foster, the real and specific problem that underlies the Grid concept is coordinated resource sharing and *problem solving* in dynamic, multi-institutional virtual organizations (Foster I, Kesslman C, Tuecke S, 2001). Therefore, cooperative problem solving is one of the most important goals of Grid. Problem Solving Environments (PSEs) are computer systems that provide necessary computational tools for reaching a batch of goals. To large-scale complex multi-discipline problems, a PSE is treated as the environment in which client users utilize Grid resources within a virtual organization. When we want to solve domain-specific problems cooperatively in fields like science, commerce and industry, we often need to access computers, software, databases and other Web resources. Problem solving in the Grid environment needs to integrate and utilize those distributed and heterogeneous Grid resources.

Nowadays there have been some research efforts on Grid-based problem solving. There exist some on-going problem-solving approaches or systems in the Grid environment. We try to list some of them as follows:

Cactus (Allen G, Benger W, Goodale T, et al, 2000) is an open source problem solving environment designed for scientists and engineers. Its modular structure facilitates parallel computation across different architectures and collaborative code development between different groups. The Cactus Code originated in the academic research community, where it has been developed and used over many years in a large international collaboration of physicists and computational scientists. The Cactus Code was originally developed to provide a framework for the numerical solution to Einstein's Equations, one of the most complex sets of partial differential equations in physics. These equations govern such cataclysmic events as the collisions of black holes or the supernova explosions of stars. The solution to these equations with computers continues to provide challenges in the fields of mathematics, physics and computer science. The modular design of Cactus enables people and institutes from all these disciplines to coordinate their research, using Cactus as the collaborating and unifying tool. Cactus was designed with the Grid requirement in mind. It provides a layer on top of the Grid, offering a programming interface which allows the user to be completely ignorant of the nature of the machine or machines that the simulation runs on.

Bioinformatics can be considered as a bridge between life science and computer science. Biology requires high and large computing power to run biological applications and to access a huge number of distributed and heterogeneous databases. Computer scientists and database communities have expertise in high performance algorithms computation and in data management. PROTEUS (Cannataro M, Comito C, Schiavo FL, Veltri P, 2003) is a software architecture allowing the building and executing of bioinformatics applications on Computational Grids. It is a Grid-based Problem Solving Environment (PSE) for bioinformatics applications. PROTEUS uses ontology to enhance the composition of bioinformatics applications. They define an ontology-based methodology to describe bioinformatics applications as distributed workflows of software components. The architecture and first implementation of PROTEUS are based on a Knowledge Grid. PROTEUS is implemented to support an application of human protein clustering.

Developing advanced applications for the emerging national-scale "Computational Grid" infrastructures is still a difficult task. Though Grid services are available that assist the application developers in authentication, remote access to computers, resource management, and infrastructure discovery, they provide a challenge because these services may not be compatible with the commodity distributed-computing technology and frameworks used previously. The Commodity Grid project is working to overcome this difficulty by creating the Commodity Grid Toolkits (CoG Kits) (Laszewski G, Foster I, Gawor J, et al, 2000) that define mappings and interfaces between the Grid and particular commodity frameworks. CoG Kits can enable new approaches to application development based on the integrated use of commodity and Grid technology.

The Grid Enabled Optimization and DesIgn Search for Engineering (GEODISE) (Xue G, Fairman MJ, Cox SJ, 2002) project is funded by the UK e-Science initiative and provides Grid-based, dynamic, and seamless access to an intelligent knowledge repository, a state-of-the-art collection of optimization and search tools, industrial strength analysis codes, and distributed computing and data resources. The GEODISE project aims to aid the engineer in the design process by making available a suite of design optimization and search tools, CFD analysis packages integrated with distributed Grid-enabled computing, data, and knowledge resources. These resources will be exposed to the user via a web-based portal. The user will be guided through the design search process by an integrated knowledge base. Components within the GEODISE system, including application servers, computational resource providers, databases and intelligent knowledge systems, are or will be constructed in the form of Web Services. Therefore, interactions between components for system operations are all conducted through the exchange of XML messages.

Therefore, the Grid technique has been applied to problem solving, especially in scientific computation, which requires a great number of computational and data resources. We can apply the technique to more relevant fields to solve domain-specific problems as the Grid technique grows more and more mature.

### 3.2.2 Problem Solving in the Semantic Grid

We can construct PSE based on the Grid to solve complex domain specific problems. The Semantic Grid as a special form of Grid can be used to support solving problems cooperatively. When the Semantic Grid becomes the PSE, it will generate many unexpected problems that we have not dealt with in traditional problem solving activities. Compared with traditional problem solving, problem solving in the Semantic Grid has the following features:

- The problems to be solved are very complex and related to several disciplines.
- The resources required to solve problems are distributed, heterogeneous and large-scale.
- Problem solving needs a large amount of domain knowledge or even semantics crossing over disciplines.

Therefore, we can give a formal definition of problem solving in the Semantic Grid as follows:

**Definition 3.1 (Problem Solving in the Semantic Grid).** *Problem solving in the Semantic Grid refers to the behavior of solving domain-specific problems cooperatively by using the semantics of domain ontology and integrating Web resources (data, services and instruments) dynamically based on the Grid infrastructure. We can represent it as an equation:* $P: G + R \xrightarrow{O} S$, *where P denotes the specific problem, G denotes the Grid, R denotes resources and S refers to the solution to P. The process of problem solving is performed with the help of the domain ontology O.*

Problem solving in the Semantic Grid is related to traditional problem solving, CDPS and MAPS. But there are distinct features (semantic) of problem solving in the Semantic Grid. The Semantic Grid infrastructure provides the ability to manage, coordinate and reuse ontologies involving domain knowledge according to specific problems. The semantics involved in ontologies are used throughout the whole process of problem solving in the Semantic Grid. We can integrate the problem-solving process of general CDPS systems or multi-agent systems. The results and effects of problem solving should be fed back to the system that evolves domain knowledge to facilitate problem solving.

In this chapter, we are not concerned with the details of the process of problem solving (e.g. how), which can be achieved by integrating specific problem-solving systems, and what we focus on is how we could use the Semantic Grid to support problem solving in a more efficient way. Moreover, the methods of ontology modeling and development are discussed in Chapter 2, so we will focus on ontology management and reuse, as well as how the Semantic Grid can support problem solving in this chapter.

## 3.3 Ontology Management for Grid-based Problem Solving

The recent advent of the Semantic Web (Berners-Lee T, Hendler J, Lassila O, 2001) has facilitated the incorporation of various large-scale on-line ontologies (Gruber T, 1993) in different disciplines and application domains; e.g. UMLS (Bodenreider O, 2004) includes 975,354 classes and 2.6 million concept names in its source vocabularies. Gene Ontology (Ashburner M, Ball CA, Blake JA, 2000) includes about 17,632 terms, 93.4% with definitions.

There is no doubt that large-scale ontologies will play a critical role in a large variety of semantic-based applications; however, including large ontologies in their complete form could imply an unnecessarily huge storage and maintenance problem. One of the possible solutions to the problem is to distribute a large domain ontology in small ontologies in a distributed environment like the Web, which can be developed and maintained independently. This calls for the ability to manage distributed ontologies universally and efficiently. There will be some unexpected challenges when dealing with multiple and distributed ontologies in semantic-based applications. For example, a user application may query an ontology class that is related to several other classes involved in different small ontologies.

In the Semantic Grid, we can utilize the features of the Grid to manage and organize the domain knowledge required for problem solving. Grid applications often involve large amounts of data and/or computing, and are not easily handled by traditional Internet and Web infrastructures. Grids are used to join various geographically distributed computational and data resources,

## 3.3 Ontology Management for Grid-based Problem Solving

and deliver these resources to heterogeneous user communities. These resources may belong to different institutions, have different usage policies and pose different requirements on acceptable requests. If we treat distributed ontologies as a type of Web resource, we can adopt the Grid technology to manage multiple independently developed *local-ontologies* in a distributed environment, which can constitute a virtual *global ontology*, which involves the domain knowledge required for problem solving in the Semantic Grid. We propose, on top of the Semantic Web technology, a Grid-oriented architecture to support ontology reuse and management in a distributed environment, like the Web. We extend the centralized ontology manipulations to the Grid-based ontology management.

### 3.3.1 Grid-based Ontology Management

As Web ontologies are the foundation of the Semantic Web, we can divide the evolution of the Semantic Web into two stages: in the first stage domain ontologies are extracted and built from heterogeneous Web sources and in this stage many ontology engineering methods are involved (e.g. ontology extraction, learning, merging, mapping, etc.); in the second stage domain ontologies are dynamically managed and reused to support semantic-based applications. There have been massive done for the first stage. However, we must also focus on issues simultaneously for the second stage. The field is still in its infancy and many problems remain unsolved or even unaddressed. Existing ontology management systems typically manage ontologies in a centralized way. In this section we present an architecture for ontology management in a distributed environment, which is a so-called *Ontology Grid*.

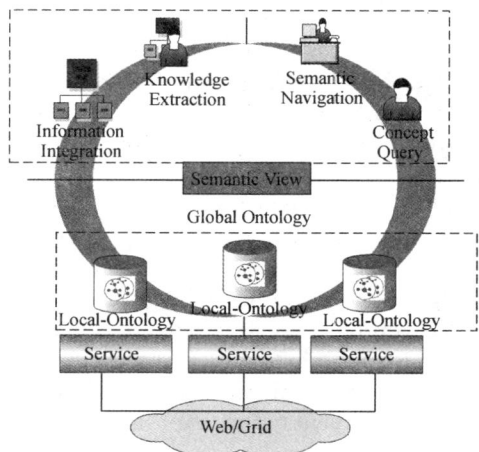

**Fig. 3.1.** The overall architecture of the Grid-based ontology management

An appropriate coordination and management of those distributed small ontologies is necessary to allow efficient use and reuse of domain knowledge. Existing ontology management approaches are inclined to manage ontologies in a centralized way, which cannot well satisfy the requirements of the Semantic Grid well. We can combine the comprehensive computational infrastructure along with the domain-specific knowledge collections to construct a Grid-based distributed ontology management infrastructure, which consists of two hierarchical layers: a core Grid service layer and a virtual semantic view layer. The former refers to the resources in the Grid and services directly implemented on the top of generic Grid services; the latter refers to a semantic-based virtual view to support high-level interaction and applications. The overall architecture of the ontology management illustrated in Fig. 3.1 clearly distinguishes between different components of the infrastructure.

The Grid has recently emerged as an integrated infrastructure for enabling resource sharing and coordinated problem solving in distributed environments. The infrastructure consists of multiple distributed Grid nodes and each node contains one or more local-ontologies. Grid nodes wrap local-ontologies as Grid services and interact with each other through a Grid service interface to exchange domain knowledge. Local-ontologies are composed from a large-scale global ontology and the contents of the ontology are generated from different independent sources. The global ontology is not a simple federation of local-ontologies but a semantic integration. Local-ontologies are integrated together by Grid services at the communication layer and by semantic relationships at the knowledge layer.

### 3.3.2 Ontology Grid Node

Grid-based ontology management consists of distributed, peer-to-peer Grid nodes for specific, small ontologies. The internal architecture of an ontology Grid node is illustrated in Fig. 3.2. The ontology Grid node is a key component of the ontology Grid and serves as an autonomous agent in the Grid. The node maintains a locally centralized knowledge-base (Local-KB) with local-ontologies. The Local-KB involves several parallel local-ontologies from different sub-domains.

The ontology Grid node also provides several Grid services to support semantic-based interaction with domain ontologies. Different nodes can interact with each other through the Grid interface.

**Direct Knowledge Service (DKS)**. For a large domain ontology like the Gene Ontology, the ontology service should provide clients with basic functions necessary for retrieving information sets from the ontology, e.g. giving a concept name and returning all the individuals of the concept. We combine all the ontology elements that can support the explanation of a concept in direct knowledge:

**Definition 3.2 (Direct Knowledge).** *Given an ontology class c, its direct knowledge $D(c)$, is a set of ontology elements that are required to understand*

## 3.3 Ontology Management for Grid-based Problem Solving

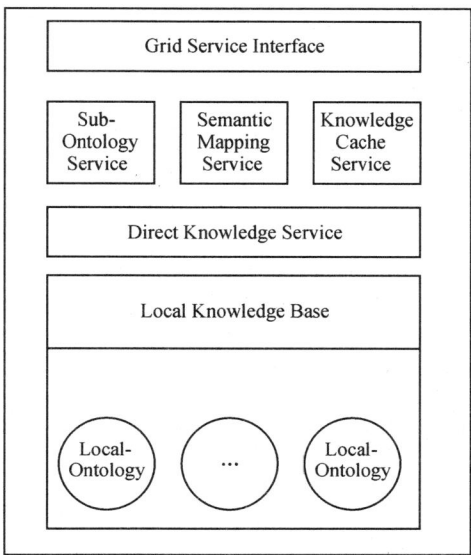

**Fig. 3.2.** The architecture of the ontology Grid node

$c$, including related classes with corresponding properties, extending instances and other attributes of $c$.

The Grid node wraps up four basic query operations as the direct knowledge service, which can be used to query direct knowledge from local-ontologies in the Local-KB directly.

- **Class-Hierarchy Query (CH)** returns all direct subclasses of a specific class.
- **Class-Instance Query (CI)** returns all direct instances of a specific class.
- **Class-Class Query (CC)** returns all related classes to a specific class.
- **Instance-Instance Query (II)** returns all related instances to a specific individual.

Combining a group of basic query operations, clients can perform some complex tasks in applications. Other high-level services can also be constructed based on the basic query service.

**Sub-Ontology Service (SOS).** Problem-solving systems would have their power restricted if the domain knowledge they possess is insufficient. Ontologies like a TCM ontology contain relatively complete domain knowledge. Although large-scale domain ontology has been distributed in many local-ontologies, a local-ontology may be still over-large for problem-solving systems. Our conjecture is that an agent specialized in a certain underlying context needs only particular aspects of the whole ontology. The notion of context is central for representing many aspects of knowledge. According to McCarthy and Buvac (McCarthy J, Buvac S, 1994; Buvac S, Fikes R, 1995), contexts in knowledge representation languages provide a means of referring to a group of related assertions (closed under entailment) about which something can be said. For example, contexts can be used to represent the beliefs of an individual or group, the information accessible to a sensor or to an agent, descriptions of situations, alternative descriptions of domain objects, or the ontology being used by an agent for a specific activity. Problem solving is always local to a subset of known information. According to (Ghidini C, Giunchiglia F, 2001), the part of what is potentially available being used while reasoning is what we call context (of reasoning).

Most existent ontology-based approaches and systems have not taken into account the context that can be defined as the locality of knowledge reference. We propose to represent those context-specific portions of knowledge from the whole ontology as sub-ontologies (Mao Y, Cheung WK, Wu Z, Liu J, 2005a), which can be reused in problem-solving systems. We can give a formal definition for sub-ontology based on the semantic structure of ontology as follows:

**Definition 3.3 (Sub-Ontology).** *Formally, a sub-ontology (SubO for short) can be represented as a triple $< C, K, O >$, where $C$ is a set of contextual classes denoting the current context, $K$ is a knowledge set relevant to $C$, and $O$ is a set of links to the SubO's source ontologies.*

Contextual class is not always top-concept in the class hierarchy tree of SubO, but at most the class related to the context. A set of contextual class is used to capture features of the current context. Concerning different implicational contexts, the same SubO may have a different set of contextual classes and it makes sense that a SubO can be reused in different contexts.

The Sub-Ontology Service is responsible for the extraction, augmentation, pruning, comparison, and merging of SubOs. The manipulations of SubOs are based on the semantic structure of ontology. Clients can use the service to retrieve SubOs from local-ontology to materialize a specific ontology view according to the dynamic application contexts and users' requirements. A database view provides exactly a self-contained portion of a resource. Similarly, we call a self-contained portion of an ontology an ontology view (Noy NF, Musen MA, 2004). An ontology view can be a virtual one and the contents are dynamically allocated from several distributed sources.

**Knowledge Cache Service (KCS).** Local-ontologies are distributed on different Grid nodes, which maintain a locally centralized knowledge-base (Local-KB) for domain-specific local-ontologies. The Local-KB involves several parallel local-ontologies from different domains, and it implies that the Ontology Grid can manage several global domain-specific ontologies at one time. The Local-KB provides manipulations with domain knowledge; however, direct access to complete local-ontologies whenever domain knowledge is required will be time-consuming and inefficient for problem-solving systems.

In computer architecture, a memory cache is a portion of memory made of high-speed static RAM instead of the slower and cheaper dynamic RAM used for main memory. Memory caching is effective in improving system performance because most programs access the same data or instructions over and over again. By keeping as much of the information as possible in cache, the computer avoids accessing the slower dynamic RAM. The principle of reference locality applies to the portions of domain knowledge currently being accessed in ontology. Some portions of a local-ontology are frequently used in problem-solving systems while some portions are rarely or never used.

The Knowledge Cache Service is responsible for organizing domain knowledge in a two-level mode, knowledge base and knowledge cache, which draws inspiration from the memory caching mechanism, to support efficient domain knowledge management and reuse. If we keep the most active SubOs for problem-solving systems in the knowledge cache of GN, the overall access speed and efficiency for problem-solving systems will be optimized. The strategy for knowledge cache utilization should maximize the number of knowledge cache access operations, in comparison with the number of direct local-ontology access operations. For a series of knowledge requests we can calculate the hit and miss ratio for the knowledge cache.

**Semantic Mapping Service (SMS).** Since a large-scale domain ontology is distributed in many small local-ontologies in different nodes, one small local ontology may contain a reference to the definition of classes or individuals in another small ontology. For example, a tourism ontology has two small ontologies: travel ontology and accommodation ontology. There is a class related to the methods of traveling to a hotel in the travel ontology and reference to the class of hotel in the accommodation ontology; however, there is no further definition of hotel in the travel ontology. So what the semantic mapping service does is to map the class reference in one local ontology to its definition in another small ontology in the same domain of interest. Besides class mapping, ontology elements including individuals and properties can also be mapped. This service is useful for applications constructed based on facts or axioms across several small ontologies.

### 3.3.3 Semantic View

Domain ontologies are, due to their complex nature, far from being a commodity and require efficient support. The Grid-based ontology management framework offers high-level semantic-based toolkits to form a virtual Semantic View (Wu Z, Mao Y, Chen H, 2004) based on the Grid services and local-ontologies in the Core Grid Layer. The Semantic View shields clients from needing to know the complexity of domain ontologies to support high-level interactions and problem solving.

**Concept Query.** Users often want to query the ontology for concepts in applications just like we do with a database. The semantic view supports the concept query for users to query relevant knowledge about a domain concept based on the DKS. Users can construct the concept query dynamically in a graphical query interface. A complex concept query can be translated into a series of basic query operations of DKS.

**Semantic Navigation.** In a large-scale domain ontology, it is usual for users to explore different aspects of ontology from ontology element to ontology element. Since a large-scale ontology is composed of multiple local-ontologies in a distributed environment, the exploring activity used to involve navigating across several local-ontologies, just like traditional navigation among different Websites. We enable semantic navigation in the semantic view, which can be performed based on SOS and SMS. On the client-side, context-specific SubOs can be visualized as semantic graphs (Mao Y, Wu Z, Chen H, 2004), with each node or arc bound to an ontology element in local-ontologies. In a semantic graph a class node is related to some other ontology elements through relationship arcs. Users can trace a target node (standing for another ontology element, say, $C_t$) of an arc in the semantic graph to view its direct knowledge. If the knowledge set of the SubO includes $D(C_t)$, it will be expanded as part of the semantic graph. If the knowledge set of the SubO doesn't include $D(C_t)$, the Ontology Grid will use SMS to search for its definition in the source ontologies the SubO belongs to. If no appropriate knowledge in the source ontologies can be mapped to $C_t$, the Ontology Grid will turn to an local-ontology node to look for portions of ontology involving relevant knowledge for $C_t$. If the knowledge search mentioned above succeeds, it means that there exists at least one local-ontology containing the relevant knowledge and it will be displayed as a new semantic graph.

**Information Integration.** The activities (e.g. medical diagnosis) of applications in a distributed environment used to require large-scale information resources more than a domain ontology, as a domain ontology only contains explicit specification of a conceptualization without more concrete and specific information. So applications must integrate more domain-specific information resources, which may be distributed on the Web, to extend the knowledge scope of ontologies for practical problem solving. Ontologies can be used to describe the semantics of the information resources with explicit content and overcome the problem of semantic heterogeneity of information sources on the Web. The semantic view provides the information integration mechanism to integrate distributed and heterogeneous information resources based on the semantics of the ontology. Distributed information resources wrap local schemas of information sources through a unified service interface and users can dynamically establish mappings from local to the ontology during the process of the semantic registration. Taking databases for example, the schema model of relational databases is very directly connected with the ontology model: users can register tables at concepts (class), fields at relationships (property) and records at individuals (instance). The mapping information of registration is maintained at a semantic registry, which can be reused for accessing and querying distributed information resources. The information resources registered at the classes within the knowledge set of an existing SubO are involved in the context of the SubO. In this way, when users or applications refer to SubOs under some contexts, they also refer to a set of registered information resources, which have been semantically interrelated in a distributed environment.

**Semantic Extraction.** Including large ontologies in their complete form could of course solve problems but imply unnecessarily huge storage and computational requirements. For a very large domain ontology, users or applications may only require specific portions of semantics from the whole ontology. This calls for the application's capability to extract semantics from a large domain ontology dynamically. In the Grid-based ontology management framework, users can extract portions of semantics from large-scale ontologies based on SOS. The semantic view can provide users with ontology views according to application contexts and user requirements. An ontology view is a set of SubOs. Each ontology view is designed as a coherent set of relevant semantics. An ontology view can be a virtual one and the contents are dynamically allocated from several local-ontologies. Whenever users or applications want to use semantics, or have to do some knowledge-based tasks, they can extract ontology view from ontologies.

## 3.4 Ontology Reuse for Grid-based Problem Solving

We have discussed the problem of distributed ontology management in the previous section, but the problem of how to reuse domain ontologies to support problem solving in the Semantic Grid remains unsolved. There is a lack of efficient mechanisms and approaches for reusing domain knowledge. Therefore we need to construct a model or framework for reusing domain knowledge to support problem solving in the Semantic Grid.

### 3.4.1 Dynamic Memory Model

Case-based reasoning (CBR) (Aamodt A, Plaza E, 1994) has grown from a rather specific and isolated research area to a field of widespread interest. CBR tries to solve new problems by adapting previously successful solutions (represented as cases) to similar problems. CBR depends on the use of a widespread repository of cases. Therefore the representation of these cases is especially important in being able to solve new cases. The representation problem in the cyclical process of CBR is the problem of deciding what to store in a case, finding an appropriate structure for describing case contents, and deciding how to organize and index the case memory for effective retrieval and reuse. There are two influential case memory models: the Dynamic Memory Model (Schank R, 1982) and the Category & Exemplar Model (Aamodt A, Plaza E, 1994).

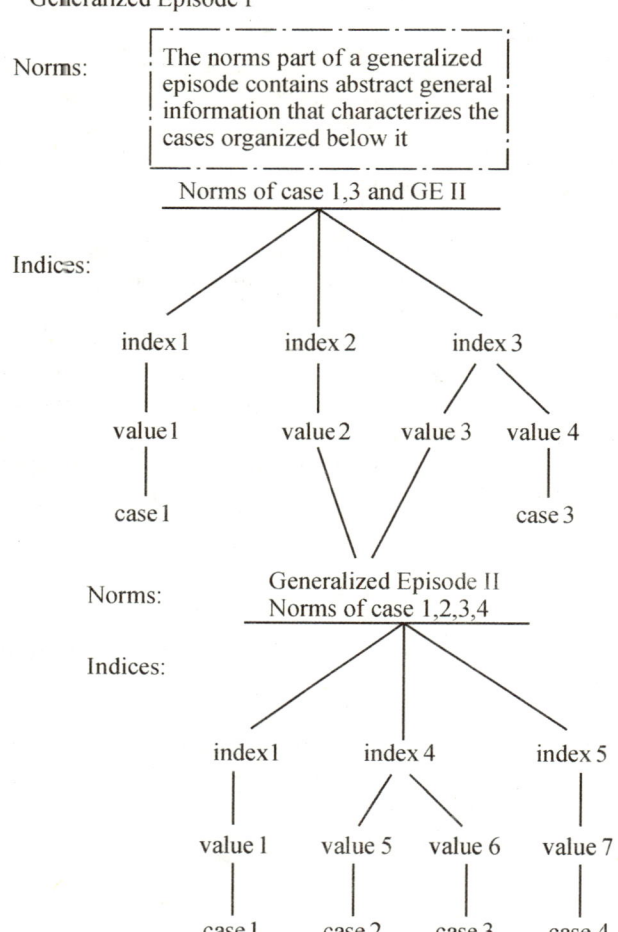

**Fig. 3.3.** A possible structure of cases and GEs in the dynamic memory model

The basic idea of the Dynamic Memory Model is to organize specific cases, which share similar properties under a more general structure, called a generalized episode (GE). A GE contains three different types of objects: norms, cases and indices. Norms are features common to all cases indexed under a GE. Indices are features which discriminate between cases within a GE. An index, which may point to a more specific GE, or directly to a case, is composed of two terms: an index name and an index value (Fig. 3.3). The entire case memory is in fact a discrimination network where a node can be a GE, an index or a case. A case is retrieved by finding the GE with most norms in common with the problem description. Indices under the GE are traversed in order to find the case that contains most of the additional problem features. Storing a new case is performed in the same way, with the additional process of dynamically creating GEs for two cases (or two GEs) that end up under the same index. The memory structure of the Dynamic Memory Model is dynamic in the sense that similar parts of two case descriptions are dynamically generalized into a GE, and the cases are indexed in the GE by their discriminative features.

### 3.4.2 Case-based Ontology Repository

The knowledge repository with SubOs can be used to improve the reuse of domain knowledge for problem solving in the Semantic Grid. If we treat the knowledge repository as a case base with different SubOs like past cases, then sophisticated case memory models can be used to construct the knowledge repository for SubOs. In this section we extend the Dynamic Memory Model to organize SubOs for domain ontology reuse.

We can directly extend the basic elements of the Dynamic Memory Model to construct the case-based framework for ontology reuse. The knowledge memory structure of the repository can be illustrated as Fig. 3.4, which is a hierarchical structure of GEs and each GE contains three different types of objects, norms, indices and cases:

- **Norm**. The norms of a GE contain a collection of features common to all cases indexed under the GE, and each feature is a domain-specific class from ontology.
- **Index**. An index includes an index name, which is unique in the knowledge memory, and an index value, which is also composed of a collection of ontology classes. As indices should discriminate among cases within a GE, features of index value are complementary to norms of the same GE. An index may point directly to a case, or to a more specific GE.
- **Case**. SubOs extracted from ontology are wrapped as cases in the knowledge memory. Each case in the ontology repository contains three elements of a SubO and features the problem-solving context by a set of domain classes.

Being different from classic CBR systems, SubOs in this ontology repository are not directly retrieved and used as solutions to problems but as domain knowledge to support problem solving (as we will see later in Section 3.5). Problem-solving systems or agents can exploit the semantic relationships involved in SubOs to solve domain-specific problems.

Based on the representation in previous section, we propose a set of operations for manipulating the ontology repository in order to reuse ontology efficiently.

**SubO Retrieval**. Starting from the root GE, the input problem description is pushed down the hierarchical structure of the discrimination

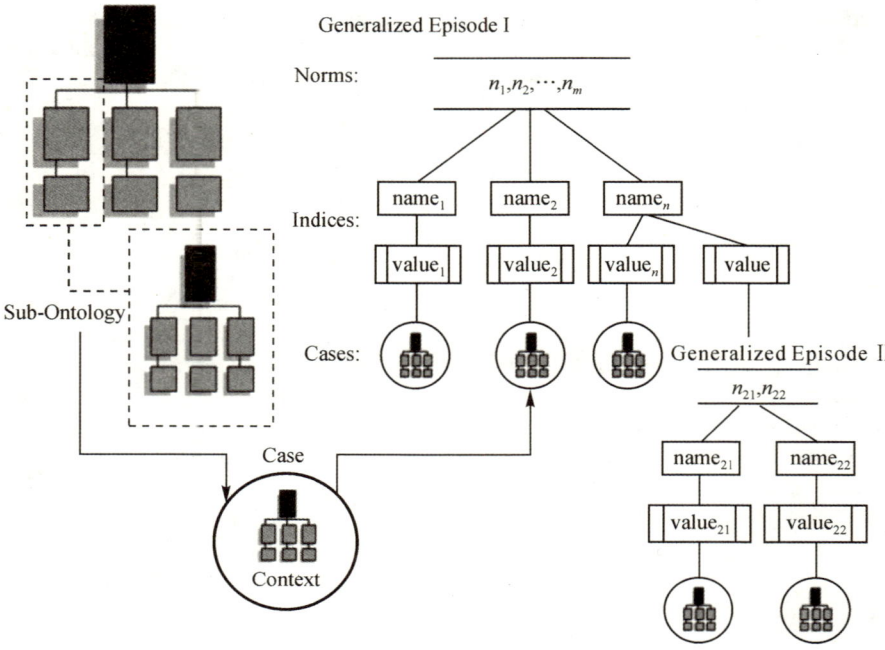

**Fig. 3.4.** The knowledge structure of the case-based ontology repository

network to retrieve the case. The input problem description $C_i$ can be represented by a tuple $< d_1, d_2, \ldots, d_n >$, norms of a GE can be represented as $< n_1, n_2, \ldots, n_m >$, and the index value can be represented as $< v_1, v_2, \ldots, v_k >$. The best matching mechanism is used to match the features of $C_i$ with the features of GE. The comparison can also be performed based on the edit distance or the Levenshtein distance (Levenshtein IV, 1966). The similarity between strings is often described as the edit distance: the number of changes (deletions, insertions, or substitutions) required to turn one string into another. However, we don't want to compare strings but two tuples. We can calculate the number of deletions, insertions, or substitution operations of features needed to turn $< d_1, d_2, \ldots, d_n >$ into $< n_1, n_2, \ldots, n_m >$. When $C_i$ matches the norms of a GE at best, cases under the GE are further distinguished based on their additional features to norms. Indices under that GE are traversed in order to find the index value $< v_1, v_2, \ldots, v_k >$ that has the shortest edit distance to the remaining list of features of $< d_1, d_2, \ldots, d_n >$. If the best matching index points to a case, it's just the required one; if the index points to a GE, the recursive process will be performed to find the case ultimately. Then the SubO wrapped in the retrieved case is reused to support problem-solving activities in the Semantic Grid.

## 3.4 Ontology Reuse for Grid-based Problem Solving

**SubO Storage.** SubOs that have supported problem-solving activities will be stored in the ontology repository. Newly extracted SubOs are wrapped as cases and storing a new case $C_n$ can be performed in a similar way to case retrieval; however, there will be some additional processes for case storage. After the best matching search, if there exists a GE whose norms match some features of $C_n$, $C_n$ will be stored under the GE. If there are no indices under the GE matching the remaining features of $C_n$, a new index will be created, with the remaining features as the index value. If there exists an index matching, the remaining features, two cases that end up under the same index will be integrated as a new GE, with their discriminative features as index values.

We can illustrate the usage of the case-based ontology repository with SubOs by a use case for reusing a large-scale TCM ontology to support TCM problem solving. Fig. 3.5 shows a small portion of the knowledge memory. A TCM formula, which can treat one or more diseases, is composed of one or more Chinese medicinal herbs. If users (say, a TCM doctor) want to reuse the TCM ontology, they can retrieve cases from the knowledge base. For example, assume the input case description $C_i$ is <*Formula, Disease, Ague, Diarrhea*> (the real-life meaning of this description can be to look for some TCM formulas that can treat ague or diarrhea), it is pushed down the hierarchical structure. As $C_i$ matches the norms of $GE_I$ at best in the knowledge base, it will be pushed in $GE_I$ and matched with indices within the GE. Indices are further distinguished by value and the case in the best-matched index will be retrieved. There are two indices (HA and SC) matching the remaining features of $C_i$ at best, with each having a feature in common with $C_i$. The current mechanism of our model will just select the index with the higher order, which is the index HA pointing to $GE_{II}$. Finally, the case <*LongHu Pellet, Headache, Diarrhea*> is retrieved from the knowledge base and the SubO (see Fig. 3.5) wrapped in the case can be reused to support the problem solving.

The SubO contains the semantic relationships that *LongHu Pellet* can be used to treat *Ague* or *Diarrhea*. SubOs that have supported the process of problem solving will be integrated into the knowledge base. Newly-arriving SubOs are wrapped with a problem-solving context as cases and stored in the knowledge memory. For example, a SubO about *LiuJunZi decoction* and *typhoid* can be represented as a case <*LiuJunZi Decoction, Typhoid*> and stored in the index BT of $GE_I$. However, there is already a case <*Baishu Drink, Typhoid*> in the index, so the two cases will be integrated in a new GE, say $GE_{III}$. The norms of the new GE can be <*Stomach-Nourishing Formula, Typhoid*>, because both *LiuJunZi decoction* and *Baishu drink* are kinds of stomach-nourishing formulas, which can be used to treat *typhoid*, according to the semantic relationships in the SubOs.

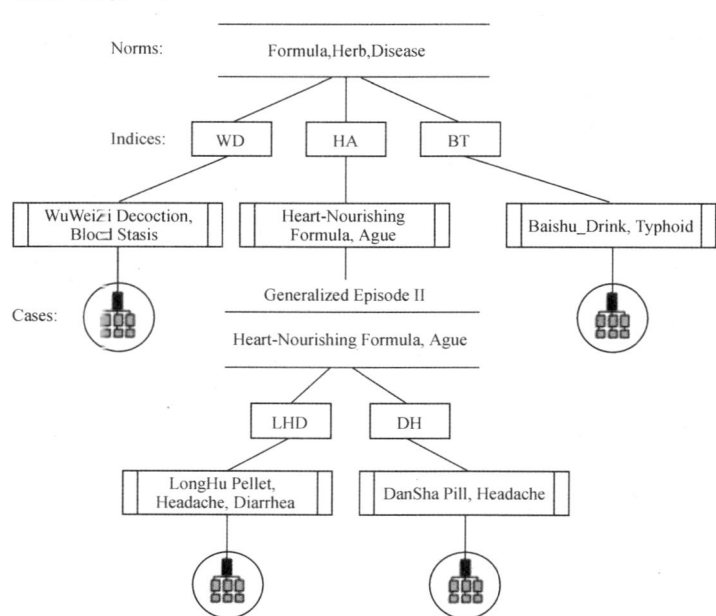

**Fig. 3.5.** A TCM use case for ontology reuse

## 3.5 Dynamic Problem Solving Based on SubO Evolution

By modeling the application components as operators and the solution as the final goal, the problem-solving process, to a certain extent, can be formulated as a task decomposition process. The process can intuitively be understood as the consecutive decomposition of a goal into sub-goals, forming a task graph eventually. In the Semantic Grid, this process can be achieved through resource matching and composition. During each of the problem-solving steps, domain knowledge is often needed for, say, service description matching so as to identify suitable service agents to fulfill sub-goals. Thus, problem-solving agents will have their problem-solving power restricted if the domain knowledge they possess is insufficient. The domain knowledge required by problem solving mainly comes from ontology. We have proposed the concept of SubO in Section 3.3. Our conjecture is that an agent specialized in a certain underlying sub-problem needs only particular SubOs from the whole ontology. This calls for the agent's capability to extract SubOs and keep on evolving them to form a specific knowledge base, emerging to be specialized in its own areas of concern. We believe that this capability is especially important for solving complex domain-specific problems where multiple ontologies corresponding to the knowledge of several domains are typically required.

Here we define sub-ontology evolution (Mao Y, Cheung WK, Wu Z, 2005b) as follows:

**Definition 3.4 (Sub-Ontology Evolution).** *The SubO evolution of a problem solving agent is defined as the process which involves autonomous extraction, integration, pruning and merging of some sub-structures of the agent's previously encountered domain ontologies, termed as sub-ontology, into its own localized repository of domain knowledge to support intelligent and efficient problem solving.*

Note that as we have mentioned before, there are various kinds of resources (data, services, etc.) involved in problem solving in the Semantic Grid. We will only focus on the most common resource in the Semantic Grid, i.e. service, in this chapter, and illustrate the problem solving mechanisms and process from the point of service.

### 3.5.1 Sub-Ontology Manipulations

As the dynamic sub-set of ontology, SubO contains context-specific domain knowledge required for problem solving. Based on the formal specification in the previous section, we propose a set of operations for manipulating SubOs from domain ontologies.

**Operations for Extraction**

**Traverse.** The traversing operation can be defined as a tuple $T = <c, R, n, O>$, where $c$ is the starting class for traversal, $n$ is the depth limit, $R$ is a set of constraint relationships and $O$ is a set of links to the source domain ontologies. The operation will return a set of facts and axioms $K$ from the ontology.

The process of traversal can be treated as traversing the semantic graph of an ontology:

- First, starting with the class $c$, explore the graph in each direction along its adjacent relationships that appear in $R$.
- The traversal will fall into several branches. For each class on the traversing path, its direct knowledge is allocated to a set, if not already in one.
- Each traversing branch or path terminates when a depth of $n$ has been reached. Assume $c_l$ is the last class in a traversing path and the classes in $D(c_i)$ are called edge classes whose definition may not be allocated incompletely.

**Extract.** The extracting operation can be defined as a tuple $E = <C, R, n, O>$, where $C$ is a set of contextual classes, $n$ is the depth of the extraction, $R$ is a set of constraint relationships, and $O$ is a set of links to the source domain ontologies. The operation will return a SubO, $B$. The process of extraction can be treated as a group of traversing operations, i.e.

each of the contextual classes, performing a traversing operation and combining resulting sets together. All classes except edge classes, whose direct knowledge is not completely included in the set, will be eliminated from the set. The final set is just the knowledge set of a SubO.

**Operations for Adjustment**
**Augment.** The augmenting operation can be defined as a tuple $A = <C', B, O>$, where $C'$ is a list of new contextual classes to be appended to $C$, $B$ is the original SubO, and $O$ is a set of links to the source domain ontologies. The operation will return an updated SubO, $B_a$.

After appending a list of contextual classes to the original SubO, the knowledge set has to be extended. Any content that can be allocated by traversing from the classes in the list should be extracted from related ontologies and integrated into the set.

**Prune.** The pruning operation can be defined as a tuple $P = <C', B>$, where $C'$ is a list of contextual classes to be eliminated from $C$, and $B$ is the original SubO. The operation will return an updated SubO, $B_p$.

After a list of contextual classes have been removed from the original SubO, the self-contained set has to be trimmed. Any content that can be allocated by traversing from the classes in the list should be removed from the set.

**Re-Context.** The re-contexting operation can be defined as a tuple $F = <C', B, O>$, where $C'$ is a new set of contextual classes to the SubO, $B$ is the original SubO, and $O$ is a set of links to the source domain ontologies. The operation will return an updated SubO, $B_r$.

Re-Contexting means the problem-solving context for a SubO has changed, which is perhaps the most complex operation in the model. If the contextual classes of a SubO changed, the content of the corresponding knowledge set needs to be changed (augmented, pruned or re-contexted) according to the new set of contextual classes.

**Merge.** The merging operation can be defined as a tuple $M = <B_1, B_2, O>$, where $B_1$ and $B_2$ are two SubOs to be merged, and $O$ is a set of links to the source domain ontologies. The operation will return a new merged SubO, $B_m$.

We can simply combine the knowledge sets of each SubO together to get $S$ of $B_m$. It is easy to prove the conjunction of knowledge sets is still self-contained, but probably with redundancy. However, there must be a mechanism to eliminate the redundancy.

**Operations for Process**
**Compare.** The comparing operation can be defined as a tuple $C = <B_1, B_2, O>$, where $B_1$ and $B_2$ are two SubOs to be compared, and $O$ is a set of links to the related domain ontologies. The operation will return a degree of similarity between the two SubOs.

The comparison can be performed based on the edit distance or the Levenshtein distance. There are two strategies for comparing two SubOs. One

3.5 Dynamic Problem Solving Based on SubO Evolution    69

is based on the edit distance of two sets of contextual classes, which is the number of changes required to turn one list of classes into another list. The other is based on the edit distance of two knowledge sets. Therefore we calculate the number of deletions, insertions, or substitutions of ontology elements needed to turn one set into another.

### 3.5.2 Terminology

Before specifying the details of the problem-solving approach, we give here some basic definitions involved.

**Definition 3.5 (Problem Description).** *A domain-specific problem can be abstracted as a description. A problem description is a collection of context-specific features about a problem and each feature is a domain class.*

Note that to identify the features of a problem-solving context always involves transforming a natural user description to an explicit semantic description of the context, which falls into the fields of human computer interaction and natural language processing. However, due to the focus of this chapter, it will not be further discussed, so we assume problem description has already been identified before problem solving.

**Definition 3.6 (Service Description).** *In the Semantic Grid, application components can be implemented as a service. Each service has a pair of input-output parameters in the service description, which are also domain classes. Here we do not consider services with multiple inputs and outputs, which can be composed by several atom services.*

**Definition 3.7 (Task).** *A domain-specific problem is composed of one or more tasks, which are also domain-specific and can be represented by a condition-goal pair. A task can be decomposed into sub-tasks and the original goal can be divided into sub-goals.*

**Definition 3.8 (Problem Solving).** *A problem is said to be solved as long as all tasks in the problem can be finished. If the condition-goal pair of a task is matched with the IO parameters of a service agent, then we can say that the task can be finished by the service. Here the realistic execution of service is not taken into account.*

### 3.5.3 Problem-Solving Environment

We can regard a distributed problem-solving environment with multi-agents as a set of application components. There are three types of agents (see Fig. 3.6): (1) service agents that can provide some specific information or functionalities as described in their service profiles (classified into information-gathering service and world-altering service in the Web Service); (2) domain ontology agents that provide access to large-scale domain ontologies; and (3) problem-solving agents that can compose and coordinate a set of service agents for solving problems. The latter two are key components in the proposed agent-oriented architecture.

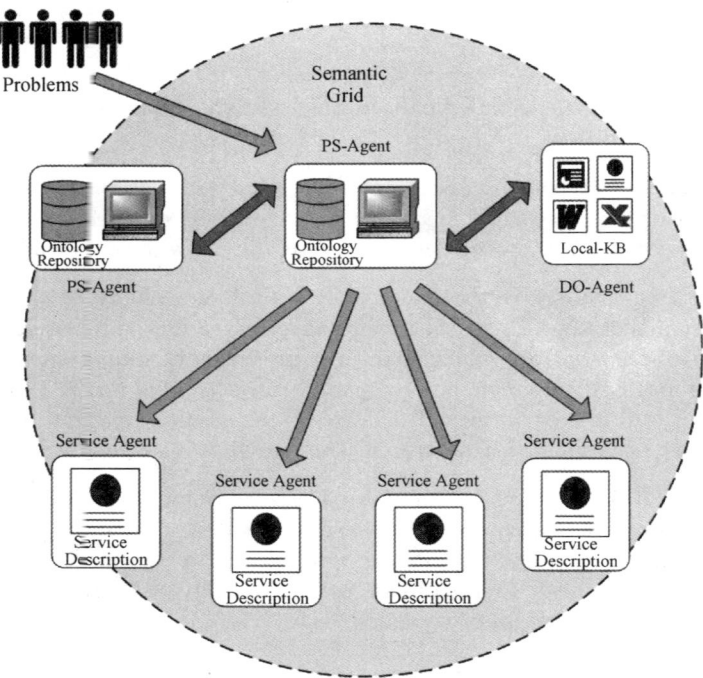

**Fig. 3.6.** The problem-solving environment with multi-agents

**Domain Ontology Agents (DO-Agent).** Each domain ontology agent is an ontology Grid node that preserves a large-scale domain-specific ontology in its Local-KB and provides a set of basic operations on the ontology. Note that we assume domain ontology is an invariant, compared with SubOs being dynamically updated. DO-Agent can provide various semantic views for knowledge consumers.

**Problem-Solving Agents (PS-Agent).** Each problem-solving agent maintains a local centralized ontology repository with SubOs from source ontologies. There is also a domain independent problem solver, which should be able to work with DO-Agent to compose service agents in a goal-directed manner, where a problem-solving ontology is installed in the PS-Agent which holds the knowledge of problem-solving *perse*, and can be represented by some extended version of OWL-S (OWL-S, 2004).

### 3.5.4 Sub-Ontology Based Problem Solving

Domain knowledge is used to support problem solving in terms of SubOs in the Semantic Grid. Our main objective is to illustrate how different aspects or views of large-scale domain ontologies, with the help of past collaborative problem-solving history, can naturally diffuse to a set of distributed PS-Agents; each becomes specialized in solving domain-specific problems via self-evolution. We do not care about the details of problem solving but how the Semantic Grid can support problem solving. The following is the detailed process (see Fig. 3.7) of the proposed sub-ontology evolution approach for problem solving in the Semantic Grid:

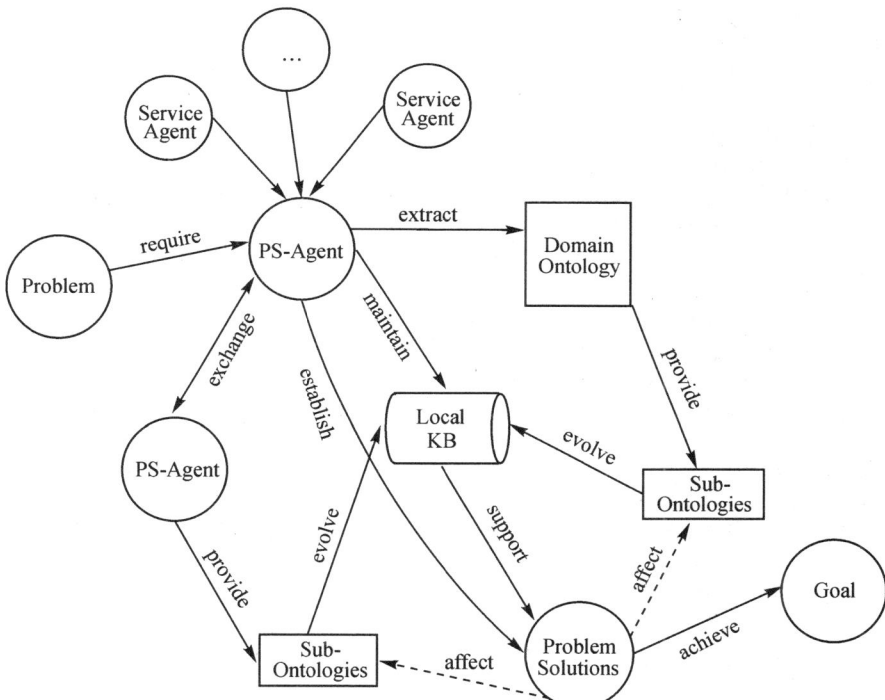

**Fig. 3.7.** The SubO-based problem solving approach

- A problem is delivered to a PS-Agent relevant to the problem description. For each task in the problem, the PS-Agent first looks for service agents that exactly match the task according to the service description. For example, a service agent with class $A$ as input and class $B$ as output directly matches the task $< A, B >$. If all tasks of the problem can be matched with a service agent, the problem is solved. If not, the PS-Agent

will use the domain knowledge it possesses to perform task decomposition and service composition.
- The PS-Agent first selects and retrieves domain-specific SubOs from its Local-KB according to the problem context. Unsolved tasks are decomposed into sub-tasks and service agents that can finish sub-tasks are composed together. There are two kinds of composition: semantic-based and literal-based. In semantic-based composition, service agents are composed according to the semantic relationships of their IO parameters and the semantics come from SubO. Transforming domain knowledge into knowledge exactly required by agents may be involved.

  For example, there exists no service agent that has $A$ as input and $B$ as output, but there exists a service agent (named $a_1$) that has $A$ as input and $C$ as output and a service agent ($a_2$) that has $D$ as input and $B$ as output. According to a SubO, $C$ is related to $D$ through a relationship $R$, so the PA-Agent may compose $a_1$ with $a_2$ to finish the task.
- If no appropriate SubOs in the Local-KB can be reused, the PA-Agent will turn to its adjacent PA-Agents (based on some P2P strategy) in the Semantic Grid to look for relevant domain knowledge that could be distributed in the Grid. If the aforementioned P2P knowledge search succeeds, it means that there exists at least one adjacent PA-Agent that specializes in solving the current problem and problem solving can proceed.
- If the P2P search fails, it implies a lack of relevant domain knowledge in the agent's proximity. The PA-Agent will try to identify a relevant DO-Agent directly to support the semantic-based service agent composition. SubOs potentially required for the composition will be extracted accordingly from the domain ontology of DO-Agent.
- The composed service agent flow obtained with the help of the SubOs will then be executed. SubOs of a PA-Agent can evolve by the SubO manipulations through a **mark mechanism**. A SubO can be divided into several parts by its contextual classes and each has an initial mark on extracting the SubO. During the process of problem solving, the parts of a SubO, which have successfully supported composing service agents to finish tasks, will gain a positive increment to their marks. As mark is accumulative, different parts will get different marks after solving plenty of problems. The parts with higher marks will be augmented while those with lower marks will be merged, pruned or even discarded.

We can illustrate the application of the SubO-based problem-solving approach through a TCM related problem.

- The application domain is TCM. Assume a user had a problem about acupuncture and submitted it to a medical agent of a TCM Semantic Grid.

3.6 The Relationship between Problem Solving and the Semantic Grid    73

- As the medical agent had never solved problems about acupuncture before, it lacked related domain knowledge and had to turn to a TCM ontology in the Grid.
- The DO-Agent in the TCM Semantic Grid managed and preserved a large-scale TCM ontology, which involved a local-ontology about acupuncture.
- The medical agent accessed the DO-Agent to extract required SubOs according to the problem-solving context and cached the SubOs in its ontology repository for future reuse.
- The medical agent allocated related resources and services (e.g., HER, TCM literature databases, TCM expert systems) in the Semantic Grid according to the semantic relationships involved in SubOs.
- Several medical agents cooperated with each other to solve the problem and generated a solution to the problem. The user verified the solution with the problem.
- The results of the problem solving were fed back to the system and the SubOs in the ontology repository of the medical agent evolved as cases in the ontology repository.
- The medical agent received a similar problem about acupuncture from another user, and it reacted to the problem immediately by reusing the domain knowledge in its local ontology repository. The problem was solved efficiently and quickly.

As the SubOs of different PA-Agents continue to evolve, a community of specialized PA-Agents will be created in the Semantic Grid. Faced with similar problem contexts next time, those PA-Agents can solve problems based on reusing the existing SubOs in their local repositories immediately. Note that consulting first the adjacent PA-Agents is to maximize the reuse of existing SubOs and in the long run results in a Semantic Grid system efficient enough, on average, for serving on-demand problem-solving requests.

## 3.6 The Relationship between Problem Solving and the Semantic Grid

The problem solving approach in this chapter is not about the fundamental infrastructure of the Semantic Grid but a high-level theory model of the Semantic Grid. As we have mentioned before, the Grid theory is close to problem solving on its emergence and cooperative problem solving is just one of the important goals of the Grid. We have introduced the infrastructure and representative model of the Semantic Grid and our ultimate goal is to utilize the Semantic Grid to solve real-life domain-specific problems. In other words, the Semantic Grid is the underlying platform for problem solving-systems and problem-solving systems are extensions to the ability of the Semantic Grid. A problem-solving system makes use of the Semantic Grid to manage and reuse domain knowledge (ontology), which is required to support

74    3 Dynamic Problem Solving in the Semantic Grid

dynamic and efficient problem solving; and the results of problem solving are fed back to problem-solving systems based on the SubO evolution mechanism to enhance the ability to solve a kind of problems. We can illustrate the relationship between the problem-solving system and the Semantic Grid.

We can construct a PSE based on the Semantic Grid infrastructure to manage and reuse domain knowledge to solve complex domain-specific problems and improve the problem-solving ability by using the SubO evolution approach.

- We can manage and reuse large-scale domain knowledge efficiently based on the distributed features of the Semantic Grid.
- We can solve complex domain-specific problems based on the service features of the Semantic Grid.
- We can improve the problem-solving ability based on the semantic features of the Semantic Grid.

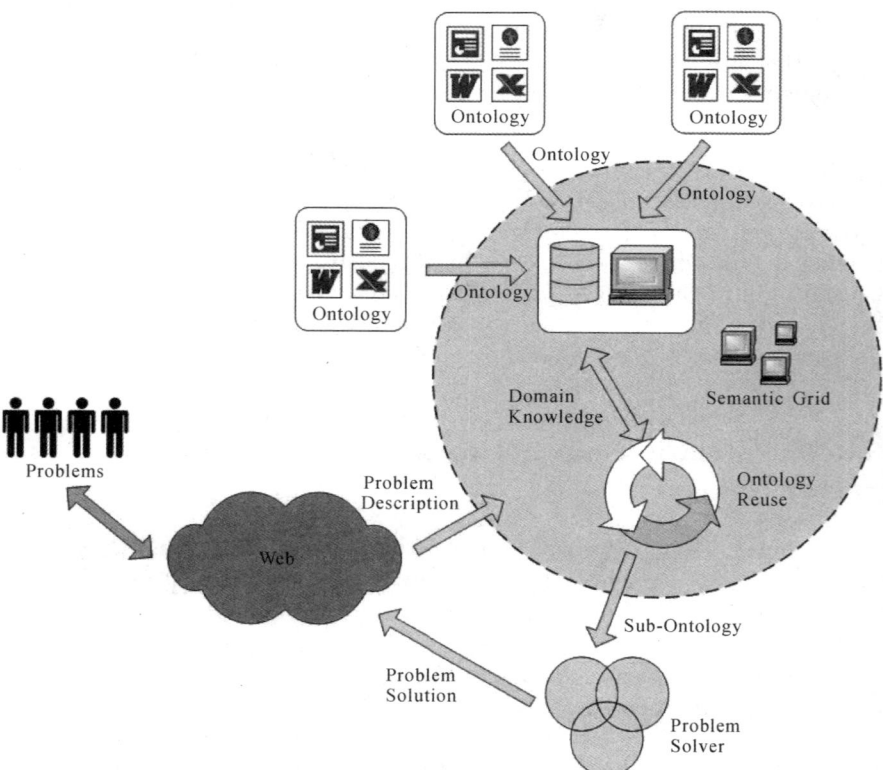

**Fig. 3.8.** The relationship between problem-solving system and Semantic Grid

## 3.7 Related Works

Problem solving in the Semantic Grid is an emerging research area and there is no unified theory or principle. However, researchers have tried to solve the problem by using different approaches from different points of view, especially in the e-Science field where the Semantic Grid emerged, and where there have been some real tools and projects.

(Houstis EN, Rice JR, 2000) reviews the current state of the problem solving environment (PSE) and imagines the future of PSE. The goal of PSE technology is to exploit the existing enormous power of hardware and algorithms for delivering cheap and fast problem solutions. They argue that a PSE consists of several components, including natural language, solvers, intelligence, and a software bus. Future PSEs will use essentially all resources of future computing technologies like net-centric facilities, dynamic and collaborative computations, knowledge discovery and learning, software reuse, human-machine interaction, etc.

(Tao F, Shadbolt N, Chen L, et al, 2004) proposes an e-Science pilot project in the domain of Engineering Design Search and Optimization (EDSO) called GEODISE. They illustrate the potential of applying Semantic Web technology in GEODISE through a semantic web based knowledge management approach. They show how ontologies and semantically enriched instances are acquired through knowledge acquisition and resource annotation. Their work shows the potential of using semantic web technology to manage and reuse knowledge in e-Science.

(Bachler M, Shum SB, Chen-Burger YH, et al, 2004) describe the CoAKTinG project that aims to advance the state of the art in collaborative mediated spaces for the Semantic Grid. They present an overview of the hypertext and knowledge based tools which have been deployed to augment existing collaborative environments, and the ontology which is used to exchange structure, promote enhanced process tracking, and aid navigation of resources before, while, and after a collaboration occurs. While the primary focus of the project has been to support e-Science, they also explore the similarities and application of CoAKTinG technology as part of a human-centred design approach to e-Learning.

(Li M, Santen P, Walker DW, et al, 2004) present a service-oriented model for the Semantic Grid called SGrid. Each Grid service in SGrid is a Web service with certain domain knowledge. A Web service oriented wrapper generator has been implemented to automatically wrap legacy codes as Grid services exposed as Web services. Each wrapped Grid service is supplemented with domain ontology and registered with a Semantic Grid Service Ontology Repository using a Semantic Services Register. Using the wrapper generator, a finite element based computational fluid dynamics (CFDs) code has been wrapped as a Grid service, which can be published, discovered and reused in SGrid.

(Majithia S, Walker DW, Gray WA, 2004) proposes a framework to facilitate automated synthesis of scientific experiment workflows in Semantic Grids based on high-level goal specification. Their framework has two main features which distinguish it from other work in this area. First, they propose a dynamic and adaptive mechanism for automating the construction of experiment workflows. Second, they distinguish between different levels of abstraction of loosely coupled experiment workflows to facilitate reuse and sharing of experiments. They illustrate the framework using a real world application scenario in the physics domain involving the detection of gravitational waves from astrophysical sources.

In summary, problem solving in the Semantic Grid is still in its infancy and most research efforts focus on models or frameworks. As the theories and technology of the Semantic Grid progress and evolve, there will be more and more real-life systems and applications for problem solving in the Semantic Grid.

## 3.8 Summary and Conclusion

In this chapter, we introduced the basic concepts and problems associated with problem solving. Considering that problem solving in the Semantic Grid needs large-scale domain knowledge (ontology), we described the approach for ontology management and reuse to support problem solving. We also presented a SubO evolution mechanism for dynamic problem solving. The results of problem solving can be fed back to the system to form domain knowledge that is more adaptive to problem solving. After we have solved the problem of ontology management and reuse, how to achieve high-level semantic-based intelligence and completely on-demand problem solving will become a *bottleneck*, which may require more theories and methods from the field of AI. As a new technology, the Semantic Grid is far from being mature, likewise problem solving in the Semantic Grid. However, there will emerge more and more problem solving systems and methods in the Semantic Grid along with the advance of the Semantic Web and Grid technology.

# References

Aamodt A, Plaza E (1994) Case-based reasoning: Foundational issues, methodological variations, and system approaches. AI Communications 7(1):39-52

Allen G, Benger W, Goodale T, et al (2000) The Cactus Code: a problem solving environment for the Grid. In Proceedings of the Ninth IEEE International Symposium on High Performance Distributed Computing 1:253-260

Ashburner M, Ball CA, Blake JA, Botstein D, et al (2000) Gene Ontology: Tool for the unification of biology. The Gene Ontology Consortium. Nat. Genet. 25:25-29

Bachler M, Shum SB, Chen-Burger YH, et al (2004) Collaboration in the Semantic Grid: a basis for e-Learning. International Conference on Intelligent Tutoring Systems Workshop 1:881-904

Berners-Lee T, Hendler J, Lassila O (2001) The Semantic Web. Scientific American 284(5):34-43

Bodenreider O (2004) Unified medical language system (umls): Integrating biomedical terminology. Nucleic Acids Research 32(D):D267-D270

Buvac S, Fikes R (1995) A declarative formalization of knowledge translation. The 4th International Conference on Information and Knowledge Management 1:340-347

Cannataro M, Comito C, Schiavo FL, Veltri P (2003) PROTEUS: A Grid based problem solving environment for bioinformatics. Workshop on Data Mining Ontology for Grid Programming (KGGI) Available at: http://www.comp.hkbu.edu.hk/~cib/2004/Feb/cib_vol3no1_article1.pdf

Durfee EH, Lesser VR, Corkill DD (1989) Trends in cooperative distributed problem solving. IEEE Transactions on Knowledge and Data Engineering KDE-1(1):63-83

Durfee EH, Lesser VR, Corkill DD (1991) Distributed problem solving. The encyclopedia of artificial intelligence (2nd Edition). John Wiley & Sons, 83-127

Ferber J (1999) Multi-agent system: an introduction to distributed artificial intelligence. Harlow: Addison Wesley Longman, 509

Foster I, Kesselman C (Eds.) (1999) The Grid: blueprint for a new computing infrastructure. Morgan Kaufmann, San Francisco, CA, 677

Foster I, Kesselman C, Tuecke S (2001) The anatomy of the Grid: Enabling scalable virtual organizations. International Journal of High Performance Computing Applications 15:200-222

Ghidini C, Giunchiglia F (2001) Local models semantics, or contextual reasoning = locality + compatibility. Artificial Intelligence 127:221-259

Gruber T (1993) A translation approach to portable ontology specifications. Knowledge Acquisition 5(2):199-220

Houstis EN, Rice JR (2000) Future problem solving environments for computational science. Mathematics and Computers in Simulation 54(4):243-257

Laszewski G, Foster I, Gawor J, et al (2000) CoG kits: A bridge between commodity distributed computing and high-performance grids. ACM Java Grande 2000 Conference 1:97-106

Levenshtein IV (1966) Binary Codes Capable of Correcting Deletions, Insertions, and Reversals. Cybernetics and Control Theory 10(8):707-710

Li M, Santen P, Walker DW, et al (2004) SGrid: A service-oriented model for the Semantic Grid. Future Generation Computer Systems 20(1):7-18

Majithia S, Walker DW, Gray WA (2004) Automating scientific experiments on the Semantic Grid. International Semantic Web Conference (ISWC):365-379

Mao Y, Cheung WK, Wu Z, Liu J (2005a) Dynamic sub-ontology evolution for collaborative problem solving. AAAI Fall Symposium v FS-05-01:1-8

Mao Y, Cheung WK, Wu Z, Liu J (2005b) Sub-ontology evolution for service composition with application to distributed e-Learning. IEEE International Conference on Tools with Artificial Intelligence 1:14-16

Mao Y, Wu Z, Chen H (2004) Semantic browser: An intelligent client for DartGrid. International Conference on Computational Science LNCS 3036:470-473

McCarthy J, Buvac S (1994) Formalizing context (Expanded Notes). Technical Note STAN-CS-TN-94-13. Stanford University, Avaiblable at: http://www-formal.stanford.edu/jmc/mccarthy-buvac-98/index.html

Nilsson N (1971) Problem-solving methods in artificial intelligence. McGraw-Hill, New York, 1-255

Noy NF, Musen MA (2004) Specifying ontology views by traversal. International Semantic Web Conference LNCS 3298:713-725

OWL-S (2004) http://www.w3.org/Submission/OWL-S/

Schank R (1982) Dynamic memory: A theory of reminding and learning in computers and people. Cambridge University Press, 240

Tao F, Shadbolt N, Chen L, et al (2004) Semantic Web based content enrichment and knowledge reuse in e-Science. International Conference on Ontologies, Databases, and Applications of Semantics for Large Scale Information Systems LNCS 3290:654-669

Wooldridge M (2002) An introduction to multiagent systems. John Wiley & Sons (Chichester, England), 1-366

Wu Z, Mao Y, Chen H (2004) Semantic view for Grid services. IEEE International Conference on Services Computing 1:329-335

Xue G, Fairman MJ, Cox SJ (2002) Exploiting Web technologies for Grid architecture. Cluster Computing and the Grid 1:272-273

# 4

# Trust Computing in the Semantic Grid

**Abstract:** Enabling trust to achieve more effective and efficient interaction is a key issue for the Semantic Grid vision. In this chapter we discuss an integrated and computational trust model based on statistical decision theory and Bayesian sequential analysis. The model helps users select an appropriate service provider within the Semantic Grid environment. The model combines a variety of sources of information to assist users in making correct decisions according to their preferences, which are expressed by prior information and utility function. It takes three types of costs (operational cost, opportunity cost and service charges) into account during the process of trust evaluation.

## 4.1 Introduction

The philosophy of the Semantic Grid is that anybody can produce information or provide services or consume and enjoy anyone else's information and services in an open environment full of uncertainty and dynamics. However there is currently a major gap between the practice and the aspiration of the Semantic Grid, in which there is a high degree of easy-to-use and seamless automation and in which there is flexible collaboration and computation on a global scale. To fully achieve this automation requires much more to be "machine-processable" and much less human intervention. The notion of agents as the entities that procure and deliver services in a dynamic, open and uncertain environment has been given more attention both for the Semantic Web and distributed systems and (Roure D, Jennings NR, Shadbolt NR, 2005) advocated the application of the ideas of agent-based computing (principally autonomous problem solvers that can act and interact in flexible ways) to achieve the necessary degree of flexibility and automation in the Semantic Grid. Multi-agent system research addresses a problem space which is closely aligned to that of the Semantic Grid. In particular, agent-based computing that brings dynamic decision-making, decentralization, coordination, and autonomous behavior needs to be brought into the conception of Grid services and evidently becomes part of the distributed scientific infrastructure and fundamental building block of the Semantic Grid vision.

Achieving the full richness of the Semantic Grid vision brings with it many significant research challenges. One of these challenges is modeling trust properly and exploring techniques for establishing computational trust and determining the provenance and quality of content and services in Grid systems. The Semantic Grid, conceived as a collection of agents, brings new opportunities to trust research. We need to face this important issue of determining how trustworthy each information source is and which service we should choose according to this trustworthiness. One solution would be to require all information in the Semantic Grid to be always consistent and absolute true. But due to its inherent magnitude and diversity of sources, this would be nearly impossible. Trust is a response to uncertainty and uncertainty can be considered as the lack of adequate information to make a decision. Uncertainty causes problems because it may prevent us from making the best decision and may even cause a bad decision to be made. Trust has been extensively studied from various disciplinary perspectives, including sociology, e-commerce, multi-agent systems, and security. However, because of the technical nature of many solutions, there are few signs of consensus emerging in this field. But some fundamental questions should be answered first, when trying to find the best way of modeling trust. These are what the exact meaning trust is from the Semantic Grid point of view, what information is relevant when evaluating trust, and how to combine information from various sources to produce final trust value. Scalable probabilistic approximation seems a direction for future research when dealing with this uncertainty.

In this chapter we try to answer these questions and employ Bayesian analysis and statistical decision theory to model trust and give trust evaluation a formal probabilistic interpretation. Our model combines prior and reputation information to produce a composite and comprehensive assessment of an agent's possible quality and quantify three types of cost: operational cost, opportunity cost and service charges (including consultant and final service) incurred when communicating or dealing with other agents.

## 4.2 Trust for the Semantic Grid

Before discussing the trust model in detail, we would like to discuss the following three aspects of trust: characteristic features of trust, the cost and utility incurred during the trust evaluation. We believe that in the best trust model various aspects should be taken into consideration, such as context, risk, cost, and task undertaken.

## 4.2.1 Characteristic Features of Trust

Firstly, we outline characteristic features of trust drawing on research by (Ding L, Zhou L, Finin T, 2003) and pay close attention to the problem of trust evaluation in an open and dynamic environment such as the Semantic Grid. Significant trust features include the following.

*Trust is context dependent.* Trust is more dependent on context. An agent may be trusted to do one task with one set of resources, yet not trusted to do a different task with the same resources. For example, you may trust a doctor to cure your diseases, but you might not trust him to fix your computer. Associating trust measurement with a specific context will inevitably increase complexity, but nevertheless is crucial for deriving meaningful trust values.

*Trust is subjective.* Trust is social knowledge that is variable from one individual to another and represents an individual value judgment, especially when selecting an appropriate service provider. For example, a high-income person may prefer expensive service with good quality, whereas a low-income person is likely to choose cheaper service with a reasonable price that he can bear.

*Trust has numerical value.* A trust relation is linked to a numerical value that represents the degree of trust. The meaning and form of the value varies with approach and application. Some representatives of value estimating are Boolean logics, multi-valued logics, fuzzy logics, classical probabilities, and discrete rankings.

*Trust is a binary and asymmetric relation.* A trust relation has two parties. They are trustor and trustee. It is asymmetric since "$A$ trust $B$" does not necessarily imply "$B$ trust $A$". Moreover, the degree of "$A$ trust $B$" is not always equal to that of "$B$ trust $A$".

*Trust is conditionally transitive.* Generally, if $A$ has trust $u$ in $B$ and $B$ has trust $v$ in $C$, then $A$ should have some trust $t$ in $C$, which is a function of $u$ and $v$. But it does not always come about, especially in security. For instance, if $A$ distrusts $B$ regarding a specific context and in turn, $B$ distrusts $C$ in that context, it is possible that $A$ will give $C$ a relatively higher rating. That is, if $A$ and $B$ hold opposite views, as $B$ and $C$ do, it may mean that $A$ and $C$ are actually close to one another. On the other hand, $A$ may distrust $C$ even more than $A$ distrusts $B$, the logic being if $A$ distrusts $B$, and $B$ cannot even trust $C$, then $C$ must be very untrustworthy. Though trust is not strictly transitive, we still believe this transitivity exists here.

*Trust is dynamic and temporal.* Since trust is learned from past observations, trust values evolve with new observation and experience. Generally, the more we take these observations, the more exactly we estimate the value of trust.

82    4 Trust Computing in the Semantic Grid

### 4.2.2 Cost and Utility

The main point of a trust model is to provide a way to operate under uncertainty, not taking too many risks, not missing too many opportunities, not deliberating too long before making commitments. Therefore, before setting up a plan of interaction between agents it is necessary to understand the risks and benefits associated with the trust evaluation. There are many different kinds of costs and benefits an agent might incur when communicating or dealing with other agents and the trust model should balance these costs and benefits. We begin by extending the viewpoint of (O'Hara K, Alani H, Kalfoglou Y, Shadbolt N, 2004) and discussing three types of costs: operational cost, opportunity cost, and service charge, and continue by introducing the utility function that is used to reflect the preferences of the agent's owner.

*Operational Cost.* Operational cost is the expense of computing and estimating trust value. In other words, this is the cost of setting up and operating the whole trust plan. Therefore, the more complex the algorithm is, the higher the cost is expected to be. If the agent is part of a network where transitivity strategy is adopted, it will incur some additional cost to analyze network structure.

*Opportunity Cost.* Opportunity cost is the cost of missing some possibility of making a better decision via further investigation. Generally, the more observations the lower the opportunity costs.

*Service Charge.* Service providers differ from each other not only in their quality of services but also in their charge. A service charge can be divided into two types that are consultant and final service charge. *Consultant service charge* (or *consultant fee*) is incurred when an agent asks for the opinions of other agents who (maybe a professional in a given domain) charge for their opinions. *Final service charge* is what will be paid to the selected provider agent who provides fee-based services.

*Utility Function.* As mentioned above, a poor person and a rich person usually have different preferences for services, as large or small scale companies do. To work mathematically with ideas of "preferences", it will be necessary to assign numbers indicating how much something is valued. Such numbers are called *utilities*, and textitutility theory deals with the development of such numbers. *Utility function*[1] can be constructed to state preferences and will be used to estimate the possible consequences of the decisions.

---

[1] Note that a gain is just a negative loss and maximizing utility is equal to minimizing loss, so lost function can simply be defined as the negative of utility function. (Milgram S, 1976) introduces a useful method for constructing utility function following a set of "rationality axioms" and recommends some standard loss functions such as squared-error loss, linear loss and "0-1" loss.

### 4.2.3 Distributed vs. Centralized

Traditionally, trust is managed and maintained by a centralized system. Typical examples are some rating systems such as *eBay* for e-businesses and security systems with a trusted third party or trusted authorities. The Semantic Grid, as a collection of agents, will be highly distributed. In such a structure the idea of a centralized authority is hard to sustain, though such authorities are useful for fostering trust. In addition, (Roure D, Jennings NR, Shadbolt NR, 2005) points out that the degree of trust of a trusted authority may drop as the number of trustees increases. Moreover another shortcoming of such an approach is that it derives values of "trustworthiness" that are not personalized for the individuals using them. So these trust models fail to capture the individuality of an agent in assessing the reliability of an interaction partner.

Much as in the development of the World Wide Web, in which there was no attempt made to centrally control the quality of information, Web services are globally distributed without centralized control or a globally agreed trust relationship. Therefore we believe that it is infeasible to do so on the Semantic Grid. Each agent should be able to make subjective judgments about other agents with respect to the services they claim to be able to supply. Given the "no central authority" nature of an open and dynamic system, agents will typically be unwilling to rely solely on a single centralized trust service.

### 4.2.4 Semantics of Information

(O'Hara K, Alani H, Kalfoglou Y, Shadbolt N, 2004) pointed out that scalable probabilistic approximation is a direction for future research. We base our model on statistical decision theory and Bayesian sequential analysis and give trust a strict mathematical interpretation in terms of probability theory. We make the assumption that the small-world phenomenon occurs in our model which hypothesizes that any pair of objects in a random network will be connected by a relatively short chain of random acquaintances (Milgram S, 1976). Mailgram's original studies indicated that any two people in the world were separated by only a small number of acquaintances (theorized to be six in the original work). Since then, studies have shown that many complex networks share the common features of the small-world phenomenon.

Consider a scenario in which a user (*initiator* agent) wants to find a service provider (*provider* agent) to fulfill a special task in the Semantic Grid, and his concern is which provider may be the most suitable for him. Assume that he maintains a list of acquaintances or neighbors (*consultant* agents), and each acquaintance has a *reliability* factor that denotes the degree to which this acquaintance's statements can be believed. Each agent also has a set of acquaintances and every pair of agents ($A$ and $B$) who are acquainted with each other are connected by two directed edges with a certain reliability factor. Note that because belief is not symmetrical, the reliability factors on two directed edges are not always equal. One represents to what degree $A$ believes $B$'s statements, the other represents to what degree $B$ believes $A$'s statements. During the process of his evaluation on the quality of different providers and in making his decision in selecting the best one among them, he can "gossip" with his acquaintances by exchanging information about their opinions on the providers' quality, termed statement. This process can be described as using the strategy of exploiting *transitivity*. The idea of this strategy is that an agent sends a message out to request opinions on the quality of agents who can provide a given service. The network of acquaintances of that agent will then either send back an opinion based on experience, or pass the message onto its acquaintances, many of whom are unknown to the first agent. The aim is to enhance the scope of an agent's knowledge by exploring the network feature of agent communities to bring in information from other, unknown, agents. We call it the reputation of a given provider agent that integrates a number of opinions from acquaintances and acquaintances of acquaintances. Besides *reputation* information, we also consider initiator agent's *prior* information based on direct experience from past interactions with the provider agent and the various relationships that may exist between them (e.g. owned by the same organization, relationships derived from relationships between the agents' owners in real life such as friendship or relatives). And then the trust can be generated by incorporating prior and reputation information, in our opinion.

When sending data across the Semantic Grid, a uniform data exchange format is required. For example, consider the situation of a user deciding which drug is appropriate for treating his influenza according to his symptoms. Two of the main factors affecting his decision are the effectiveness and price of the drug. We assume that the influenza has four symptoms: headache, fever, cough and snivel, and it has five distinct scales (serious, heavy, moderate, slight and normal) to describe each symptom. The symptoms of a particular patient can be represented in the format of RDF statement as follows.

```
<rdf:Description rdf:about="symptoms">
  <headache>slight</headache>
  <fever>normal</fever>
  <cough>moderate</cough>
  <snivel>heavy</snivel>
</rdf:Description>
```

In our system each user has an agent that is responsible for tracing and recording the owner's private information and preferences, communicating or dealing with agents of other local systems, and assisting its owner to solve problems and make decisions. In this case the agent will send the above RDF statement to the corresponding agents of the systems that are able to reason with this statement and give the suggestions of available drugs. The RDF statement should be rewritten in the formats that can be understood by other

## 4.2 Trust for the Semantic Grid

intelligent systems or database systems. We give the following examples to illustrate that these conversions are convenient for some systems.

CLIPS (C Language of Integrated Production Systems) is an expert system language which supports three types of programming paradigms: rule-based, object-oriented, and procedural. For CLIPS, we have

```
(assert (symptoms
  (headache slight)
  (fever normal)
  (cough moderate)
  (snivel heavy)))
```

The system developed by CLIPS language just needs the following deftemplate

```
(deftemplate symptoms "An example deftemplate")
  (slot headache)
  (slot fever)
  (slot cough)
  (slot snivel))
```

For Prolog language, we may have

```
assertz(symptom(headache, slight))
assertz(symptom(fever, normal))
assertz(symptom(cough, moderate))
assertz(symptom(snivel, heavy))
```

And for database system, we may get

```
select Medicine.name, Medicine.price,
   Prescription.effective
where Medicine.mid=Prescription.mid and
   Prescription.pid=Symptom.pid and
   Symptom.headache='slight' and
   Symptom.fever='normal' and
   Symptom.cough='moderate' and
   Symptom.snivel='heavy'
-- mid is medicine ID and pid is prescription ID.
```

To realize the above conversions we need a sharing ontology for a given domain and define the semantic mappings from local data schema or ontologies to these global ontologies. A semantic registration service helps in establishing these mappings through a uniform visual interface, and Chapter 5 will discuss the conversion rules and semantic mappings in detail. But here we can mention that Protégé, a well-known ontology editor, is built on CLIPS; therefore the above semantic mappings could be created easily and conveniently. Query or inference results will be returned to users in semantically wrapped RDF format, like

```
<rdf:Description rdf:about="drug A">
  <effective>0.75</effective>
  <price>79</price>
```

```
</rdf:Description>
<rdf:Description rdf:about="drug B">
  <effective>0.69</effective>
  <price>62</price>
</rdf:Description>
```
After the agent receives the responses from other agents, it should combine these responses (for this case, the responses are available drugs as well as their effectiveness for treating this case of influenza) to help its owner make the correct decision in choosing the most appropriate drug. It is the time when knowledge fusion happens.

## 4.3 Closed Trust Model

In our model the quality of a provider agent can be considered to be an unknown numerical quantity, and will represent it by $\theta$ (possibly a vector) and it is possible to treat $\theta$ as a random quantity with a probability distribution. Consider the situation of an agent $A$ trying to make an estimate of trust value for agent $B$. $A$ holds some prior information (subjective) of $B$, represented by distribution $\pi(\theta)$ (for either the continuous case or discrete case), and requests $A$'s acquaintance to give opinions on $B$'s quality. After $A$ receives the assessments of $B$'s quality from its acquaintances, $A$ takes these statements as samples of $\theta$. The outcome of these samples is a random variable and will be denoted by $\boldsymbol{X}$ (Often $\boldsymbol{X}$ will be a vector). A particular realization of $\boldsymbol{X}$ will be denoted by $x$ and $\boldsymbol{X}$ will be assumed to be either a continuous or a discrete random variable, with density $f(x|\theta)$. Then we can compute "posterior distribution" of $\theta$ given $x$, denoted $\pi(\theta|x)$. Just as the prior distribution reflects beliefs about $\theta$ prior to investigation in $B$'s reputation, so $\pi(\theta|x)$ reflects the update beliefs about $\theta$ after (posterior to) observing the sample $x$. In other words, the posterior distribution combines the prior beliefs about $\theta$ with the information about $\theta$ contained in the sample, $x$, to give a composite picture of the final beliefs about $\theta$. We take the posterior distribution of $\theta$, $\pi(\theta|x)$, as the estimate of $B$'s trust. If we want to take another investigation on $B$'s quality for more accuracy, $\pi(\theta|x)$ will be used as prior distribution for the next stage of investigation instead of the original $\pi(\theta)$.

When several similar provider agents exist, $A$ needs to decide which one should be selected. At that time the preferences of agent $A$'s owner should be considered properly in making this decision. Therefore, *utility function* should be constructed for agent $A$'s owner, which is represented by $U_A(r)$, to express his preferences, where $r$ represents rewards of the consequences of a decision. Suppose that $\pi(\theta|x)$ is the posterior distribution of provider agent $B$, the expected utility of function $U_A(r)$ over $\pi(\theta|x)$, denoted as $E^{\pi(\theta|x)}[U_A(r)]$, is possible gain of consequence of selecting $B$. If there are several provider agents to be considered, we simply select one that will result in the most expected utility of the decision.

## 4.3 Closed Trust Model

By treating an agent as a node, the "knows" relationship as an edge and remembering that trust is an asymmetric relation, a directed graph emerges. To facilitate the model description, agents and their environment are to be defined. To clarify the idea of our trust model, we begin with a simple illustration. Consider the scenario that agent $A$ is evaluating the trust value of $B$ and $C$ for doing business. The set of all consultant agents that $A$ requests for this evaluation as well as $A, B, C$ can be considered as a unique society of agents $\boldsymbol{N}$. In our example (see Fig. 4.1), $\boldsymbol{N}$ is $A, B, C, D, E, F, G, H, I, J, K$ and is called a "closed society of agents" with respect to $A$.

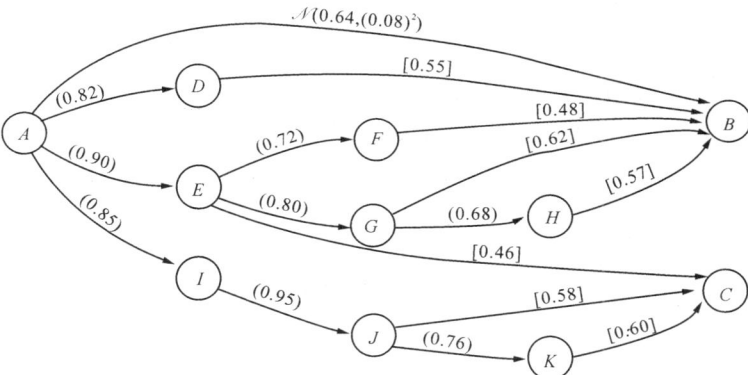

**Fig. 4.1.** A "closed society of agents" with respect to agent $A$

Decisions are more commonly called *actions* and the set of all possible actions under consideration will be denoted by $\mathcal{A}$. In our example, the initiator agent $A$ is trying to decide whether to select agent $B$ (action $b$) or $C$ (action $c$) as business partner ($\mathcal{A} = b, c$). Service charges of $B$ and $C$ are 250 and 210 units respectively ($SC_B = 250, SC_C = 210$, where $SC$ denotes service charge). We will treat quality of service, $\theta$, as a continuous variable here, and the unknown quantity $\theta$ that affects the decision process is commonly called the *state of nature*. See Fig. 4.1, a notion on an edge between the initiator and the consultant agent or between the two consultant agents represents the reliability factor, and between the consultant and the provider agents is the assessment of service quality and between the initiator and the provider agent is prior information. As shown in Fig. 4.1, the agent $A$ feels that $\theta_B$, the service quality of $B$, has a normal prior density, $\mathcal{N}(0.64, (0.08)^2)$ (the subscript denotes which provider agent is being taken into consideration). We also suppose that the prior density of $\theta_C$ is $\mathcal{N}(0.5, (0.15)^2)$ here. The probable distribution of $\boldsymbol{X}$ that represents the assessments of service quality from consultant agents will, of course, depend upon the unknown state of nature $\theta$. Therefore, we assume that $\boldsymbol{X}$ is another continuous random variable with density $f(x|\theta) \sim \mathcal{N}(\theta, (0.05)^2)$. We also assume that users can be divided into three types, "*Rich*", "*Bourgeois*", and "*Poor*", and agent $A$'s owner is "*Bourgeois*". The curves of their utility functions are shown in Fig. 4.2. We use polynomial regression up to fourth degrees to get a fitted model of utility curves and we have

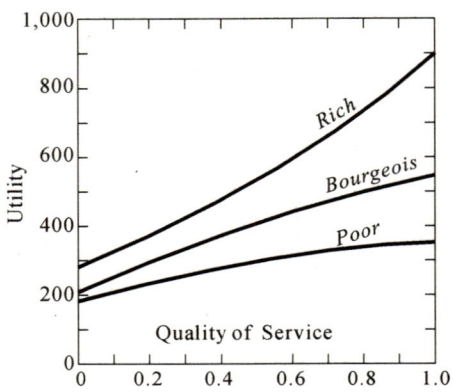

**Fig. 4.2.** Utility function

$$U_{Rich}(r) = 280.2 + 334.1r + 705.7r^2 - 944.1r^3 + 524.5r^4$$
$$U_{Bourgeois}(r) = 208.4 + 459.8r - 17.95r^2 - 99.84r^3$$
$$U_{Poor}(r) = 179 + 294.1r - 77.62r^2 - 80.03r^3 + 34.97r^4$$

Note that $\theta$ and $X$ have joint (subjective) density

$$h(x,\theta) = f(x|\theta)\pi(\theta) \tag{4.1}$$

and in making a decision it is clearly important to consider what the possible states of nature are. The symbol $\Theta$ will be used to denote the set of all possible states of nature. So, $X$ has marginal (unconditional) density.

$$m(x) = \int_\Theta f(x|\theta)\pi(\theta)d\theta \tag{4.2}$$

it is clear that (providing $m(x) \neq 0$)

$$\pi(\theta|x) = \frac{h(x,\theta)}{m(x)} \tag{4.3}$$

In discrete situations the formula for $\pi(\theta|x)$ is commonly known as Bayes's theorem.

Assume $X \sim \mathcal{N}(\theta, \sigma^2)$, where $\theta$ is unknown but $\sigma^2$ is known. Let it be prior information, $\pi(\theta)$, a $\mathcal{N}(\mu, \tau^2)$ density, where $\mu$ and $\tau^2$ are known. Note

## 4.3 Closed Trust Model

that the marginal distribution of $\overline{X}$, $m(x)$ is $\mathcal{N}(\mu, \sigma^2 + \tau^2)$ and the posterior distribution $\theta$ of given $x$ is $\mathcal{N}(\mu(x), \rho)$, where

$$\mu(x) = \frac{\sigma^2/n}{\tau^2 + \sigma^2/n}\mu + \frac{\tau^2}{\tau^2 + \sigma^2/n}\overline{x} \qquad (4.4)$$

$$\rho = \frac{\tau^2 \sigma^2}{n\tau^2 + \sigma^2} \qquad (4.5)$$

We take the assessments of $B$'s quality from consultant agents as sample of $\theta_B$ and combine this sample information $(x)$ and prior information into posterior distribution of $\theta_B$ given $x$. In order to answer the question of which sample information should be used with higher priority we propose the following order rules: (1) The sample from the agent with shorter referral distance should be used first; (2) If the samples come from the agents that have the same referral distance, that with a larger reliability factor is prior to that with smaller one; (3) If Rule 1 and Rule 2 still do not work, the priority will be given to the sample that results in less utility.

Now, we can evaluate trust value of $B$ for $A$ by using the above formulas and information. Firstly, we use the sample information from $D$ through the path $A \rightarrowtail D \rightarrowtail B$, and the posterior distribution $\pi_B(\theta|x = 0.55) \sim \mathcal{N}(0.5753, (0.0424)^2)$, where

$$(0.05^2/(0.08^2 + 0.05^2)) \times 0.64 + (0.08^2/(0.08^2 + 0.05^2)) \times 0.55 = 0.5753$$
$$(0.08^2 \times 0.05^2/(0.08^2 + 0.05^2)) \times 0.55 = 0.0424^2$$

However, the reliability factor has not been considered during the process of calculating this posterior distribution. We used the following formula to rectify above $\pi_B(\theta|x = 0.55)$, where $p_{old}$, $p$ and $p_{new}$ represent the parameter of prior distribution, the posterior distribution before rectification and the posterior distribution after rectification respectively ($p$ is mean or variant for normal distribution), and $R$ is reliability factor.

$$p_{new} = p_{old} + (p - p_{old}) \times R \qquad (4.6)$$

Hence, after rectification, $\mu_B = 0.64 + (0.5753 - 0.64) \times 0.82 = 0.5869$ and $\tau_B = 0.08 + (0.0424 - 0.08) \times 0.82 = 0.0492$. Then the posterior distribution $\pi_B(\theta|x = 0.55)$ is $\mathcal{N}(0.5869, (0.0492)^2)$ (see the first row in the Table 4.1). The residual calculating process of $B$ and the whole calculating process of $C$ are shown in Table 4.1 and Table 4.2. Note that we employ multiplying to merge two, or more than two, reliability factors. For example, the reliability factor of the edge $A \rightarrow E$ is 0.9 and that of $E \rightarrow G$ is 0.8, then the value of reliability factor on the path $A \rightarrow G$ is 0.72 (0.9 × 0.8). The reason behind using multiplying is that the statement is true only if the agents that propagate this statement all tell the truth and it is considered to be free for any two agents to lie or not to lie. After obtaining the final posterior distribution of $B$

90  4 Trust Computing in the Semantic Grid

and $C$, we can compare the result of the expectation of $U_A(r)$ over $\pi_B(\theta|x)$ minus $SC_B$ with that of the expectation of $U_A(r)$ over $\pi_C(\theta|x)$ minus $SC_C$, and simply select the agent that possibly will produce more utility. Expected utility of $B$ and $C$ are (Simpson method is used to solve definite integral):

Table 4.1. The process of evaluating $B$'s trust

| No. | Sources of Opinions | $\mu_B(x)$ | $\rho_B$ | Utility |
|---|---|---|---|---|
| 1 | None | 0.6400 | 0.0800 | 217.78 |
| 2 | D | 0.5790 | 0.0454 | 198.80 |
| 3 | D, G, F | 0.5656 | 0.0311 | 194.45 |

Table 4.2. The process of evaluating $C$'s trust

| No. | Sources of Opinions | $\mu_C(x)$ | $\rho_C$ | Utility |
|---|---|---|---|---|
| 1 | None | 0.5000 | 0.1500 | 207.54 |
| 2 | E | 0.4644 | 0.0497 | 197.65 |
| 3 | E, J | 0.5157 | 0.0371 | 216.79 |

Utility of $B$

$$= \int_{-\infty}^{+\infty} U_A(r\pi_B(\theta|x))d\theta - SC_B$$

$$= \int_{-\infty}^{+\infty} (208.4 + 459.8\theta - 17.95\theta^2 - 99.84\theta^3) \frac{1}{\sqrt{2\pi} \times 0.0285} e^{-\frac{(\theta - 0.5663)^2}{2 \times 0.0285^2}} d\theta - 250$$

$$= 194.72$$

Utility of $C$

$$= \int_{-\infty}^{+\infty} U_A(r\_\pi_C(\theta|x))d\theta - SC_C$$

$$= \int_{-\infty}^{+\infty} (208.4 + 459.8\theta - 17.95\theta^2 - 998.84\theta^3) \frac{1}{\sqrt{2\pi} \times 0.0321} e^{-\frac{(\theta - 0.5370)^2}{2 \times 0.0321^2}} d\theta - 210$$

$$= 224.46$$

hence (224.46 > 194.72), action $c$ should be performed, which means that $C$ is more appropriate than $B$ in the eyes of $A$.

## 4.4 Open Trust Model

The above discussion has a pre-condition, namely that the "closed society of agents" must be defined first, but it is nearly impossible for an inherent open and dynamic Web. Our idea is that at every stage of the procedure (i.e., after every given observation) one should compare the (posterior) utility of making an immediate decision with the "expected" (preprosterior) utility that will be obtained if more observations are taken. If it is cheaper to stop and make a decision, that is what should be done. To clarify this idea, we transform Fig. 4.1 to the structure of a tree, shown in Fig. 4.3. The top of the tree is an initiator agent, a non-leaf node represents a consultant agent and a node with leaf represents a provider agent.

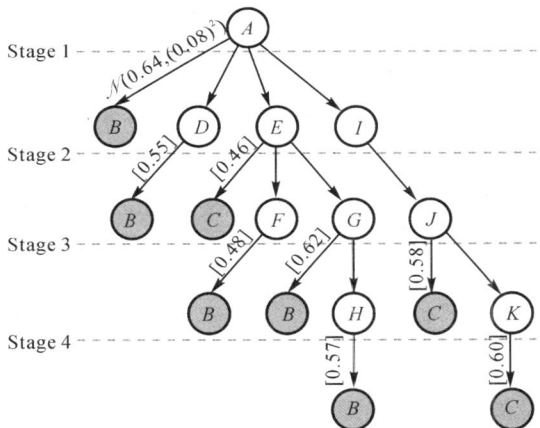

**Fig. 4.3.** The process of trust evaluating

The goal of preposterior analysis is to choose the means of investigation which minimizes the overall cost. This overall cost consists of the decision loss (opportunity cost) and the cost of conducting the observation (consultant fee). Note that these two quantities are in opposition to each other. To lower the decision loss it will generally be necessary to carry out a larger observation, whereby the cost of consultant services will be increased. In this section we propose an approach to balance these two costs.

We continue the above example used in the illustration of the closed trust model. As shown in Fig. 4.3, we begin at Stage 1 when $A$ only holds the prior information of $B$ and has no information about $C$ (even the existence of $C$, but it is more likely that an agent with the prior distribution of $\mathcal{N}(0.5, (0.15)^2)$ and the expected service charge of 210 is close by in the network). Agent $A$ either can make an immediate decision (to select $B$) or can send a request to its acquaintances for their opinions by extending the tree of

Fig. 4.3 down to the next layer. Suppose that the cost of consultant services is determined by how much agents will be requested at the next stage and the consultant service charge is the constant of 1 for each time (for example, at Stage 1, Agent $A$ can ask Agents $D, E$ and $I$ for their opinions, so the cost of the consultant fee for Stage 1 will be 3). When preposterior and Bayesian sequential analysis are performed in our sample, we use the 1-step look ahead procedure for simplicity.

The utility of an immediate decision is the larger of

$$\int_{-\infty}^{+\infty} U_A(r)\pi_B(\theta|x)d\theta - SC_B = 217.78$$

here, $\pi_B(\theta) \sim \mathcal{N}(0.64, (0.08)^2)$, and

$$\int_{-\infty}^{+\infty} U_A(r)\pi_C(\theta|x)d\theta - SC_C = 207.54$$

here, $\pi_C(\theta) \sim \mathcal{N}(0.5, (0.15)^2)$. (Note that $C$ is not known at this stage, we use a subscript of $C$ in the above equation just for convenience). Hence the utility of an immediate decision is 217.78. If the request message is sent and $x$ observed, the posterior density $\pi_B(\theta|x)$, is $\mathcal{N}(\mu(x), \rho)$, where

$$\mu_B(x) = \frac{0.05^2}{0.08^2 + 0.05^2} \times 0.64 + \frac{0.08^2}{0.08^2 + 0.05^2}(x) \cong 0.1798 + (0.7191)x$$

$$\rho_B = \frac{0.08^2 \times 0.05^2}{0.08^2 + 0.05^2} \cong 0.0018$$

However, we do not know which $x$ will occur, but we know the relevant distribution for $\boldsymbol{X}$ is the "predictive" or marginal distribution, $m_B(x)$, which in this situation is $\mathcal{N}(0.64, (0.08)^2 + (0.05)^2)$. Note that if $x < 0.5914$ is observed, the expected utility of $\pi_B(\theta|x)$ is less than 207.54, so we prefer to select $C$ instead of $B$. Hence the expected utility of not making an immediate decision is

$$\int_{-\infty}^{0.5914} 207.54 m_B(x)dx + \int_{0.5914}^{+\infty}(\int_{-\infty}^{+\infty} U_A(r)\pi_B(\theta|x)d\theta - SC_B)m_B(x)dx - 3$$
$$= 219.24$$

This is no other than the opportunity cost (3 is the consultant fee in above equation). Because $219.24 > 217.78$, then further investigation would be well worth the money. In other words $A$ should send the request to its acquaintances for their opinions. The residual process of Bayesian sequential analysis is shown in Table 4.3 and remember that further exploiting should be terminated immediately along the path on which a cycle is detected.

As shown in Table 4.3, at Stage 3, the expected utility of $C$ begins to be larger than that of $B$, and because $216.79 > 214.78$, making an immediate

Table 4.3. The process of Bayesian sequential analysis

| Stage | Agent B | | | | Agent C | | | | Consultant Fee | Utility | | Decision |
|---|---|---|---|---|---|---|---|---|---|---|---|---|
| | Prior Distribution | | Marginal Distribution | | Prior Distribution | | Marginal Distribution | | | Immediate Decision | Further Investigation | |
| | $\mu_B$ | $\tau_B$ | $\mu_{x|B}$ | $\sigma_{x|B}$ | $\mu_C$ | $\tau_C$ | $\mu_{x|C}$ | $\sigma_{x|C}$ | | | | |
| 1 | 0.6400 | 0.0800 | 0.6400 | 0.0943 | 0.5000 | 0.1500 | - | - | 3 | 217.78 | 219.24 | Continue |
| 2 | 0.5790 | 0.0454 | 0.5790 | 0.0675 | 0.4644 | 0.0497 | - | - | 3 | 198.80 | 199.36 | Continue |
| 3 | 0.5656 | 0.0311 | - | - | 0.5157 | 0.0371 | 0.5157 | 0.0623 | 2 | 216.79 | 214.78 | Stop |

decision is more profitable. Therefore $A$ should stop investigating and select $C$ as a decision. The advantage of sequential analysis should be clear now. It allows one to gather exactly the correct amount of data needed for a decision of the desired accuracy.

## 4.5 Experiments

In this section we develop a simulation system to measure some properties of our trust models. We present three sets of experiments. The goal of the first experiment is to see if our trust models help users to select the appropriate providers that match their preferences better. We compare the performance of the closed and open models in terms of precision and consultant fee. The second experiment is to examine the effect that varying the accuracy of the survey has on the overall performance of the system and, finally, we want to see what quality of agent population is necessary for the system to work well.

For the sake of simplicity each agent in our system plays only one role at a time, either the role of service provider or the role of consumer (including initiator and consultant agent). The number of providers and consumer agents are equal. Every consumer agent keeps two lists. One is the list of a "neighbor" that recorded all acquaintances to which a reliability factor is attached. The other is the provider list that recorded the known providers and the corresponding prior information. The number of the total items in the above two lists is defined as "the degree of outgoing".

We expect the information on the Semantic Grid to be of varying quality, so we assign to each consumer agent $i$ a quality $\gamma_i \in [0, 1]$. A consumer's quality determines to what degree a statement passed or issued by the consumer is true. Unless otherwise specified, the quality of a consumer is chosen from a Gaussian distribution with $\mu = 0.8$ and $\sigma = 0.15$. The higher a consumer's quality, the more his messages were likely to be trusted. So, for any pair of consumer $i$ and $j$ where $i$ trusts $j$:

$t_{ij}$ = uniformly chosen from $[\max(\gamma_j - \delta, 0), \min(\gamma_j + \delta, 1)]$

Where $\gamma_j$ is the quality of consumer $j$ and $\delta$ is a noise parameter that determines how accurate consumers were at estimating the qualities of other consumers, and for these experiments we let $\delta = 0.2$. We also generate randomly each provider agent's quality that is represented by distribution $\pi(\theta)$ (the mean of $\theta$ is chosen from a Gaussian distribution $\mathcal{N}(0.5, (0.20)^2)$ and the variant of $\theta$ is chosen from a Gaussian distribution $\mathcal{N}(0.08,(0.02)^2)$, (see Section 4.4 for more details and its corresponding final service charge), and assume that the consultant service charge is the constant of 1 each time. Unless otherwise specified, the probable distribution of $X$ that represents the assessments of service quality from consultant agents (the accuracy of the survey) is $\mathcal{N}(\theta,(0.05)^2)$.

As mentioned above, we assume that the consumers are divided into three types, "*Rich*", "*Bourgeois*" and "*Poor*", and which type a consumer belongs to is decided randomly during the experiment. The curves of the consumers' utility functions are shown in Fig. 4.2.

Let $G$ be the set of all provider agents in an experiment, and $S_i$ is the set of the providers "reachable" by consumer $i$ (A provider is reachable if there is at least one path from consumer $i$ to the provider), so, $recall_i = |S_i|/|G|$. The symbol $M_i$ is used to denote the maximum utility that a provider in $G$ can bring consumer $i$ and let $O_i$ be the utility that is produced by a provider selected by $i$ using a certain trust model, so $precision_i$ can be defined as $O_i/M_i$. Unless otherwise specified the maximum path length is 10 in our experiments. The program will terminate and generate the results when reaching this maximum. We run each configuration 10 times and use the means for the final experimental results.

**Varying the Number of Agents**. We explore the effect of varying the number of agents for the closed and open trust models introduced earlier. As shown in Fig. 4.4, we find that the precision differed only slightly between the closed and open models, except between 500 and 1,000 agents and to our surprise, the open model begins to outperform the closed model when the number of agents reaches 1,000. Through careful investigation we believe this is because the closed model will meet with more noise in the network than the open model when the number of agents grows. We also find that the average precision of the open model decreases slightly when the number of agents grows from 100 to 1,000. So the results of the experiment show that the open trust model is robust for the population of agents.

As shown in Table 4.4 and Fig. 4.4, we find that the average consultant fee of the open trust model, which incurred during the process of trust evaluating is significantly lower than that of the closed trust model, though two models differ only slightly in terms of precision. This also means that the open model has less runtime for trust evaluation. Furthermore, the average consultant fee of the closed model dramatically goes up after 200 agents. Otherwise, that of the open model increases comparatively smoothly (since the maximum path length is 10 in our experiments, the average consultant fee of the closed model does not increase significantly after 1,000 agents. If the experiment were not restricted to this maximum, it would be larger than the numerical value shown in Table 4.4). This is because if more investigation is not profitable, the open model will terminate exploration and make an immediate decision.

## 4.5 Experiments

Therefore the open model has computational scalability that may not be the case for the closed model.

**Table 4.4.** Average consultant fee of closed model vs. open model during the process of trust evaluation

| Number of Agents | Average Consultant Fee | | Number of Agents | Average Consultant Fee | |
|---|---|---|---|---|---|
| | Closed Model | Open Model | | Closed Model | Open Model |
| 100 | 1048.36 | 11.23 | 600 | 2044.53 | 13.23 |
| 200 | 1948.54 | 12.85 | 700 | 2034.93 | 13.08 |
| 300 | 2075.07 | 13.61 | 800 | 2267.41 | 13.38 |
| 400 | 2062.19 | 13.27 | 900 | 2287.80 | 13.57 |
| 500 | 2302.92 | 13.14 | 1,000 | 2581.62 | 13.31 |

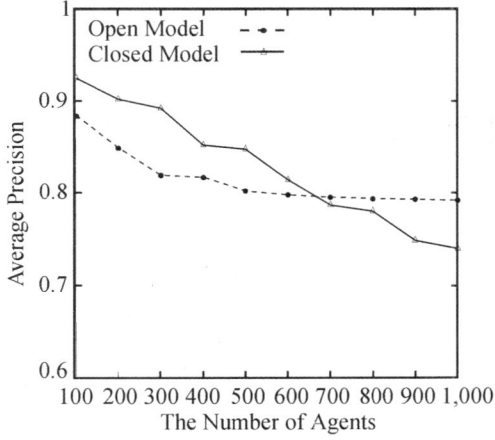

**Fig. 4.4.** Effect of the number of agents on the precision

We also want to know how the average recall was affected by the number of agents and just explore this for the closed trust model here. As shown in Fig. 4.5, we saw that the average recall decreased significantly when the number of agents increased. The high correlation between the precision of the closed model and the average recall was observed. The reason is that lower recall will prevent agents from finding the most suitable service in the whole network.

**Varying the Accuracy of the Survey.** It is necessary to know the effect that the accuracy of consultant agents' assessments of service quality has on the average precision of the systems. We explore this by varying the variant of $X$ (the accuracy of the survey) from 0.02 to 0.12. We set the number of agents to 100 here. As shown in Fig. 4.6, we find that the more

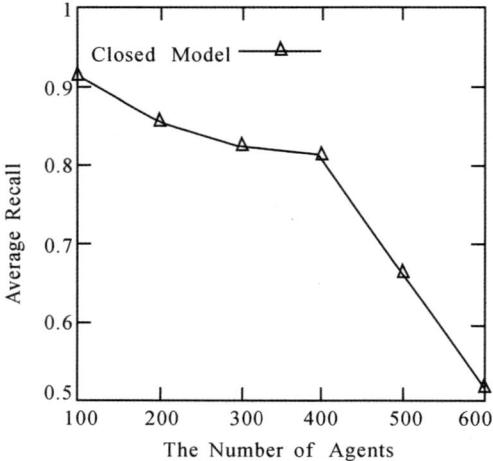

**Fig. 4.5.** Effect of the number of agents on the recall

accurate the assessment, the more exactly we estimate value of trust. So, the exactness of the closed and open trust models all depends on the accuracy of the survey, but the average precision of our models decreases slightly when the accuracy of the survey decreases.

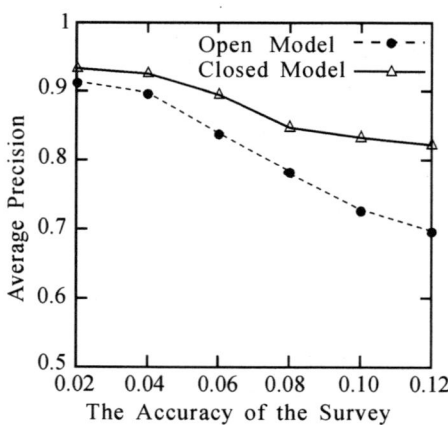

**Fig. 4.6.** Average precision for various accuracy of the survey

**Varying the Population Quality.** It is important to understand how the average precision is affected by the quality of agent population. We explore this by varying the mean quality of agents and set the number of agents at 100. To measure the robustness of the model to bad agents, we select agent qualities from six Gaussian distributions with means from 0.4 to 0.9 and the same variant of 0.15. We vary the fraction of agents drawn from each distribution. Overall, as shown in Fig. 4.7, we find that the system using the closed and open models differs only slightly in terms of precision, and the better the agent population, the higher the average precision is, which makes sense because in this case the agent should get a more accurate estimate of the provider's quality.

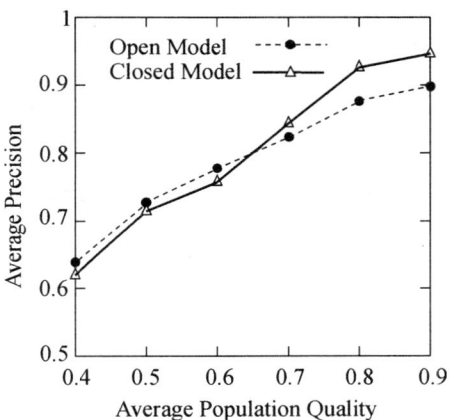

**Fig. 4.7.** Average precision for various qualities of agent population

The results show that the closed and open trust models are robust to the quality of the agent population and the accuracy of the survey and the open trust model is robust to the number of agents. Also, the open model outperforms the closed model in terms of precision and consultant fee after the number of agents exceeds 1,000. We believe the reason that underlies these results is: the closed model uses the transitivity strategy to prune its searches and is affected by the length of a chain of recommendations, falling as the chain gets longer. This pruning is likely to result in the loss of too much investigation. However, the idea of the open model is that at every stage of the procedure (after every given observation) one should compare the posterior Bayesian risk (or utility) of making an immediate decision with the "expected" posterior Bayesian risk (or utility) that will be obtained if more elaborate observations are taken. If it is cheaper to stop and make a decision, that is what should be done. Experimental results also show that the open model will stop mostly before pruning all its searches and its precision is not worse than the closed model. Furthermore, the open model scales well with any social network size, as only tiny subsets of relatively constant size are visited and have computational scalability.

## 4.6 Related Work

Trust is a response to uncertainty and uncertainty can be considered as the lack of adequate information to make a decision. Uncertainty is a problem because it may prevent us from making the best decision and may even cause a bad decision to be made. A number of theories have been proposed to deal with uncertainty. These theories include classical probability, Bayesian probability, Hartley theory based on classical sets, Shannon theory based on probability, Dempster-Shafer theory, and Zadeh's fuzzy theory. Unfortunately, determining the best conclusion may not be easy, although a lot of methods have been proposed for dealing with uncertainty (Giarratano J, Riley G, 1996).

Real situations are very often uncertain or vague in a number of ways. Due to lack of information the future state of the system might not be known completely. This type of uncertainty (stochastic character) has been handled appropriately by probability theory and statistics, in which the events (elements of sets) or the statements are well defined. Zimmermann calls this type of uncertainty or vagueness stochastic uncertainty in contrast to the vagueness concerning the description of the semantic meaning of the events, phenomena or statements themselves, which they call fuzziness in (Zimmermann HJ, 1985). Application of fuzzy set theory can be found in artificial intelligence, control engineering, decision theory, and others. However, membership functions of fuzzy set generally are supposed "to be given". Therefore, much empirical research and modeling efforts are still needed on connectives and on the measurement of membership functions to be able to use fuzzy set theory adequately as a modeling language. Moreover, so far fuzzy set theory has not yet been proven to be computationally able to solve large and complex problems efficiently.

A Bayesian network is a directed acyclic graph that represents a probability distribution. Nodes represent random variables and arcs represent probabilistic correlation between the variables. The key feature of Bayesian networks is the fact that they provide a method for decomposing a probability distribution into a set of local distributions. Naïve use of Bayesian network technology would involve building one large network to represent a domain. For large systems this is impracticable from an engineering standpoint. Although large domain models can often be decomposed into a collection of independent smaller networks it is desirable, for systems that need to address a broad range of problems, to be able to assemble the needed model components dynamically. The lack of modularity in the representation also makes reuse of models difficult. A second limitation is that a Bayesian network is essentially a propositional representation of a domain: each node represents a multi-valued propositional variable. Thus it is not possible to express general relationships among concepts without enumerating all the potential instances in advance. This pre-enumeration is again impracticable when the system faces a broad range of dynamic decision situations (Haddawy P, 1999).

Another method of dealing with uncertainty uses certainty factors, originally developed for the MYCIN expert system. Although MYCIN was successful in diagnosis, there were difficulties with the theoretical foundations of certainty factors. One problem was that the certainty factors' values could be the opposite of conditional probabilities. The second problem is that in general $P(H|e) \neq P(H|i)P(i|e)$, where $i$ is some intermediate hypothesis based on evidence $e$, and yet the certainty factor of two rules in an inference chain is calculated as independent probabilities by $CF(H, e) = CF(H, i)CF(i, e)$. Moreover, the combining function for certainty factors can be described as heuristic with no reasonable explanation in terms of mathematics.

Given its importance, a number of computational models of trust and reputation also have been developed in security, e-commerce and multi-agents systems. Probably the most widely used trust models are those on $eBay^2$ and $Amazon^3$ Auctions. Both of these are implemented as a centralized rating system so that their users can rate and learn about each other's reputation. For example, on eBay sellers receive feedback (+1, 0, -1) for their reliability in each auction and their trust is calculated as the sum of those ratings over the last six months. Both approaches are completely centralized and require users to explicitly make and reveal their ratings of others. However, it is questionable if the ratings reflect the trustworthy behavior of sellers, since in the online marketplaces it is very likely for users to misbehave, and trick with malice. What makes it worse is that these systems are not convenient for users for receiving a personalized set of trusts according to their preferences.

Social network analysis techniques are used in (Golbeck J, Parsia B, Hendler J, 2003) to measure trust over a Friend of a Friend (FOAF[4]) network, extended with trust relations. This work describes the applicability of social network analysis to the Semantic Web, particularly discussing the multi-dimensional networks that evolve from ontological trust specifications. But this work uses a simple function to calculate trust and does not make further deep investigation of algorithms for calculating trust. So, it is nearly impossible to apply in the real world. A similar approach for exploring the web of trust is described in (Richardson M, Agrawal R, Domingos P, 2003), where users provide trust values for a number of other users, which are used to measure trust. It takes advantage of the link structure of the web and generalizes this idea to the Semantic Web by having each user specify which others he/she trusts, and leveraging this "web of trust" to estimate a user's belief in statements supplied by any other user. It formalizes some of the requirements for such a calculus, and describes a number of possible models for carrying it out. But it does not considers the different types of cost to

---

[2] http://www.ebay.com
[3] http://www.amazon.com
[4] http://www.foaf-project.org

operate a trust computation. Moreover, the algorithm for evaluating trust in this method is just heuristic and there is no reasonable explanation in terms of mathematics.

The algorithms, as in (Gil Y, Ratnakar V, 2002), rely on manually-set trust opinions, which once more shifts the problem of trust to the source of the opinions. It addresses the issue of the web of trust by regarding whether to trust the content of a web resource by depending on its source and describes work on TRELLS to enable users to annotate the rationale for their decisions, hypotheses, and opinions as they analyze information from various sources. But TRELLS does not propose an approach to formalize and evaluate the credibility factor of a statement that is supported or unsupported by two or more different sources with different reliability factors.

(Ramchurn SD, Jennings NR, Sierra C, Godo L, 2003) develop a trust model based on confidence and reputation and show how it can be concretely applied, using fuzzy sets, to guide agents in evaluating past interactions and in establishing new contracts with one another. But this model is rather complex and cannot be easily used in today's electronic communities. The main problem with their approach is that every agent must keep rather complex data structures, which can be laborious and time-consuming. Also it is not clear how the agents get needed information and how well the model will scale when the number of agents grows.

(Maximilien EM, Singh MP, 2003) propose using a centralized agent to measure the reputation of Web services by monitoring and collecting client feedback, and making the information available to other agents. Relying on centralized institutions to measure trust takes the burden off the interactive agents when deciding which agents to trust. However, such systems raise the question of how trustworthy the sources of their trust information are in the first place, and why such trust warehouses should be trusted at all. We argue against these centralized units for measuring trust because of their scalability limitations and the implicit trust measurement mechanisms they adopt.

(Huynh D, Jennings NR, Shadbolt NR, 2004) present FIRE, a trust and reputation model that integrates interaction trust, role-based trust, witness reputation, and certified reputation to generate a comprehensive assessment of an agent's possible performance. But this work assumes that all agents are honest in exchanging information, uses a static parametric model that can not dynamically adjust itself to the change of environment, and has no learning abilities. Therefore it can not be used in a real open multi-agents system.

(Wang Y, Vassileva J, 2003) propose a Bayesian network-based trust model for a file sharing peer-to-peer application which enables an agent to consider its trust in a specific aspect of another agent's capability or in a combination of multiple aspects. According to this model peers make recommendations to each other, by exchanging and comparing their Bayesian networks. After this comparison the agents update their trust ratings of each other, depending on whether they share similar preferences, on the assumption that an agent with similar preferences is more likely to give suitable recommendations than others. However, the model's mathematical formulation for the calculation of trust can at best be described as intuitive – without justifications and their experiment uses a very simple naïve Bayesian network, which cannot represent complex relationships. Furthermore, this model is applicable in a small-size network and does not scale well with any social network size because maintaining and comparing a more complex Bayesian network for each agent will be computationally intractable.

## 4.7 Summary and Conclusion

Grid application areas are shifting from scientific computing toward industry and business applications. To meet those needs and achieve a pervasive, worldwide Semantic Grid, an enhancement of the computational trust model should be designed to support and enable computers and people to acquire, represent, exchange and integrate available data and information efficiently and conveniently. We make the assumption that in the future there is likely to be a service-rich environment, necessitating the selection between similar services being offered by different providers. Though we use a discrete example to illustrate our approach, it is convenient to extend our approach to a continuous case (even more convenient to treat).

The Semantic Grid is very heterogeneous, dynamic and uncertain. If it is to succeed, trust will inevitably be an issue. After three aspects of this issue (characteristic features of trust, the cost and utility incurred when evaluating trust, and advantages and disadvantages of a centralized and distributed system) have been discussed, two trust models have been formalized. Our work's contributions are: (1) Closed and open trust models have been proposed based on statistical decision theory and Bayesian sequential analysis. And these models give trust a strict mathematical interpretation in terms of probability theory and lay the foundation for trust evaluating in the Semantic Grid; (2) The utility and three types of costs, operational cost, opportunity cost and service charge incurred during the process of trust evaluating have been proven sufficient and an approach is proposed to balance the cost and utility; (3) Our approach enables a user to combine a variety of sources of information to cope with the inherent uncertainties in the Semantic Grid and each user receives a personalized set of trusts, which may vary widely from person to person. However, our proposed approach goes beyond representations of trust, trust evaluating algorithms, and formal analysis as in other approaches. Experiment results show that our model has computational scalability and is able to select the appropriate service provider for users effectively and efficiently.

For the future a formal robust analysis for our model should be made properly. But we can mention that robustness can be dealt with more easily in Bayesian analysis. Service quality is multi-faceted. For instance, the file providers' capability can be presented in various ways, such as the download speed, file quality and file type. We would like to consider multi-valued trusts and will add the approach to generate the utility function automatically for a user, according to his or her history of behavior and preferences.

## References

Ding L, Zhou L, Finin T (2003) Trust based knowledge outsourcing for Semantic Web agents. Int. IEEE/WIC Web Intelligence (WI) 1:379-387

Giarratano J, Riley G (1996) Expert systems principles and programming (3rd Edition). PWS Publishing Company

Gil Y, Ratnakar V (2002) Trusting information sources one citizen at a time. The First International Semantic Web Conference (ISWC) LNCS 2342:162-176

Golbeck J, Parsia B, Hendler J (2003) Trust networks on the Semantic Web. Proceedings of Cooperative Intelligent LNCS 2782:238-249

Haddawy P (1999) An overview of some recent developments in Bayesian problem solving techniques. Introduction to the special issue of AI Magazine 20(2):11-19

Huynh D, Jennings NR, Shadbolt NR (2004) Developing an integrated trust and reputation model for open multi-agent systems. The 7th International Workshop on Trust in Agent Societies 1:65-74

Maximilien EM, Singh MP (2003) An ontology for Web service ratings and reputations. Workshop on Ontologies in Agent Systems, Second International Joint Conference on Autonomous Agents and Multi-Agent Systems:25-30

Milgram S (1976) The small world problem. Psychology Today 1:61

O'Hara K, Alani H, Kalfoglou Y, Shadbolt N (2004) Trust strategies for the Semantic Web. Workshop on Trust, Security and Reputation on the Semantic Web, Available at: http://sunsite.informatik.rwth-aachen.de/Publications/CEUR-WS/Vol-127/paper5.pdf

Ramchurn SD, Jennings NR, Sierra C, Godo L (2003) A computational trust model for multi-agent interactions based on confidence and reputation. Workshop on Deception, Fraud and Trust in Agent Societies 1:69-75

Richardson M, Agrawal R, Domingos P (2003) Trust management for the Semantic Web. The 2nd International Semantic Web Conference LNCS 2870:351-368

Roure D, Jennings NR, Shadbolt NR (2005) The semantic grid: Past, present, and future. Int. IEEE 93(3):669-681

Wang Y, Vassileva J (2003) Bayesian network-based trust model. IEEE /MIC International Conference on Web Intelligence 1:372-378

Zimmermann HJ (1985) Fuzzy set theory and its application. Kluwer-Nijhoff Publishing, 28-31

# 5
# Data Integration in the Semantic Grid

**Abstract:** Integrating legacy relational databases is important for both Grid and Semantic Web applications. This chapter elaborates on several issues relevant to data integration in the Semantic Grid environment. Specifically, the chapter presents an intelligent framework with a formal mapping system to bridge the gap between a relational data model and semantic web languages. It also studies the problem of reasoning and query answering using views based upon the formal mapping system.

## 5.1 Introduction

The Semantic Web technology has been a promising paradigm for future information systems with rich semantics (Hendler J, Tim BL, Miller E, 2002). Many advanced information systems are applying ontologies as the semantic backbone to support intelligent data and knowledge management. The Semantic Grid applications typically draw upon semantic web languages to represent and describe the information semantics of grid resources, to enable intelligent resource discovery and ease the process of service inter-operation and resource sharing.

One of the most important resources in typical grid applications is the database, for which the semantic heterogeneity issue is far more protruding than any other types of grid resources. Moreover, as essential components of modern information systems, relational databases (RDB) hold a magnificent amount of data everywhere. While relational database integration has been a long-studied database research topic, it presently calls for a more efficient and intelligent framework that possesses enough expressive power, and flexible architecture to share semantics and integrate legacy databases across organization boundaries as the sharing scale gets larger and larger (Fensel D, Baader F, Rousset MC, Wache H, 2001).

This chapter is devoted to the issue of data integration in the Semantic Grid. In particular, we emphasize the integration of a legacy relational database (RDB) in the Semantic Grid environment, as RDB is the dominant storage media for almost all data management systems. Specifically we study the model difference between the underlying logical formalisms of the semantic web language and relational data, and propose a mapping formalism to bridge the gap between the OWL ontologies and schemata of the relational data model (RDM). In the framework the semantic web ontologies serve as the semantic mediator among database providers in a typical Semantic Grid environment. Based upon the formal mapping system we present a semantic query process approach to rewriting ontological queries as SQL queries.

Based upon fundamental approaches, a suite of semantic tools and applications have also been developed to help in managing, querying and searching within the Semantic Grid environment. The system consists of a visualized semantic mapping tool, a semantic query answering interface, a semantic search engine, and a suite of back-end grid services including the ontology service, semantic registration service and semantic query service.

This toolkit and its applications are introduced in more detail in Chapter 8. This chapter only considers the fundamental issues. Firstly we introduce related work and prerequisite knowledge for better understanding the rest of this chapter. Then we discuss the details of our basic approaches, technologies and the corresponding implementations. We note that for formal discussion we focus attention on the $\mathcal{SHIQ}$ (Horrocks I, Patel-Schneider PF, Harmelen FV, 2003) description logic language, which is the underlying formalism for semantic web ontology languages.

### 5.1.1 Related Work

There are two major aspects of the related work: one falls into the Semantic Web context, and the other is related to classic data integration.

#### 5.1.1.1 Semantic Web Context

Integrating relational databases and structured data are always a hot research topic in the Semantic Web community (Korotkiy M, Top JL, 2004; Jos LA, Corchuelo R, Ruiz D, Toro R, 2007; Chen HJ, Wang YM, Wu ZH, et al, 2006). In one of the earliest documents describing the Semantic Web vision, Tim Berners-Lee firstly discussed the relationship and differences between the RDF and the RDB models (Tim BL, 1998).

D2R Server[1] uses the D2RQ mapping language to capture mappings between relational database schemata and OWL/RDFS ontologies. The central object in D2RQ is the *ClassMap* which represents a mapping from a set of entities described within the database, to a class or a group of similar classes of resources. Each *ClassMap* has a set of property bridges, which specify the

---

[1] http://sites.wiwiss.fu-berlin.de/suhl/bizer/d2r-server/

mapping from a relational table column to class property. D2R Server allows applications to query RDB using the SPARQL via a query rewriting approach. A similar mapping mechanism and rewriting approach is adopted in the SquirrelRDF project[2], RDF Gateway[3]. Virtuoso[4] recently released a declarative meta schema language for mapping SQL data to RDF ontologies. This functionality is referred to as "RDF Views" which is similar to the $\mathcal{SHIQ}$-$\mathcal{RDM}$ view proposed in this chapter.

However, the formal foundations and expressiveness of their mapping systems and rewriting techniques are not clear, and the mapping specifications are all based upon manually edited text files. Our approach is based upon the notion of "answering and rewriting queries using views" which has well-studied formal foundations for complex mapping expressiveness and query answering, and owns a handful of practical rewriting techniques. Besides, we offer a set of convenient tools such as the visualized semantic mapping tool and semantic query and search tool which are not provided by these systems.

Richard (Richard C, 2005) reports a relational algebra for SPARQL and describes an approach to translate SPARQL into SQL, the project SPASQL[5]. But they only consider syntax-level translation, and do not discuss query rewriting on the basis of view-based mapping for heterogenous database integration.

Yuan An and colleagues (An Y, Borgida A, Mylopoulos J, 2005) present a tool which could automatically infer the Local-as-View (LaV) mapping formulas from simple predicate correspondences between relational schema and formal ontologies. Although a completely automatic approach to define semantic mapping is difficult, it would be a great enhancement to our visualized tool if some candidate mapping suggestions could be provided beforehand. That will be our future work.

Dejing Dou and colleagues (Dou DJ, LePendu P, 2006) propose an ontology-based framework called OntoGrate for relational database integration. The mappings are defined by using bridge-axioms, and the queries are described by a language called WEB-PDDL which will be rewritten into SQL queries for data retrieval.

Piazza (Halevy AY, Ives ZG, Madhavan J, et al, 2004) is a P2P-based data integration system with consideration of semantic web vision. The current system is implemented with the XML data model for its mapping language and query answering.

### 5.1.1.2 Classic Database Integration Context

Closely relevant areas from classic AI and database communities are referred to as *logic-based data integration* (Calvanese D, Giacomo DG, 2005; Ullman

---

[2] http://jena.sourceforge.net/SquirrelRDF
[3] http://www.intellidimension.com
[4] http://virtuoso.openlinksw.com
[5] http://www.w3.org/2005/05/22-SPARQL-MySQL

JD, 2000) and *ontology-based data integration* (Wache H, Vogele T, Visser U, et al, 2001; Natalya FN, 2004; Calvanese D, Giacomo DG, Lemo D, et al, 2004; Goasdoue F, Rousset MC, 2003; Arens Y, Hsu CN, Knoblock CA, 1997; Mena E, Kashyap V, Sheth AP, Illarramendi A, 1996; Stevens RD, Baker PG, Bechhofer S, et al, 2000). A popular approach is to take advantage of description logics formalism to define global ontology to mediate a set of heterogeneous data sources (Calvanese D, Giacomo DG, Lemo D, et al, 2004). Calvanese and colleagues (Calvanese D, Giacomo DG, Lemo D, et al, 2004) propose a specific DL language called $\mathcal{ALCQI}$ for ontology-based database integration. The conjunctive query answering in the $\mathcal{ALCQI}$-mediated integration system is decidable. They also propose the DL-Lite, a specifically tailored restriction of $\mathcal{ALCQI}$ that not only ensures tractability of query answering, but also keeps enough expressive power to capture the fundamental aspects of conceptual data models.

Within the traditional database community a substantial number of works have been written on data integration over the past couple of decades (Lenzerini M, 2002; Halevy AY, Rajaraman A, Ordille JJ, 2006). Among them the most typical approach to query mediation is usually referred to as *answering or rewriting queries using views* (Halevy AY, 2001; Levy AY, Ordille RA, 1996; Abiteboul S, Duschka O, 1998). Most previous works have been focused on the relational case (Pottinger R, Halevy AY, 2001), and XML case (Yu C, Popa L, 2004; Deutsch A, Tannen A, 2003; Manolescu I, Florescu D, Kossmann D, 2001). In this context several general query rewriting algorithms, the *bucket algorithm* and the *inver-rule algorithm* (Halevy AY, 2001; Qian X, 1996), and a more scalable rewriting algorithm called MiniCon (Pottinger R, Halevy AY, 2001), have been proposed for rewriting queries using views. Actually our algorithm absorbs ideas from both of them, whereas we have our own features. In general the *triple group* can be viewed as a bucket for a later rewriting combination. On the one hand our algorithm generates a bucket for a triple group rather than generating a bucket for each subgoal or each individual triple. On the other hand we take the key idea of an inverse-rule algorithm to construct a set of rules that actually invert the view definitions.

### 5.1.2 Preliminaries

#### 5.1.2.1 $\mathcal{SHIQ}$ Description Logic

We focus our attention on a specific ontology language, $\mathcal{SHIQ}$ (Horrocks I, Patel-Schneider P, Harmelen FV, 2003), which belongs to the well-studied family of DL languages as the underlying formalism for the web ontologies. Chapter 2 gives a comprehensive overview of the ontology languages.

**Syntax.** Given $\mathcal{R}$ as a finite set of transitive and inclusion axioms with normal role names $N_R$, an $\mathcal{SHIQ}$-role is either some $R \in N_R$ or an *inverse role* $R^-$ for $R \in N_R$. TransR and $R \sqsubseteq S$ represent the transitive and inclusion axioms, respectively, where $R$ and $S$ are roles. A simple role is an $\mathcal{SHIQ}$-role

**Table 5.1.** Semantics of $\mathcal{SHIQ} - \mathcal{KB}$

| Interpretation of Concepts |
|---|
| $(\neg C)^{\mathcal{I}} = \Delta^{\mathcal{I}} \setminus C^{\mathcal{I}}$ |
| $(C \sqcap D)^{\mathcal{I}} = C^{\mathcal{I}} \cap D^{\mathcal{I}}, (C \sqcup D)^{\mathcal{I}} = C^{\mathcal{I}} \cup D^{\mathcal{I}}$ |
| $(\exists R.C)^{\mathcal{I}} = \{x \in \Delta^{\mathcal{I}} \mid R^{\mathcal{I}}(x, C) \neq \emptyset\}$ |
| $(\forall R.C)^{\mathcal{I}} = \{x \in \Delta^{\mathcal{I}} \mid R^{\mathcal{I}}(x, \neg C) = \emptyset\}$ |
| $(\leqslant nS.C)^{\mathcal{I}} = \{x \in \Delta^{\mathcal{I}} \mid \sharp R^{\mathcal{I}}(x, C) \leqslant n\}$ |
| $(\geqslant nS.C)^{\mathcal{I}} = \{x \in \Delta^{\mathcal{I}} \mid \sharp R^{\mathcal{I}}(x, C) \geqslant n\}$ |
| Interpretation of Axioms |
| $(C \sqsubseteq D)^{\mathcal{I}} = C^{\mathcal{I}} \subseteq D^{\mathcal{I}}, (R \sqsubseteq S)^{\mathcal{I}} = R^{\mathcal{I}} \subseteq S^{\mathcal{I}}$ |
| $(\mathsf{Trans} R)^{\mathcal{I}}$ |
| $= \{\forall x, y, z \in \Delta^{\mathcal{I}} \mid R^{\mathcal{I}}(x, y) \cap R^{\mathcal{I}}(y, z) \to R^{\mathcal{I}}(x, z)\}$ |
| $\sharp R$ is the number restriction of a set $R$ and $R^{\mathcal{I}}(x, C)$ is defined as $\{y \mid \langle x, y \rangle \in R^{\mathcal{I}} and y \in C^{\mathcal{I}}\}$. |

that neither its sub-roles nor itself is transitive. Let $N_C$ be a set of *concept names*, the set of $\mathcal{SHIQ}$-concepts is the minimal set such that every concept $C \in \mathcal{N}_C$ is an $\mathcal{SHIQ}$-concept and for $C$ and $D$ are $\mathcal{SHIQ}$-concepts, $R$ is a role, $S$ a simple role and $n$ a positive integer, then $(\neg C), (C \sqcap D), (C \sqcup D)$, $(\exists R.C), (\forall R.C), (\leqslant nS.C)$ and $(\geqslant nS.C)$ are also $\mathcal{SHIQ}$-concepts. Therefore we have a knowledge base where $\mathcal{KB}$ is a triple $(\mathcal{R}, \mathcal{T}, \mathcal{A})$ where (1) a TBox $\mathcal{T}$ is a finite set of axioms representing the concept inclusions with the form $C \sqsubseteq D$; (2) an ABox $\mathcal{A}$ is a finite set of axioms with individual names $N_I$ and the form $C(x), R(x, y)$ that consists of equality-relations $x$ is (un)equal to $y$.

**Semantics.** The semantics of $\mathcal{KB}$ is given by the interpretation $\mathcal{I} = (\Delta^{\mathcal{I}}, ^{\mathcal{I}'})$ that consists of a non-empty set $\Delta^{\mathcal{I}}$ (the domain of $\mathcal{I}$) and the function $^{\mathcal{I}'}$ in the Table 5.1 . It is well known that $\mathcal{KB}$ is satisfiable with respect to interpretation $\mathcal{I}$ iff $\mathcal{KB}^I$ is satisfiable in first order logic. The satisfiability checking of $\mathcal{KB}$ in expressive Description Logic (DL) is performed by reducing the subsumption and the reasoning over TBox and role hierarchy can be reduced to reasoning over only role hierarchy (Horrocks I, Patel-Schneider PF, 1999). The interpretation $\mathcal{I}$ is the model of $\mathcal{R}$ and $\mathcal{T}$ if for each $R \sqsubseteq S \in \mathcal{R}$, $R^{\mathcal{I}} \subseteq S^{\mathcal{I}}$ and for each $C \sqsubseteq D \in \mathcal{T}, C^{\mathcal{I}} \subseteq D^{\mathcal{I}}$.

### 5.1.2.2 Answering Queries Using Views

A data integration system is usually made up of three major components: source schemata, target global schema, and mappings between them. There are two main approaches for specifying the mapping: in the local-as-view (LaV) approach the source structures are defined as views over the target or global schema; on the contrary, in the global-as-view (GaV) approach each global concept is defined in terms of a view over the source schemata. A more general approach is called global-local-as-view (GLaV) which combines the expressivity of both LaV and GaV.

108    5 Data Integration in the Semantic Grid

Answering queries using views (Halevy AY, 2001) aims to find efficient means for answering queries posed by the global schema on the basis of the mapping specification and source data. In LaV there are two approaches in query processing: Query rewriting computes a rewriting of the query in terms of the views and then evaluates the rewriting procedure; query answering procedure directly answers the query based on the materialized view extensions. In GaV, existing systems deal with query processing by simply unfolding each global concept in the query with its definitions, w.r.t., the sources.

The queries in actual applications are usually conjunctive queries. A view is a named query. If the view results are pre-computed and stored, we refer to them as materialized views. In this chapter we consider the conjunctive query for $\mathcal{SHIQ}$ as defined as below.

**Definition 5.1 (Conjunctive Queries).** *Let $N_V$ be a countably infinite set of variables disjointed from $N_C$, $N_R$, and $N_I$. An atom is an expression $A(v)$ (concept atom) or $R(v, v')$ (role atom), where $A$ is a concept name, $R$ is a role, and $v, v' \in N_V$. A conjunctive query $q$ is a non-empty set of atoms in the form: $q(\bar{X}) : e_1(\bar{X}_1, \bar{Y}_1), \ldots, e_n(\bar{X}_n, \bar{Y}_n)$, where*

- *$q$ belongs to a new alphabet $\mathcal{Q}$ of queries that is disjointed from $N_C$, $N_R$, $N_I$ and $N_V$.*
- *$e_1(\bar{X}_1, \bar{Y}_1), \ldots, e_n(\bar{X}_n, \bar{Y}_n)$ are called the subgoals in the query body, and are either a concept atom in the form of $A(v)$ or a role atom in the form of $R(v, v')$.*
- *$\bar{X}_1, \ldots, \bar{X}_n$ are either variables from $N_V$ or constants from $N_I$, and $\bar{X} \subseteq \bar{X}_1 \cup \ldots \cup \bar{X}_n$ are called distinguished variables. $\bar{Y}_1, \ldots, \bar{Y}_n$ are called existential variables.*

The *distinguished variables* must have a value binding as to query evaluation. Instead, *existential variables* do not have to bind to any instance or data values.

In the following sections we propose a formal mapping system between $\mathcal{SHIQ}$ description logic model and the relational data model $\mathcal{RDM}$. We then discuss the fundamental aspects of *answering queries using $\mathcal{SHIQ}$-$\mathcal{RDM}$ mapping views*. Finally we present a novel algorithm for rewriting SPARQL queries as SQL queries using $\mathcal{SHIQ}$-$\mathcal{RDM}$ views.

## 5.2 Semantic Mapping in the Semantic Grid

### 5.2.1 The Mapping Issue

As the semantic web languages become more and more popular, there has been an ongoing increase of interest and endeavor in transforming and integrating legacy relational databases with semantic web languages (Stephens S, Morales A, Quinlan M, 2006; Martone ME, Gupta A, Ellisman MH, 2004).

## 5.2 Semantic Mapping in the Semantic Grid

For example, life science researchers are trying to transform legacy neuroscience relational databases into RDF/OWL format to enable integrative query answering and reasoning (Lam YK, Marenco L, Shepherd GM, Miller PL, Cheung KH, 2006). However, experience in building such applications has revealed a gap between semantic web languages and a relational data model.

To understand the differences and the problems specifically, consider the following example. For a bookstore application, one might require each book to have at least one author. In a relational database this could be captured by a foreign key constraint stating that, for each tuple in the book table, an associated tuple in the author table must exist. Such a constraint would be used to ensure data integrity during database updates. In an OWL knowledge base the same requirement could be captured by an *owl:someValuesFrom* restriction asserting that for all books they have at least one author. However, the key difference is that the OWL restriction would not be used to check data integrity. One can add a new book into the knowledge base without specifying an author for that book and the knowledge base system would not consider it as an error, rather that book would be simply inferred to as having some unknown authors. As a matter of fact the OWL knowledge base considers the restriction as a kind of TBox knowledge for reasoning.

More issues arise while mapping legacy relational databases to OWL ontologies. Most available approaches merely consider the mappings between tables/columns and classes/properties, with no consideration of database integrity constraints which are actually important information and knowledge. A problem comes up while doing query answering and reasoning. For the same example, if new books with no authors explicitly specified are transferred into the OWL knowledge base (OWL-KB) and one issues a query of all books having at least one author, the OWL-KB would simply discard all of those newly added books.

There are certain differences between the underlying logical formalisms of ontologies and relational schemata, and it is not straightforward to bridge the gap between them without developing a not only theoretically well-found but also a practically applicable approach.

In the next sections we propose a mapping formalism to bridge the gap between the OWL ontologies and schemata of a relational data model (RDM), and present an approach to rewriting $\mathcal{SHIQ}$ conjunctive queries as SQL queries on the basis of the mapping system. In particular we consider a special mapping called *Constraint Mapping* between RDM integrity constraints and $\mathcal{SHIQ}$ axioms. By including an extra reasoning process in the view, the OWL TBox knowledge and the constraints information are incorporated into the view definitions, thus enabling the query rewriting algorithm to answer more types of queries.

## 5.2.2 Basic Mapping System

The basic mapping system consists of a mapping formalism between a target $\mathcal{SHIQ}$ ontology and a set of source relational schemata that employs the form of LaV (i.e., each relational predicate is defined as a view over the ontology).

**Definition 5.2 ($\mathcal{SHIQ}$-$\mathcal{RDM}$ View).** An $\mathcal{SHIQ}$-$\mathcal{RDM}$ view is in this form: $\mathfrak{R}(\overline{X}) : -\mathfrak{B}(\overline{X'}, \overline{Y'})$ where

- $\mathfrak{R}(\overline{X})$ is called the head of the view, and $\mathfrak{R}$ is a relational predicate.
- $\mathfrak{B}(\overline{X'}, \overline{Y'})$ is called the body of the view, and is an $\mathcal{SHIQ}$ conjunctive query over the ontology.
- The $\overline{X} \subseteq \overline{X'}$ is the set of distinguished variables, $\overline{Y'}$ is the set of existential variables.

**Definition 5.3 ($\mathcal{SHIQ}$-$\mathcal{RDM}$ Mapping System).** An $\mathcal{SHIQ}$-$\mathcal{RDM}$ mapping system $\mathcal{MS}$ is a triple $(\mathcal{S}, \mathcal{T}_r, \mathcal{M}_r)$, where

- $\mathcal{S}_r$ is a source $\mathcal{RDM}$;
- $\mathcal{T}$ is the target $\mathcal{SHIQ}$ ontology consisting of a set of named concepts and roles, and several $\mathcal{SHIQ}$ axioms such as the role inclusion;
- $\mathcal{M}_r$ is the mapping between $\mathcal{S}_r$ and $\mathcal{T}$ of the form $q_s \leadsto q_r$, where $q_s$ and $q_r$ are queries over $\mathcal{S}_r$ and $\mathcal{T}$, respectively, and $\leadsto_r \in \{\sqsubseteq, \sqsupseteq, \equiv\}$.

Fig. 5.1 is an $\mathcal{SHIQ}$-$\mathcal{RDM}$ mapping scenario consisting of the target FOAF ontology[6] and two source relational data sources "$zju$" and "$ycmi$". Fig. 5.2 illustrates the corresponding $\mathcal{SHIQ}$-$\mathcal{RDM}$ views. Note we use RDF triple syntax to describe the concept atoms and role atoms. Within the view definitions, $?y_1, ?y_2$ are existential variables, and all other ones are distinguished variables. In practice, we use a skolem function such as $y_1 = F(?en)$ to generate the instance values for existential variables while answering queries.

## 5.2.3 Constraint Mapping

Database integrity constraints such as *Primary Key, Foreign Key,* and *Cardinality Constraint* are actually important information. However, most of the available mapping approaches merely consider the mappings between tables/columns and classes/properties disregarding the knowledge captured in constraints. We propose a special mapping called "constraint mapping" between database integrity constraints and $\mathcal{SHIQ}$ axioms. We then show in the next section an approach to incorporating these $\mathcal{SHIQ}$ axioms and description logic reasoning into query rewriting using views to enable the algorithm to answer more types of queries. Table 5.2 illustrates the set of constraint mapping rules for generating $\mathcal{SHIQ}$ axioms.

---

[6]The FOAF project: http://www.foaf-project.org/.

5.2 Semantic Mapping in the Semantic Grid    111

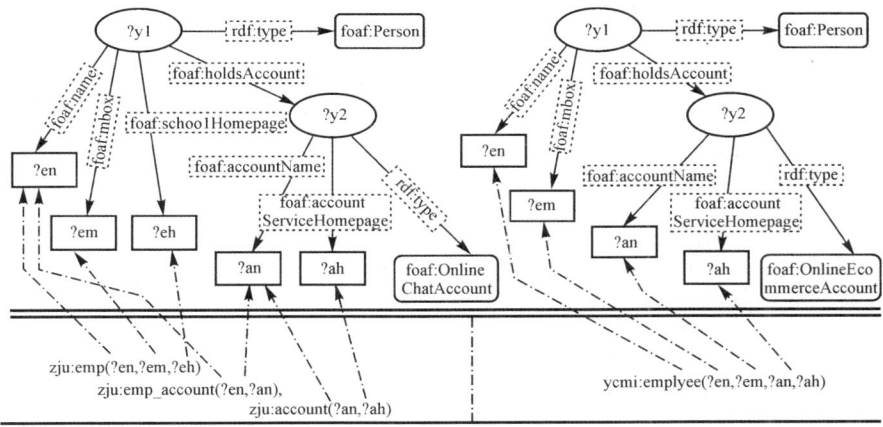

**Fig. 5.1.** $\mathcal{SHIQ}\text{-}\mathcal{RDM}$ mapping scenario

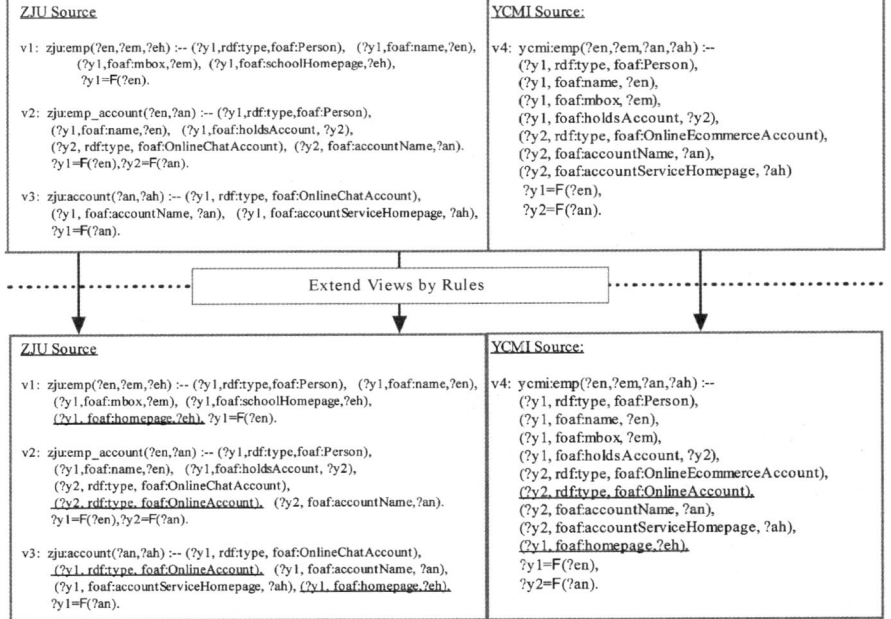

**Fig. 5.2.** $\mathcal{SHIQ}\text{-}\mathcal{RDM}$ view examples (The underscored triples are generated due to applying the extension rules.)

**Table 5.2.** Constraint Mapping. $T_1$, $T_2$ are relational tables, and are mapped to class $A, C$ respectively.

| Primary Key Constraint : $T_1$ $\Rightarrow$ Axiom: $A \sqsubseteq \exists hasPK.\top \sqcap \leqslant 1 hasPK.\top$ |
|---|
| Formal Semantics: $\forall x : [A(x) \mapsto \exists y : hasPK(x,y)]$ AND $\forall x, y_1, y_2 : [A(x) \wedge hasPK(y_1) \wedge hasPK(y_2) \mapsto y_1 \approx y_2]$ |
| Foreign Key Constraint: $T_1, T_2$ $\Rightarrow$ Axiom: $A \sqsubseteq \exists R.C$ |
| Formal Semantics: $\forall x : [A(x) \mapsto \exists y : R(x,y) \wedge C(y)]$ |
| $\leqslant n$-Cardinality Constraint: $T_1, T_2$ $\Rightarrow$ Axiom: $A \sqsubseteq \leqslant nR.C$ |
| Formal Semantics: $\forall x : [A(x) \mapsto \sharp R^{\mathcal{I}}(x, C) \leqslant n\}]$ |
| $\geqslant n$-Cardinality Constraint: $T_1, T_2$ $\Rightarrow$ Axiom: $A \sqsubseteq \geqslant nR.C$ |
| Formal Semantics: $\forall x : [A(x) \mapsto \sharp R^{\mathcal{I}}(x, C) \geqslant n\}]$ |
| $n$-Cardinality Constraint: $T_1, T_2$ $\Rightarrow$ Axiom: $A \sqsubseteq \leqslant nR.C \sqcap \geqslant nR.C$ |
| Formal Semantics: $\forall x : [A(x) \mapsto \sharp R^{\mathcal{I}}(x, C) = n\}]$ |

As shown in the example, suppose *?en* is the primary key of table *zju:emp(?en,?em,?eh)*, *zju:emp(?en,?an)* has a foreign key relationship with *zju:account(?an,?ah)* on *?an*, and the database requires that all persons have exactly two accounts. We could generate the following $\mathcal{SHIQ}$ axioms.

*Example 5.4 (Generated $\mathcal{SHIQ}$ Axioms).*

1. foaf:Person $\sqsubseteq$ $\exists$foaf:name $\sqcap$ $\leqslant$1foaf:name
2. foaf:Person $\sqsubseteq$ $\exists$foaf:holdsAccount.foaf:Account
3. foaf:Person $\sqsubseteq$ $\leqslant$2foaf:holdsAccount.foaf:Account
4. foaf:Person $\sqsubseteq$ $\geqslant$2foaf:holdsAccount.foaf:Account

## 5.3 Semantic Query Processing in the Semantic Grid

### 5.3.1 Answering Queries Using $\mathcal{SHIQ}$-$\mathcal{RDM}$ Views

The mapping system provides the formal foundation for query answering and reasoning. As SPARQL[7] is emerging as the standard query language for semantic web ontologies we use it to encode the conjunctive $\mathcal{SHIQ}$ queries in our framework. In the following we use a specific SAPRQL query as a running example for discussion. In our discussion we have also considered some special features of SPARQL, for example the *OPTIONAL* predicate in the example specifies that if the optional part does not lead to any solutions, the variable *?eh* in the optional block can be left unbound.

*Example 5.5 (SPARQL Query Example).*

---

[7] We refer readers to W3C SPARQL specification: http://www.w3.org/TR/rdf-sparql-query/ for SPARQL syntax and (Perez JA, Arenas M, Gutierrez C, 2006) for semantics and complexity. Note, in using SPARQL, we use RDF triple syntax to describe the concept atoms and role atoms in the query body.

## 5.3 Semantic Query Processing in the Semantic Grid

```
Q1: SELECT ?en ?em ?eh ?an ?ah where
    ?y1 rdf:type foaf:Person.
    ?y1 foaf:name ?en.
    ?y1 foaf:mbox ?em.
    OPTIONAL ?y1 foaf:homepage ?eh.
    ?y1 foaf:holdsAccount ?y2.
    ?y2 rdf:type foaf:OnlineAccount.
    ?y2 foaf:accountName ?an.
    ?y2 foaf:homepage ?ah.
```

Given an $\mathcal{SHIQ}$ ontology, a set of source relational instances $\mathcal{I}$, a set of $\mathcal{SHIQ}$-$\mathcal{RDM}$ views, plus a set of constraint mappings $\mathcal{CM}$, the central problem we are interested in is how to compute answers to $\mathcal{SHIQ}$ queries such as $Q_1$.

One approach is to materialize the views by transforming the relational instances to yield an $\mathcal{SHIQ}$ data instance $G$ based upon the mappings. We should then be able to directly evaluate $Q_1$ on $G$. In detail, we propose two phases for the materialization process: 1)Reasoning over views; 2)Transforming data.

#### 5.3.1.1 Reasoning over Views

In this process, a set of rules based on $\mathcal{SHIQ}$ TBox axioms, including the axioms generated by constraint mappings, are applied to the original view definitions. We formally specify these rules as follows.

**Definition 5.6 (View Reasoning Rules).**
Let $x, x_1, x_2, y$ denote either variable names from $N_V$ or constant names from $N_I$, let $A(x)$ and $R(x_1, x_2)$ denote concept atom and role atom respectively, and let $\mathcal{B}$ denote the set of atoms in the view body.

1. $\subseteq_C$-rule: **IF** a)$A \subseteq A'$, b) $A(x) \in \mathcal{B}$ c)$A'(x) \notin \mathcal{B}$ **THEN** ADD $A'(x)$ into $\mathcal{B}$.
2. $\subseteq_R$-rule: **IF** a)$R \subseteq R'$, b) $R(x_1, x_2) \in \mathcal{B}$, c)$R'(x_1, x_2) \notin \mathcal{B}$ **THEN** ADD $R'(x_1, x_2)$ into $\mathcal{B}$.
3. $\exists$-rule: **IF** a)$A \subseteq \exists S.C$, b)$A(x) \in (B)$, c)There is no $y$ such that $S(x,y) \in \mathcal{B}$ and $C(y) \in \mathcal{B}$ **THEN** ADD both $S(x,y)$ and $C(y)$ into $(B)$ where $y$ is a new existential variable.
4. $\forall$-rule: **IF** a)$A \subseteq \forall S.C$, b)$A(x_1) \in \mathcal{B}$, c)There is a $x_2$ such that $S(x_1, x_2) \in \mathcal{B}$ and $C(x_2) \notin \mathcal{B}$ **THEN** ADD $C(x_2)$ into $\mathcal{B}$.
5. $\geqslant_n$-rule: **IF** a)$A \subseteq \geqslant nS.C$, b)$A(x) \in \mathcal{B}$, c) $x$ has no $n$ $S$-related $y_1, ..., y_n$ such that $C(y_i) \in \mathcal{B}$ and $y_i \neq y_j$ for $1 \leqslant i \leqslant j \leqslant n$ **THEN** ADD into $\mathcal{B}$ with $n$ new role atom $S(x, y_i)$ and $n$ new concept atom $C(y_i)$ for all $1 \leqslant i \leqslant n$.

6. $\leqslant_n$-rule: **IF** a)$A \sqsubseteq \leqslant nS.C$, b)$A(x) \in \mathcal{B}$, c) $x$ has more than $n$ S-related $y$ such that $C(y) \in \mathcal{B}$, d)There are two S-related $y_1, y_2$ such that $C(y_1) \in \mathcal{B}$ and $C(y_2) \in \mathcal{B}$ with $y_1 \neq y_2$ **THEN** Replace all concept atoms $A'(y_2) \in \mathcal{B}$ with $A'(y_1)$ and all role atoms $R'(x, y_2) \in \mathcal{B}$ with $R'(x, y_1)$.
7. Inv-rule: **IF** a) $R^-$ is the inverse role of $R$, b)$R(x_1, x_2) \in \mathcal{B}$, **THEN** ADD $R^-(x_2, x_1)$ into $\mathcal{B}$.

For example, supposing the $\mathcal{SHIQ}$ ontology has the axioms in Example 5.7, we can get the extended view definitions as illustrated in Fig. 5.2, if applying these axioms together with the axioms generated by constraint mappings (c.f. Example 5.4).

*Example 5.7 (TBox Axioms)*.

1. foaf:OnlineChatAccount $\sqsubseteq$ foaf:Account
2. foaf:accountServiceHomepage $\sqsubseteq$ foaf:homepage

### 5.3.1.2 Transforming Data

Next, all relational instances are transformed into $\mathcal{SHIQ}$ data instances based on the extended views. Fig. 5.3 illustrates examples of the relational instances and a target $\mathcal{SHIQ}$ data instances graph. The evaluation of $Q_1$ on this target instance produces the tuples in Table 5.3.

**Table 5.3.** Query answers after evaluating $Q_1$ on the target $\mathcal{SHIQ}$ data instance $G$ in Fig. 5.3. Note for kei the variable ?eh is left unbound, namely, is nullable because of the "OPTIONAL" predicate in the query, but other variables MUST have a binding.

| Person.name | Person.mail-box | Person.homepage | Account.name | Account.homepage |
|---|---|---|---|---|
| kei | kei@ale.edu | NULL | kei@ebay.com | http://ebay.com |
| huajun | huajun@zju.edu.cn | http://.../huajun | huajun@amazon.com | http://amazon.com |
| huajun | huajun@zju.edu.cn | http://.../huajun | huajun@msn.com | http://msn.com |
| huajun | huajun@zju.edu.cn | http://.../huajun | chenhj@gmail.com | http://gmail.com |

An important notion is the *blank node IDs* generated in the target data instances. As shown in Fig. 5.3, _:$bn_1$, _:$bn_2$ are both newly generated blank node IDs corresponding to the variables ?$y_1$, ?$y_2$ in $v_1$. In general, a new blank node ID is generated in the target instance corresponding to each existential variable ?$y \in \Upsilon$ in the view. This treatment of the existential variable is in accordance with the RDF semantics[8], since blank nodes can be viewed as existential variables.

In practice these blank node IDs are generated by some *skolem function* which takes one or more distinguished variables as input parameters. For example, $y_1 = F(?en)$ is such a kind of function. The skolem function is also

---
[8]W3C RDF Semantics: http://www.w3.org/TR/RDF-mt/

## 5.3 Semantic Query Processing in the Semantic Grid    115

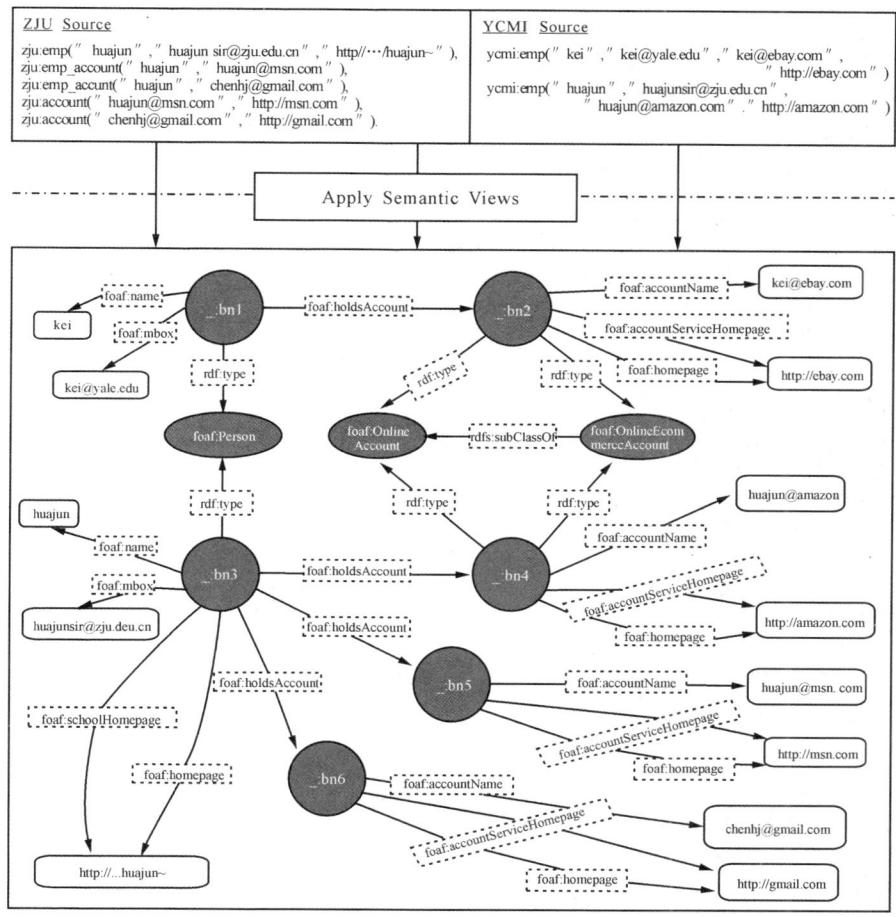

**Fig. 5.3.** Target $\mathcal{SHIQ}$ data instances

useful for merging instances stemming from different sources. For example, for the person name *huajun*, the same blank node ID $\_:bn_3$ is generated for both *ycmi* and *zju* sources.

*Remark 5.8 (RDF(s) Blank Node and Incomplete Semantics).* In many practical cases the data semantics of the relational database is incomplete. Take the *ycmi:emp* table as an example, it implies the semantics saying "for each person, *there is an* online account whose account name is...". The *"There is an..."* semantics is actually lost. This kind of semantics can be well captured by *RDF Blank Node*, since blank nodes are treated as simply indicating the existence of an entity without identifying it. The incomplete problem (Imielinski T, Lipski JR, 1984; Meyden RVD, 1998) has been considered as an important issue related to view-based data integration, and it is more acute for semantic web applications because apparently the Web is an open-ended system that is highly dynamic and extensible. Actually the $\mathcal{SHIQ}$ data instance graph, which is a RDF graph, is similar to the *conditional table* (Imielinski T, Lipski JR, 1984) introduced in database literatures to model incomplete databases. A *conditional table* is a database instance which might have existential variables as entries in its tuples. Similarly, the RDF graph might have blank nodes which could be viewed as existential variables. From this point of view we argue that blank node is an important representation construct for data integration in the Semantic Web.

Theorem 5.9 is about the theoretical complexity of the query answering problem.

**Theorem 5.9.** *Let $\mathcal{V}$ be a set of $\mathcal{SHIQ}$-$\mathcal{RDM}$ view definitions, $\mathcal{I}$ be a set of relational database instance, $\mathcal{T}$ be a $\mathcal{SHIQ}$ TBox, Q be a SPARQL query defined over $\mathcal{T}$, then the problem of computing the query answer with respect to $\mathcal{V}, \mathcal{I}, \mathcal{T}, Q$ is decidable and co-NP-complete regarding data complexity, and can be decided in time exponential in the size of $\mathcal{I}$ and double exponential in the size of the query Q.*

PROOF:
The basic idea here is to reduce the problem of answering conjunctive queries using $\mathcal{SHIQ}$-$\mathcal{RDM}$ views to the problem of conjunctive query answering for $\mathcal{SHIQ}$ description logic.

Let $n$ be the total number of tuples in $\mathcal{I}$ and let $k$ be the maximal number of triples in the view definitions. If we apply the view definitions onto $\mathcal{I}$, for each tuple in $I$, there could be at most $k$ triples generated in target data instance $G$, which is actually an $\mathcal{SHIQ}$ ABox. Therefore, by at most $nk$ step, a target $\mathcal{SHIQ}$ ABox $G$ with at most $nk$ triples can be generated. And the problem becomes one of evaluating the conjunctive query $Q$ directly on the $\mathcal{SHIQ}$ ABox $G$, w.r.t, the $\mathcal{SHIQ}$ TBox $\mathcal{T}$.

Since the steps of this process are polynomial in size of $\mathcal{I}$, the problem of answering conjunctive queries using $\mathcal{SHIQ}$-$\mathcal{RDM}$ views is polynomially reducible to the problem of conjunctive query answering for $\mathcal{SHIQ}$ description logic.

The new results from (Glimm B, Horrocks I, Lutz C, Sattler U, 2007) reveal that conjunctive query entailment in $\mathcal{SHIQ}$ is data complete for co-NP, and can be decided in time exponential in the size of the knowledge base and double exponential in the size of the query. □

### 5.3.2 Rewriting SPARQL Queries Using $\mathcal{SHIQ}$-$\mathcal{RDM}$ Views

In many practical cases the access to data source is limited. The query approach based upon view materialization becomes inapplicable. In this section we present an inference-enabled algorithm to rewrite SPARQL queries as SQL queries on the basis of the $\mathcal{SHIQ}$-$\mathcal{RDM}$ views. It could be generally

## 5.3 Semantic Query Processing in the Semantic Grid

divided into three stages: 1) Reasoning over views; 2) Splitting views into smaller mapping rules; 3) Rewriting queries using mapping rules.

### 5.3.2.1 Step 1: Reasoning over View

The first step is the same as the one for view materialization presented in the previous section. This extra reasoning process is necessary and essential because it directly incorporates the constraints information and TBox knowledge into the view definitions, and enables the rewriting algorithm to answer more types of query. For example, obviously $Q_1$ can not be answered by using the original views because the query makes a reference to foaf:OnlineAccount and foaf:homepage, which do not appear in any original view definitions at all. In another example, by incorporating Axioms 3,4 in Example 5.4 into the view, the system can answer the query of all persons who have exactly two accounts. Most importantly, because all TBox knowledge and constraints information has been encoded into the views as new *concept atoms or role atoms*, it greatly facilitates the implementation and improves the performance of the query rewriting algorithm since the algorithm does not need to consider the TBox knowledge and the constraints information anymore while doing query translation. Fig. 5.2 illustrates the examples of extended views after applying the extension rules.

### 5.3.2.2 Step 2: Splitting Views

In the second step, the views are turned into a set of smaller rules called *Class Mapping Rules*, denoted by $\mathcal{CMR}$. The purpose is to make it easier to match and replace the bodies of queries and views in the later on rewriting process.

**Definition 5.10 (Class Mapping Rule $\mathcal{CMR}$).** *A $\mathcal{CMR}$ rule is in the form*
$$t_1(\bar{X}_1), ..., t_n(\bar{X}_n) : -A(x), R_1(x, y_1), ..., R_m(x, y_m) \text{ where}$$

- $t_1(\bar{X}_1), .., t_n(\bar{X}_n)$ *are relational predicates.*
- $A(x)$ *is a concept atom,* $R_1(x, y_1), ..., R_m(x, y_m)$ *are role atoms.*

Intuitively, a $\mathcal{CMR}$ rule defines a mapping from the relational predicate to a subset triples (triple group) of the view body.

**Definition 5.11 (Triple Group).** *A triple group is a set of triples that have the same subject. A triple group represents a fragment of the view body which can later be matched and combined more easily. For example, the first four triples of v4 can be considered as a triple group, the next three triples can be viewed as another triple group. In Example 5.12, R1 defines the mapping from ycmi:emp(?en, ?em, ?an) to the first triple group, and R2 defines the mapping to the second triple group.*

*Example 5.12 (Class Mapping Rule Examples).*

```
R1: ycmi:emp(?en,?em,?an):-
        (y1,rdf:type,foaf:Person),
        (y1,foaf:name,?en), (y1,foaf:mbox,?em).
R2: ycmi:emp(?an,?ah):-
        (y2,rdf:type,foaf:OnlineEcommerceAccount),
        (y2,rdf:type,foaf:OnlineAccount),
        (y2,foaf:accountName,?an),(y2,foaf:homepage,?ah).
        (y2,foaf:accountServiceHomepage,?ah),
R3: zju:emp(?en,?em,?eh):-
        (y1,rdf:type,foaf:Person),
        (y1,foaf:name,?en), (y1,foaf:mbox,?em),
        (y1,foaf:schoolHomepage,?eh),(y1,foaf:homepage,?eh).
R4: zju:emp_account(?en,?an):-
        (y1,rdf:type,foaf:Person),
        (y1,foaf:name,?en), (y1,foaf:holdsAccount,F(?an)).
R3-4: zju:emp(?en,?em,?eh), zju:emp_account(?en,?an):-
        (y1,rdf:type,foaf:Person),
        (y1,foaf:name,?en),(y1,foaf:mbox,?em),
        (y1,foaf:schoolHomepage,?eh),
        (y1,foaf:homepage,?eh),(y1,foaf:holdsAccount,F(?an)).
```

---

**Algorithm 1** Generating Class Mapping Rules
---
**Require:** Set of $\mathcal{SHIQ\text{-}RDM}$ view $\mathcal{V}$
1: Initialize mapping rules list $\mathcal{M}$,
2: **for all** $v$ in $\mathcal{V}$ **do**
3:     Partition the triples in $v$ into triple groups.
4:     Let $T$ be the set of triple groups generated for $v$
5:     **for all** triple group $t$ in $T$ **do**
6:         create new mapping rule $m$
7:         $\mathfrak{R}(m) = \mathfrak{R}(v)$
8:         $\mathfrak{C}(m) = t$
9:         add $m$ to $\mathcal{M}$
10:     **end for**
11: **end for**
12: Merge rules if they describe the same class.
13: Output mapping rule list $\mathcal{M}$

---

Algorithm 1 illustrates the rule generation process. In general, for each view the algorithm firstly partitions the view body into triple groups. Next, the algorithm generates one class mapping rule for each *triple group*. Sometimes we need to merge the rules, for example R3 and R4 are merged into the R3-4 because they are both descriptions for foaf:Person class.

### 5.3.2.3 Query Rewriting Using Class Mapping Rules

In this phase the Algorithm 2 transforms the input $\mathcal{SHIQ}$ query using the $\mathcal{CMR}$ mapping rules, and outputs a set of valid rewritings that only refer to a set of view heads. The key to the query rewriting is to find out the *applicable class mapping rules*, namely those mapping rules that are capable of providing (partial) answers, and then replace the query body with the rule heads to yield candidate rewritings.

In detail, the rewriting algorithm starts by looking at the body of the query and partitions the body into *triple groups*, as Algorithm 1 does. Next it begins to look for rewritings for each triple group by trying to find an *applicable mapping rule*.

---

**Algorithm 2** Query Rewriting

**Require:** Set of mapping rule $\mathcal{M}$, sparql query $q$
1: Initialize rewriting list $Q$
2: Let $T$ be the set of triple groups of $q$
3: Add $q$ to $Q$
4: **for all** triple group $t$ in $T$ **do**
5:    Get all class mapping rules applicable to $t$, denoted by $\mathcal{AM}$
6:    **for all** $q$ in $Q$ **do**
7:       remove $q$ from $Q$
8:       **for all** $m$ in $\mathcal{AM}$ **do**
9:          **for all** *optional* triple $t_o$ in $t$ **do**
10:             Let $\bar{x}$ be a variable in $t$
11:             **if** and $\bar{x}$ is in the head of $q$ and $\bar{x}$ is not bound by any data value **then**
12:                 $\bar{x}$ = **NULL**
13:             **end if**
14:          **end for**
15:          Replace $t$ of $q$ with head of $m$
16:          Add $q$ to $Q$
17:       **end for**
18:    **end for**
19: **end for**
20: Output rewriting list $Q$

---

**Definition 5.13 (Applicable Class Mapping Rule).** *Given a triple group $t$ of a query $Q$, a mapping rule $m$ is an applicable class mapping rule $\mathcal{AM}$ with respect to $t$, if a) there is a triple mapping $\varphi$ that maps every triple in $t$ to a triple in $m$, and b) variables in $t$ appearing in the query head also appear in the head of $m$.*

**Definition 5.14 (Triple Mapping).** *Let $t_1$, $t_2$ denote RDF(s) triples and let $\mathsf{Vars}(t_i)$ denote the set of variables in $t_i$. $t_1$ is said to be mapped with $t_2$ if*

120    5 Data Integration in the Semantic Grid

there is a functional variable mapping $\varphi$ from $\mathsf{Vars}(t_1)$ to $\mathsf{Vars}(t_2)$ such that $t_2 = \varphi(t_1)$.

If the system finds an $\mathcal{AM}$, it replaces the triple group with the head of the mapping rule, and generates a new partial rewriting. After all triple groups have been replaced, a candidate rewriting is yielded. If a triple $t$ in $Q_i$ is *OPTIONAL* and no triple in the mapping rule is mapped to $t$, the variable in $t$ is set to NULL as default value.

Fig. 5.4 depicts the rewriting process for query $Q_1$ using the mapping rules in Example 5.12. Because of the space limitation, only two candidate rewritings are illustrated here.

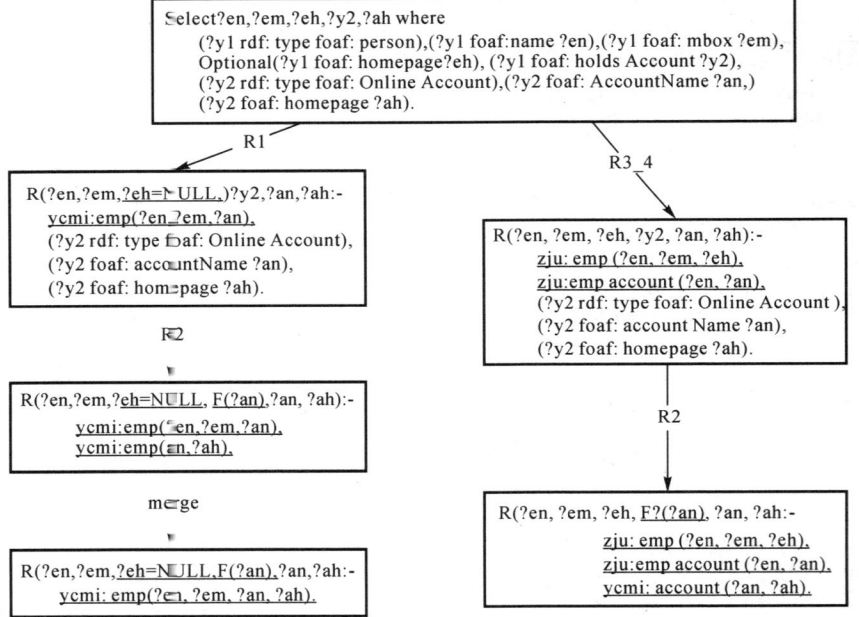

**Fig. 5.4.** The query rewriting example

Given the algorithms, we give an analysis on the complexity of the algorithm. Let $n$ be the number of triple groups in $Q_1$, let $m$ be the number of mapping rules, and it is not difficult to see that in the worst cases the rewriting can be done in time $O(m^n)$. We sketch the analysis as follows. For each triple group the possible number of applicable mapping rules is $m$. Therefore, in the worst case there might exist $m^n$ combinations of possible rewritings for $Q_1$. The worst case experiment in the evaluation section reflects the correctness of this statement. We note that all rewriting algorithms in LaV settings are limited because a complete algorithm must produce an exponential number of rewritings (Halevy AY, 2001).

### 5.3.2.4 Proof of the Soundness of the Rewriting Algorithm

PROOF: We say that a query $Q_1$ is contained in the query $Q_2$, denoted by $Q_1 \subseteq Q_2$, if the answer to $Q_1$ is a subset of the answer to $Q_2$. To show soundness we need to show that every rewriting $R$ that is obtained by the rewriting algorithm is contained in $Q$, i.e. $R \subseteq Q$. Since $R$ is the union of conjunctive query rewritings, we show that for each conjunctive rewriting $r \in R$, there is a containment mapping from $Q$ to $r$.

**Lemma 5.15.** *The Query $Q_2$ contains $Q_1$ if and only if there is a containment mapping from $Vars(Q_2)$ to $Vars(Q_1)$.*

Lemma 5.15 follows from (Chandra AK, Merlin PM, 1977), if we view triples as subgoals.

A conjunctive rewriting has the form: $H(\bar{X}) : -R_1(\bar{X}_1), R_2(\bar{X}_2), ..., R_k(\bar{X}_k)$ where $R_i(1 \leqslant i \leqslant k)$ is relational predicate. Note, because of the OPTIONAL predicate in $Q$, it is possible that $\bar{X}$ is not a subset of the union of $R_k(\bar{X}_k)$.

Given a conjunctive rewriting $r$, the expansion of $r$, denoted by $r'$ is the query in which the relational atoms are replaced by the RDF triples in the body of the class mappings rules that are used to generate $r$. We denote this rule set as $M$. To show there is a containment mapping from $Q$ to $r$, we would like to show that there exists a containment mapping from $Q$ to $r'$.

Firstly, the mapping of the head is straightforward. Let us consider the body: given a non-optional triple $t$ in $Q$, by the definitions of the triple mapping and the applicable class mapping rule, we know that there must exist a mapping rule $m \in M$, which includes $\varphi(t)$, where $\varphi$ is the triple mapping that maps every non-optional triple in a triple group $g$ of query $Q$ to a triple in $m$. We then know that for each non-optional triple $t$ in $Q$, there must exist a triple $t'$ in $r'$ such that $t' = \varphi(t)$. Thus, we could conclude that there exists a containment mapping from $Q$ to $r'$. By Lemma 5.15 we conclude $r' \subseteq Q$. Since $r$ is equivalent to $r'$ we continue to get the result of $r \subseteq Q$. Since every $r \in R$, $r \subseteq Q$, we finally get $R \subseteq Q$. □

### 5.3.2.5 Proof of the Completeness of the Rewriting Algorithm

PROOF: To show completeness[9] we need to prove that the rewriting algorithm generates all possible rewritings and there is no other rewriting except the ones generated by the algorithm. Formally speaking, let $P$ be the set of rewritings of $Q$ using $V$ and let $R$ be the rewritings produced by the algorithm. The algorithm is complete if $P \subseteq R$.

Since both $R$ and $P$ are unions of conjunctive queries, it suffices to show that if $p'$ is a conjunctive rewriting in $P$, then there exists a conjunctive rewriting $r'$ in $R$, such that $p' \subseteq r'$.

---

[9]Note: this is not to prove the completeness of query answering using views, which is actually a different problem.

Let $p''$ be the expansion of $p'$ by expanding the body of $p'$ with the view definitions.

**Proposition 5.16.** *If $p'$ is part of a rewriting of $Q$, then there exists a containment mapping $\varphi$ from $Q$ to the expansion $p''$ of $p'$.*

We will use $\varphi$ to show that given $p' \in P$, we can construct a conjunctive rewriting $r'$ based on our algorithm such that $r'$ contains $p'$.

We proceed as follows: For each subgoal $g_i \in p'$, we look at the view definition $v_i$ for $g_i$, and for each view $v_i$, we generate the class mapping rules by the approach mentioned before. Let $M$ be the set of mapping rules generated for $p'$. We note $M$ satisfies the following two properties:

- Property 1. $triples(Q) \subseteq triples(m_1) \cup ... \cup triples(m_i) \cup ... \cup triples(m_k)$, where $m_i \in M$ denotes individual mapping rule, and $triples(m_i)$ denotes the set of triples in the body of $m_i$. This is because $\varphi$ is a containment mapping by Proposition 5.16.
- Property 2. For every $i \neq j$, $triples(m_i) \cap triples(m_j) = \emptyset$ because of the way we construct the mapping rules.

By Property 1 we know that, for each non-OPTIONAL triple $t \in triples(Q)$, we can find a mapping rule $m$ in $M$ such that $\varphi$ maps $t$ to a triple $t' \in triples(m)$. We can group the triples in $Q$ by using the mapping rule they are mapped. Let $G$ be such a set of triple groups. We then get the following assertion.

**Proposition 5.17.** *Given a triple group $g_i \in G$, there is a class mapping rule $m_i \in M$ such that there exists a triple mapping $\varphi_i$ from $triples(g_i)$ to $triples(m_i)$.*

At this point, we have constructed a set of class mapping rules. By Properties 1 and 2, if we apply these rules to $Q$, we get a valid rewriting $r'$. We note that $r'$ has the same subgoals with $p'$. By Lemma 5.15, since there is a containment mapping from $r'$ to $p'$, we get $p' \subseteq r'$.□

## 5.4 Summary and Conclusion

This chapter proposes an $\mathcal{SHIQ}$-$\mathcal{RDM}$ view-based mapping system for relational database integration in the Grids and the Semantic Web. The fundamental issues including answering and rewriting SPARQL queries using $\mathcal{SHIQ}$-$\mathcal{RDM}$ view, are discussed. The ultimate goal of the presented approach is to realize the "web of structured data" vision by semantically interconnecting legacy databases, which allowed a person or a machine to start in one database, and then moved around an unending set of databases which were connected by rich semantics. As will be seen in the following chapters, some of the approaches introduced in this chapter have been implemented in a practical toolkit and applied in real-life applications.

# References

Abiteboul S, Duschka O (1998) Complexity of Answering Queries Using Materialized Views. Proc. 17th ACM SIGACT-SIGMOD-SIGART Symp. Principles of Database Systems. pp.254-263

An Y, Borgida A, Mylopoulos J (2005) Inferring complex semantic mappings between relational tables and ontologies from simple correspondences. International Semantic Web Conference. pp. 6-22

Arens Y, Hsu CN, Knoblock CA (1997) Query Processing in the SIMS Information Mediator. In Book: Readings in Agents. Morgan Kaufmann. pp.82-90

Calvanese D, Giacomo DG (2005) Data Integration: A Logic-based Perspective. AI Magazine. v25(1):59-70

Calvanese D, Giacomo DG, et al (1998) Description Logic Framework for Information Integration. Proc. of the Sixth International Conference on Principles of Knowledge Representation and Reasoning. pp.2-13

Calvanese D, Giacomo DG, Lemo D, et al (2004) What to ask a Peer: Ontology-based Query Reformulation. Proc. of the Ninth International Conference on Principles of Knowlege Representation and Reasoning. pp.469-478

Chandra AK, Merlin PM (1977) Optimal Implementation of conjunctive queries in relational databases. In: Proc. Ninth Annual ACM Symposium on Theory of Computing, 77-99

Chen HJ, Wang YM, Wu ZH, et al (2006) Towards a Semantic Web of Relational Databases: a Practical Semantic Toolkit and an In-Use Case from Traditional Chinese Medicine. Proc. of International Semantic Web Conference. 177-193

Deutsch A, Tannen A (2003) MARS: A system for publishing XML from mixed and redundant storage. Proc. of International Conference on VLDB. pp.220-230

Doan AH, Halevy AY (2005) Semantic Integration: Research in the Database Community. AI Magazine. v26(1):83-90

Dou DJ, LePendu P (2006) Ontology-based Integration for Relational Databases. Proc. of Annual ACM Symposium on Applied Computing. pp.254-263

Fensel D, Baader F, Rousset MC, Wache H (2001) Heterogeneous information resources need semantic access. Journal of Data Knowl. Eng, v36(3):211-213

Glimm B, Horrocks I, Lutz C, Sattler U (2007) Conjunctive Query Answering for the Description Logic $\mathcal{SHIQ}$. Proc. of International Joint Conference on Artificial Intelligence, 399-404

Goasdoue F, Rousset MC (2003) Querying Distributed Data through Distributed Ontologies: A Simple but Scalable Approach. IEEE Intelligent Systems. v18(5): 60-65

Halevy AY (2001) Answering Queries Using Views: A Survey. Journal of Very Large Database. v10(4):270-294

Halevy AY, Ives ZG, Madhavan J, et al (2004) The Piazza Peer Data Management System. IEEE Transactions on Knowledge and Data Engineering. v16(7):787-798

Halevy AY, Rajaraman A, Ordille JJ (2006) Data Integration: The Teenage Years. Proc. of 32nd International Conference on Very Large Data Bases. pp.9-16

Hendler J, Tim BL, Miller E (2002) Integrating Applications on the Semantic Web, Journal of the Institute of Electrical Engineers of Japan, v122(10): 676-680

Horrocks I, Patel-Schneider PF (1999) Optimizing Description Logic Subsumption. Journal of Logic and Computation. v9(3):267-293

Horrocks I, Patel-Schneider PF, Harmelen FV (2003) From SHIQ and RDF to OWL:the Making of a Web Ontology Language. Journal of Web Semantics. v1(1):7-23

Imielinski T, Lipski JR (1984) Incomplete Information in Relational Databases. Journal of ACM. v31(4):761-791

Jos LA, Corchuelo R, Ruiz D, Toro R (2007) From Wrapping to Knowledge. IEEE Transactions on Knowledge and Data Engineering. v19(2):310-323

Korotkiy M,Top JL (2004) From Relational Data to RDFS Models, Proc. of International Conference on Web Engineering. pp430-434

Lenzerini M (2002) Data integration: A theoretical perspective. In Proc. of the 21st ACM SIGACT SIGMOD SIGART Symp. on Principles of Database Systems. pp.233-246

Lam YK, Marenco L, Shepherd GM, Miller PL, Cheung KH (2006). Using web ontology language to integrate heterogeneous databases in the neurosciences. AMIA Annu Symp Proc. 464-468

Levy AY, Ordille RA (1996) Querying heterogeneous information sources using source descriptions. Proc. of International Conference on VLDB. pp.251-262

Manolescu I, Florescu D, Kossmann D (2001) Answering XML Queries on Heterogeneous Data Sources. Proc. of International Conference on VLDB. pp.241-250

Martone ME, Gupta A, Ellisman MH (2004) e-Neuroscience: challenges and triumphs in integrating distributed data from molecules to brains. Nature Neuroscience. v7:467-472

Mena E, Kashyap V, Sheth AP, Illarramendi A (1996) OBSERVER:An Approach for Query Processing in Global Information Systems based on Interoperation across Pre-existing Ontologies. Proc. of Conference on Cooperative Information Systems. pp.14-25

Meyden RVD (1998) Logical Approaches to Incomplete Information:A Survey. In Logics for Databases and Information Systems. p307-356

Natalya FN (2004) Semantic Integration: A Survey of Ontology-Based Approaches. SIGMOD Record, Special Issue on Semantic Integration, v33(4):65-70

Perez JA, Arenas M, Gutierrez C (2006) Semantics and Complexity of SPARQL. Proc. of International Semantic Web Conference. pp.30-43

Pottinger R, Halevy AY (2001) MiniCon: A Scalable Algorithm for Answering Queries Using Views. Journal of Very Large Database. v10(2-3):182-198

Qian X (1996) Query folding. Proc. of International Conference on Data Engineering. pp.48-55

Richard C (2005) A Relational Algebra for SPARQL. HP Technical Reports. HPL-2005-170, http://www.hpl.hp.com/techreports/2005/HPL-2005-170.html

Stevens RD, Baker PG, Bechhofer S, et al (2000) Tambis: Transparent access to multiple bioinformatics information sources. Bioinformatics. v16(2):184-185

Stephens S, Morales A, Quinlan M (2006) Applying Semantic Web Technologies to Drug Safety Determination. IEEE Intelligent Systems. v21(1):82-86

Tim BL (1998) Relational Databases on the Semantic Web. http://www.w3.org/DesignIssues/RDB-RDF.html

Ullman JD (2000) Information Integration Using Logical Views. Journal of Theoretical Computer Science. v239(2):189-210

Wache H, Vogele T, Visser U, et al (2001) Ontology-based integration of information – a survey of existing approaches. In Proc. of IJCAI01 Workshop: Ontologies and Information Sharing. pp.108-117

Yu C, Popa L (2004) Constraint-based XML Query Rewriting for Data Integration. Proc. of the ACM SIGMOD International Conference on Management of Data. pp371-382

# 6

# Service Flow Management in the Semantic Grid

**Abstract:** How to carry out collaboration efficiently in the Grid environment becomes a hot topic in research and development of the Grid. Service flow management is one of key technologies for solving the problem. In this chapter we expatiate on the background of service flow management. And then we present the research framework for service flow management and introduce some important issues in the framework. After that we analyze some key issues in service flow management and propose corresponding solutions in our prototype of service flow management—Dartflow.

## 6.1 Introduction

Service flow (service composition) is a process that is composed of several services involving data transfer, message exchange and logical combination according to business processes. It is a new form of workflow combined with Web service and grids.

Workflow is a part of the computer supported cooperative work (CSCW) (WFMC, 1995). It realizes the flow management, flow analysis and flow regeneration by decomposing a business flow into well-defined activities, roles and rules. Workflow technology has been widely adopted by electronic business, electronic government affairs and manufacture, and it has greatly accelerated the process of business flows. Recently, enterprise business processes are not limited to a single enterprise itself, but overspread to multi-organizations even wide area networks as international cooperation becomes prevalent. And Web Service plays an important role in distributed flow management among organizations.

Web Service is an application that is based on open standards and can be invoked through the Web. With the incessant development of the Web service, service-oriented computing (SOC) has become an important computing paradigm on the Internet (Papazoglou MP, 2003). More and more enterprises and organizations encapsulate their business functions and processes into web services and publish them over the internet to find possible customers and partners, as the standards for Web services are constantly improving and the enterprise-level platforms for Web services are continually maturing. Web service, as a new distributed application, is widely applied to electronic business, finance, tourism and scientific computing, to accomplish various operations. Hence, how to seamlessly integrate Web services that are dispersed over the internet, to form a powerful service flow that meets business needs, and how to manage the large-scale service flows that are distributed, multi-organizations and loosely coupled, have become the key to accelerate the evolution of workflow and the Web service.

Meanwhile, service flow management has also become an important problem yet to be solved as the development of grid technology and the implementation of grid applications. Cooperation is an important goal for grid technology. Cooperation in the Grid is the cooperation among services since any resources and systems can be deemed as services in a grid environment. The key to collaborate and co-compute in a grid environment is to realize the seamless integration and cooperation of services. And service-based flow management is the key technology to solve service cooperation; hence it becomes pivotal to achieve cooperation using grid technology.

## 6.2 Research Framework of Service Flow Management

Service flow management targets at composing services into processes and executing processes to realize different business goals. It involves many research issues such as service discovery, composition, verification, execution and monitoring. All of these topics construct the research framework for service flow management (shown in Fig 6.1).

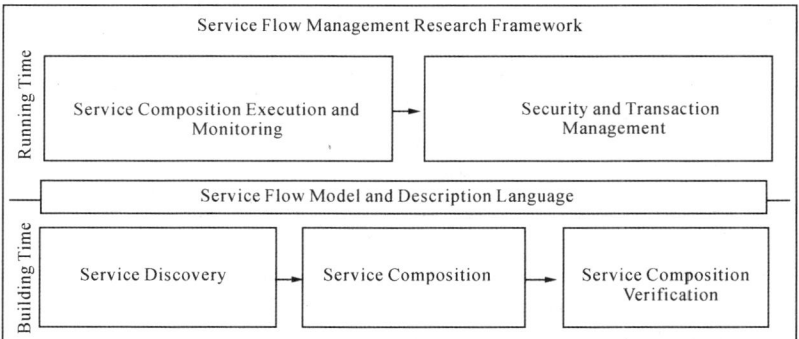

**Fig. 6.1.** Service flow management research framework

According to the lifecycle of service flow management, the research topics covered by the research framework can be divided into two phases: the building phase and running phase. The former involves issues such as service discovery, service composition, service composition verification and service flow model and description language, while the latter includes service composition execution, monitoring and security and transaction management. Because the issues covered in the running time have not attracted much attention, although there exist several research works and standard establishment efforts focus on web service security and transactions such as WS-Security and WS-Transaction, we only give a detailed description of the issues involved in the building time, i.e., service discovery, service composition, and service composition verification.

### 6.2.1 Service Matchmaking and Discovery

Service is the core element in service flow. In order to construct a service flow it is important to discover target services in an efficient and fast way. At present it is an active research area. It originates from the issue of software component reuse and discovery in software engineering and distributed computing, and information (data or web) retrieval in knowledge and data engineering. During the past few years much effort has been placed on the area of service discovery in both industrial research and academic research.

As an industrial initiative to create an Internet wide registry of Web service, UDDI has become a *de facto* standard specification for registering, integrating and discovering services. It allows businesses to register and search for Web services. However, UDDI provides limited search facilities allowing only a keyword-based search for services based on names, comments and descriptions. It fails to recognize the similarities and differences between the capabilities provided by services. Thus, service discovery in UDDI does not yield a satisfactory recall rate and precision for users.

To address the limitation in UDDI, the emerging approaches from academic research rely on semantic web technology. At present, many semantic-based service discovery methods are proposed in the literature, for example, the process-ontology based method (Klein M, Bernstein A, 2004), OWL-S-based service capability matchmaking method (Paolucci M, Kawamura T, Payne TR, Sycara K, 2002), the process-model based method (Brogi A, Corfini A, Popescu R, 2005) and description logic based methods (Benatallah B, Hacid MS, Leger A, Rey C, 2005). Based on related ontology languages and inference engines, semantic web services provide machine understandable descriptions of what services do and how they achieve their goals. Semantic-based service discovery utilizes the process of semantic matchmaking to check whether an advertised service satisfies a user's request for a service by computing the similarity degree between the description for the service and the one for the request. If the similarity degree exceeds some threshold value specified by the user, the service is returned; otherwise it is excluded from the result set. Given an advertised service description and a request description both enhanced by semantics, semantic matchmaking is carried out between their inputs, outputs, preconditions and effects, respectively. Due to the accurate and unambiguous description of a service's functionalities and a user's request, semantic-based service discovery methods tend to get a good recall rate and precision. The recall rate is the proportion of relevant services that are retrieved and the precision rate is the proportion of retrieved services that are accurately matched.

### 6.2.2 Service Composition

Service composition is the process of composing atomic services into a composite service. As it has the ability of one business to provide value-added services through composition of basic web services, possibly offered by different companies, at present service composition has become the focus for both industry and academy in the area of business process management, service-oriented computing and artificial intelligence. A large number of service composition methods are proposed (Rao J, Su X, 2004; Dustdar S, Schreiner W, 2005).

Researchers from different fields suggested various methods for Web Service composition based on their own perspectives. We can classify these methods in terms of the different classification standards. For instance, according to the degree of automation, the methods can be separated into manual service composition method, semi-automatic service composition method and automatic service composition method; and according to the dynamic degree of service composition, the methods can also be separated into static service composition method and dynamic service composition method. We classify those methods into the business process driven service composition methods and on-line task solving oriented methods. The former is mainly based on process management techniques such as workflow technology, and the latter focuses on artificial intelligence theory, such as logical reasoning, task planning, and theorem proof. However, these two methods have their own limitations: 1) for the business process-driven service composition method, most of the composition work is based on the fixed business process model. Though the dynamic of the service composition has been improved by introducing the concepts of service dynamic binding, service templates and service community, these methods still can't deal with the dynamic business processes whose contents can't be fixed on in the modeling-phase, for example some sub-processes need to be re-organized and re-established according to run-time information. So the current fixed-process-based service composition method is difficult for meeting the needs of business processes; 2) the on-line task-solving oriented methods are mainly based on artificial intelligence theory and formal methods, which calls for pretreatment and formal conversion for service and tasks. These methods have high complexity, and once the associated service set of the composition becomes huge, the search and reasoning processes for the service composition will become extremely difficult and slow, and are unable to satisfy the response time expected by the users. Besides, these methods have a fairly high degree of automation, so the accuracy and usability of the service built by these service composition methods need further examination.

### 6.2.3 Service Composition Verification

Web service composition combines autonomic services into a service process according to a certain business logic. Generally speaking, componential atomic services are from different organizations or institutions. To ensure the composite service works properly and eventually reaches the business objectives, it is required that the service process conform to the business logic and also the atomic services within the composition collaborate and interact with each other normally, thereby each atomic service is successfully invoked and data is correctly transferred between each atomic service. Accordingly, it is vital to validate the service process before putting it into use. Presently the topic of Web service combination is widely studied (Martens A, 2005; Bultan T, Fu X, Hull R, Su J, 2003; Foster H, Uchitel S, Magee J, Kramer J, 2004). Most of the work is based on a formal methodology, such as Petri-net, automata theory and process algebra. After a deep investigation of the related research and bibliography, we can split the topic of service composition verification into two subjects, one is the validation of the correctness of the process logic within the combined services, and the other is the validation of the compatibility of all componential services.

The validation of service composition is similar to that of traditional workflow. Much research continues to adopt the process validation method and mechanism in the workflow, primarily focusing on validating the status reachability, the terminability, the liveness and the free-deadlock of the process, etc. The other topic in the validation of Web service composition is to validate the compatibility of each componential service. The primary objective is to validate whether services interact with each other normally. We split the topic into three aspects: 1) the grammatical compatibility between services; 2) the semantic compatibility between services; 3) the behavior compatibility between services. Grammatical compatibility refers to the state in which interactive services can normally interact with each other on the semantic level, for example the output of the former service meets the specification of the input of the latter one in message quantity and message structure. It focuses on validating the grammatical information such as the format and quantity of the interface message. Semantic compatibility refers to the state in which the interactive services are in accordance with each other in the service function, parameter meaning, message content and so on. For example, if the function of the invoked service meets users' requirements at the semantic level, again the output content of the former service semantically accords with the input content of the latter one. Behavior compatibility is a new topic in the validation of service composition. Its primary objective is to validate whether services in a composition can successfully interact with each other without violating any business logic.

## 6.3 Service Matchmaking in DartFlow

With the widespread adoption of SOA, enterprises are encouraged to develop and publish more and more services. As the number of services has increased, so has the need for a sophisticated discovery mechanism. Service discovery is for retrieving services advertised in a repository that match a user's goal. It has been a well-recognized challenge in the application of SOA. In DartFlow, a service flow management platform introduced later, we propose a semantic service matchmaking mechanism (Deng S, Wu J, Li Y, Wu Z, 2006).

### 6.3.1 An Extended Service Model

A web service is a self-contained, self-describing, modular application that can be published, located, and invoked across the Web. Most services can provide a group of functions. For example, a stock service can provide the stock query and exchange functions. Currently the prevalent service description languages support multiple functional units in a service. WSDL, as the *de facto* standard service description language, can specify multiple operation elements in it. Every operation element can be regarded as a functional unit. OWL-S, as the specification of SWS, is an ontology language for Web services with three main parts: the service profile that provides public information for advertisements and discoveries, the process model that tells "how the service works" in detail, and the grounding that tells "how to access the service". OWL-S can specify multiple atomic processes in it. Every atomic process can be treated as a functional unit, too. But neither WSDL nor OWL-S provides a mechanism to describe and publish the relations among different functional units inside a service. Moreover, there exists another deficiency in WSDL and OWL-S. Both of them lack a mechanism for service providers to describe the dependencies between inputs and outputs within a functional unit of a service. In fact, in a functional unit there is such an output which is only dependent on part of the inputs. Thus a mechanism is needed for service providers to describe and publish which inputs are necessary for each output of a functional unit. In DartFlow we propose a formal service model that extends the service profile of OWL-S and provides feasible and convenient mechanisms to depict and publish the relations among different functional units and interface dependency information through the assignable-relation concept and the full/partial dependency concept, respectively. A functional unit of a service is an atomic operation for service consumers to invoke. This concept is like the operation element of WSDL or the atomic process element in the OWL-S.

**Definition 6.1.** *A functional unit $U$ is a 6-tuple: $U = (N, I, O, P, E, \psi)$ where:*
*(1) $N$ is the functional unit name.*
*(2) $I = \{i_1, i_2, \cdots, i_n\}$ is the set of inputs.*
*(3) $O = \{o_1, o_2, \cdots, o_n\}$ is the set of outputs. $I \cup O$ is called interface set of the service. $\forall e \in I \cup O$ is expressed using a domain-dependent ontology class with some properties.*
*(4) $P$ is the precondition.*
*(5) $E$ is the effect.*
*(6) $\psi$ is the dependency function from the output set to the input power set.*

For an output $o \in O$, $\psi(o) = \phi \in 2^I$, meaning that $o$ depends on input set $\phi$. $\phi$ can be regarded as an extension to OWL-S, which allows service providers to depict and publish the interface dependency information. The meaning of dependency between outputs and inputs is defined in Definition 6.2 below. Although the concepts of precondition and effect also exist in OWL-S, they are used to depict the precondition and effect of the whole service. We argue that the granularity is too coarse to describe each atomic process in OWL-S. Thus we transfer the concepts of precondition and effect from a whole service to each functional unit.

**Definition 6.2.** *Given an output $o$ and an input $i$ of a functional unit $U$, $o$ depends on $i$ (denoted by $o \prec I$) if and only if $i$ must be provided in order to get $o$ in the service invocation.*

**Definition 6.3.** *Given a functional unit $U = (N, I, O, P, E, \psi)$ and $o \in O$, if $o \prec I$ or $\psi(o) = I$, $o$ is a fully-dependent output. If $\psi(o) \subset I$, $o$ is a partially-dependent output.*

As Fig. 6.2 shows, both outputs $o_1$ and $o_2$ depend on $i_1$ and $i_2$ while $o_3$ depends on only $i_1$. So $o_1$ ad $o_2$ are fully-dependent outputs and $o_3$ is a partially-dependent output. We represent a fully-dependent output as a dot-filled rectangle and a partially-dependent output as a fork-filled rectangle as shown in Fig. 6.2.

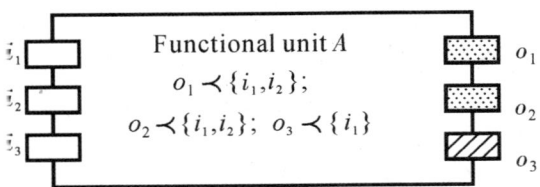

**Fig. 6.2.** A functional unit definition

## 6.3 Service Matchmaking in DartFlow

**Definition 6.4.** *For two functional units $U_1 = (N_1, I_1, O_1, P_1, E_1, \psi_1)$ and $U_2 = (N_2, I_2, O_2, P_2, E_2, \psi_2)$, and an output o and an input i where $o \in O_2$ and $i \in I_1$, we say that o is assignable to i (denoted by $o \mapsto i$) if and only if: (1) The message structure and type of o are compatible with those of i, and (2) o and i use the same ontology concepts or o is a SubClassOf i. The first condition ensures that o can be assigned to i at the syntax level while the second condition ensures that o can be assigned to i at the semantic level.*

**Definition 6.5.** *A Web service S is a 6-tuple: $S = (\eta, \sigma, \rho, \pi, \delta, \zeta)$ where
(1) $\eta$ is a service name;
(2) $\sigma$ depicts some general information about the Web service in natural language for human reading, such as the functional description;
(3) $\rho$ is a provider description of the service, which contains information about the service provider such as the provider name and the corresponding method;
(4) $\pi$ is a category name of the service based on a taxonomy;
(5) $\delta = \{U_1, U_2, \ldots, U_n\}$ is a set of functional units of the service;
(6) $\zeta : U_i.O \to 2^{\bigcup U_j.I}$ where $1 \leqslant i,j \leqslant n$ and $j \neq i$, is a function to indicate which inputs of other functional units can be assigned with an output of the current functional unit $U_i$.*

For an output $o \in U_1.O$, if $\zeta(o) = \{i_1, i_2\}$, where $i_2 \in U_2.I$, $i_3 \in U_3.I$, $\{U_1, U_2, U_3\} \subseteq \delta$ we say that $o$ of $U_1$ can be assigned to $i_2$ of $U_2$ as well as $i_3$ of $U_3$. Fig. 6.3 shows an example service that has two functional units with names $A$ and $B$ respectively. In $A$, $o_1$ is a fully-dependent output and $o_2$ is a partially-dependent output. In $B$, both of $o_2$ and $o_3$ are partially-dependent outputs while $o_1$ is fully-dependent. The assignable-relations and $B.O.o_2 \mapsto A.I.i_1$ and $B.O.o_3 \mapsto A.I.i_2$ indicate that $o_2$ of $B$ can be assigned to $i_1$ of $A$ and $o_3$ of $B$ can be assigned to $i_2$ of $A$.

Note that a service specification based on Definition 6.5 is used not only for service matchmaking algorithms but also for service providers to publish their services. It has the same purpose as the service profile of OWL-S and covers all the content of the service profile. But it differs from the service profile in that it provides additional mechanisms for service providers to depict and publish the interface dependency and assignable relation information among interfaces. The extended service profile ontology for OWL-S is illustrated in Fig. 6.4.

Compared with the standard service profile ontology of OWL-S, the extended one has three new ontology classes named functional unit, partially-dependent output and assignable relation, respectively. Each new class has several properties. For example, an assignable relation has one source output and one destination input. This means that the output can be assigned to the input. The relation among profile classes is as follows: a service profile can have several functional units and assign relations. Each unit can have one or more partially-dependent outputs.

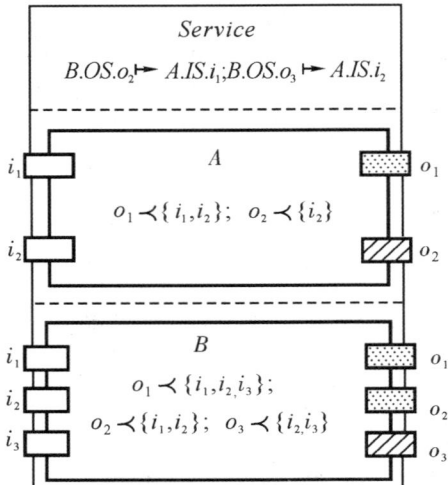

**Fig. 6.3.** A service example

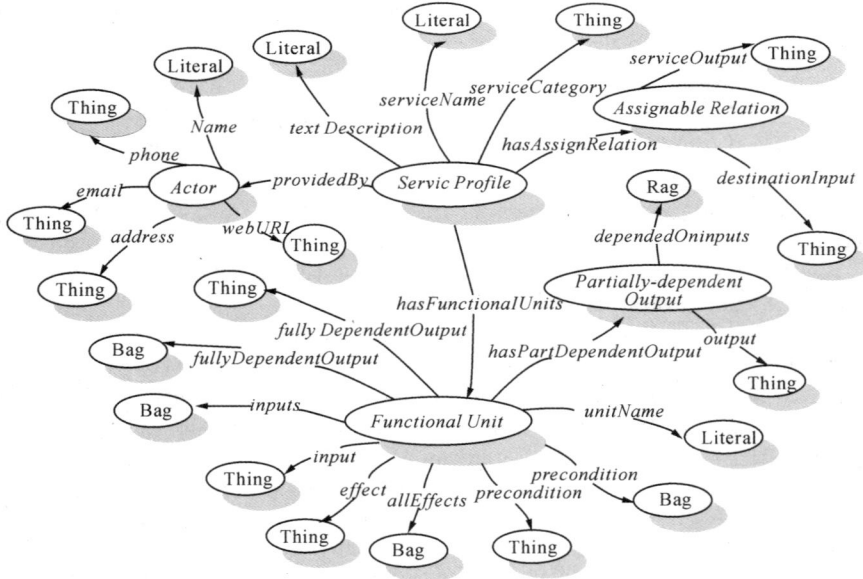

**Fig. 6.4.** A service example

### 6.3.2 Service Matchmaking

The matchmaking method in DartFlow is capable of composing functional units inside a service to fulfill requests; and also it takes into account the

## 6.3 Service Matchmaking in DartFlow

interface dependencies implied in a functional unit. Before introducing it, we present some important definitions and assistant algorithms.

**Definition 6.6.** *Given a service $S = (\eta, \sigma, \rho, \pi, \delta, \zeta)$, two functional units $U_1 = (N_1, I_1, O_1, P_1, E_1, \psi_1)$ and $U_2 = (N_2, I_2, O_2, P_2, E_2, \psi_2)$, $U_1$ can be concatenated to $U_2$ (denoted by $U_1 \ominus U_2$) if and only if:*

*(1) $|U_2.O_2| \geqslant |U_1.I_1|$, and;*
*(2) For $\forall i \in U_1.I_1, \exists o \in U_2.O_2$, the relation $o \mapsto i$ holds.*

This definition defines the conditions under which two functional units can be concatenated together. Condition 1 ensures that the number of $U_1$ inputs is not larger than the number of $U_2$ outputs[1]. Condition 2 ensures that for any input of $U_1$ there exists one output of $U_2$ which can be assigned to the input. According to Definition 6.6, $A$ can be concatenated to $B$ (denoted by $B \ominus A$) in Fig. 6.3. The concatenation relation between two operational units is illustrated in Fig. 6.5. For three units $A$, $B$ and $C$, if both $A$ and $B$ can be concatenated to $C$, we denote it as $C \ominus A, B$.

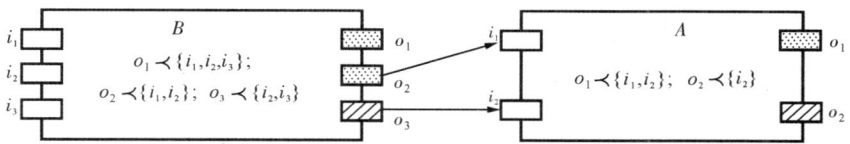

**Fig. 6.5.** The concatenation relation between two operational units

**Definition 6.7.** *Given a service $S = (\eta, \sigma, \rho, \pi, \delta, \zeta)$, and a function $\chi : \delta \rightarrow 2^\delta$, and $\chi$ is a joint function if and only if for $\forall u \in \delta, v \in \chi(u)$ the relations $u \ominus v$ and $u \notin \chi(u)$ hold when $\chi(u) \neq \phi$.*

For a functional unit in a service, the joint function is used to find out which other functional units can be concatenated to it. Based on Definition 6.6, the joint function can be implemented through $FINDSUBSEQUENCE$ algorithm, listed below, with the time complexity $O(m \times n \times k)$, where $m = |\delta|, n = |u \cdot I|$ and $k = |u \cdot O|$.

Algorithm: $FINDSUBSEQUENCE$
Input: A service $s = (\eta, \sigma, \rho, \pi, \delta, \zeta)$ and a functional unit service request $u \in \delta$
Output: $\chi(u)$

---

1. FOR $i = 1$ to $|\delta|$ DO
2.    IF $u_i \neq u$ AND $|u_i.I| \leqslant |u.O|$ THEN

---

[1] In order to be simple, we do not consider the interface dependency while composing functional units within a service.

```
3.      WHILE j ⩽ |u_i.I| DO
4.          IF ∃o_k ∈ u.O AND o_k → i_j (1 ⩽ k ⩽ |u.O| and i_j ∈ u_i.I) THEN
5.              j + +
6.          END IF
7.      END WHILE
8.      IF j = |u_i.I| + 1 THEN
9.          χ(u).add(u_i)
10.     END IF
11. END IF
12. END FOR
13. RETURN χ(u)
```

---

In general a service request specifies its input/output requirements, optional QoS criteria and additional information such as the service category name and description in its specification. In fact, the input/output requirements are the critical factors for matchmaking algorithms. For the purpose of simplicity, we currently discuss only the input/output requirements in a service request.

**Definition 6.8.** *A service request is a 2-tuple:* $R = (I^r, O^r)$, *where*

*(1)* $I = \{i_1^r, i_2^r, \ldots, i_m^r\}$, *is the set of inputs and;*
*(2)* $O = \{o_1^r, o_2^r, \ldots, o_n^r\}$, *is the desired set of outputs.*

**Definition 6.9.** *Given a functional unit* $U = (N, I, O, P, E, \psi)$ *and a service request* $R = (I^r, O^r)$, *we say that the functional unit matches the request (denoted by* $U \perp R$*) if and only if:*

*(1)* $O \supseteq O^r$, *and*
*(2)* $\forall o \in O$ *and* $o \in O^r$, $\psi(o) \subseteq I^r$

The first condition ensures that the functional unit can provide all the desired outputs specified in the request. The second one indicates that for any output of the functional unit, which is also specified in the request, all of its dependent inputs can be provided by the request. If a functional unit satisfies these two conditions, it fulfills the request. In a service there maybe exists more than one functional unit matching the request. In this case, we select the one with the greatest matching degree as the target for the request.

**Definition 6.10.** *Given a functional unit* $U = (N, I, O, P, E, \psi)$ *and a service request* $R = (I^r, O^r)$, *where* $U \perp R$ *holds, the matching degree of* $U \perp R$ *(denoted by* $\omega(U \perp R)$*) is computed as follows:* $\omega(U \perp R) = \frac{|O^r|}{|O|} \times \frac{|I|}{|I^r|}$.

The *MATCHUNIT* algorithm is used to check whether a functional unit matches the service request, and computes the matching degree for the functional unit if there is a match. Its time complexity is $O(m \times n \times p \times q)$ where $m = |I|, n = |O|, p = |I^t|, q = |O^r|$.

## 6.3 Service Matchmaking in DartFlow

Algorithm: $MATCHUNIT$
Input: a functional unit service request $U = (N, I, O, P, E, \psi)$ and a service request $R = (I^r, O^r)$
Output: $\omega(U \perp R)$

---

1. FOR $i = 1$ to $|O^r|$ DO
2.    IF $u_i \neq u$ AND $|u_i.I| \leqslant |u.O|$ THEN
3.       WHILE $j \leqslant |O|$ DO
4.          IF $o_j = o_i^r$ OR $o_j \in SubClassOf(o_i^r)$ THEN
5.             BREAK
6.          ELSE
7.             $j++$
8.          END IF
9.       END WHILE
10.       IF $j = |O| + 1$ THEN
11.          RETURN 0
12.       ELSE
13.          LET $\psi(o_j) = \{d_{i_1}, d_{i_2}, \ldots, d_{i_m}\}$
14.          FOR $k = 1$ to $m$ DO
15.             WHILE $t \leqslant |I^r|$ DO
16.                IF $i_t^r = d_{i_k}$ OR $i_t^r \in SubClassOf(d_{i_k})$ THEN
17.                   BREAK
18.                ELSE
19.                   $t++$
20.                END IF
21.             END WHILE
22.             IF $t = |I^r| + 1$ THEN
23.                RETURN 0
24.             END IF
25.          END FOR
26.       END IF
27.    END IF
28. END FOR
29. RETURN $\frac{|O^r|}{|O|} \times \frac{|I|}{|I^r|}$

**Definition 6.11.** *For a service $S = (\eta, \sigma, \rho, \pi, \delta, \zeta)$, a service request $R = (I^r, O^r)$, and an ordered functional unit sequence $f = <u_1, u_2, \ldots, u_m>$ $(u_i \in \delta, 1 \leqslant i \leqslant m \leqslant |\delta|)$, $f$ is a matching sequence for $R$ if and only if:*

*(1) for any two elements $u_i$ and $u_{i+1}$ $(1 \leqslant i \leqslant m - 1)$ in $f$, $u_i \ominus u_{i+1}$ holds, and*

*(2) $R.I^r \supseteq u_1.I$ holds, and*

*(3) $R.O^r \subseteq u_m.O$ holds.*

A matching sequence is a composition of functional units that fulfills request $R$. Sometimes, although no functional unit alone can fulfill a request, the composition of several ones can. Thus service matchmaking algorithms need to check whether there exists a matching sequence to fulfill the request when no single functional unit can provide the requested function.

**Definition 6.12.** *The length of a matching sequence $f$ (denoted by $\ell(f)$) is defined as the number of functional units in $f$.*

**Definition 6.13.** *For a service $S$ and a service request $R$, we call $f_S(R) = \{f_1, f_2, \ldots, f_n\}$ the matching sequence set, which is the set of all the matching sequences for $R$ in $S$.*

**Definition 6.14.** *For a service $S$ and a service request $R$ and a matching sequence $f$, we call $f$ an optimal matching sequence for $R$ (denoted by $f_S^o(R)$), if and only if $\forall f \in f_S(R)$, $\ell(f) \geqslant \ell(f_S^o(R))$ holds.*

The $MATCHSEQUENCE$ algorithm is used to find the optimal matching sequence for a service request in a service. Its time complexity is $O(2^n)$, where $n$ is the number of functional units in a single service and it is not too large for most services.

Algorithm: $MATCHSEQUENCE$
Input: A service $S = (\eta, \sigma, \pi, \delta, \zeta)$ and a functional unit service request $R(I^\gamma, O^\gamma)$
Output: $f_s^o(R)$

```
1.  LET f_s(R) be an empty list
2.  SET SS be the set of permutations for δ, in which every
    permutation has more than one element
3.  FOR each SEQ ∈ SS DO
4.        LET SEQ =< u_1, u_2, u_3, ..., u_m >
5.        IF u_1.I ⊃ R.I^γ OR U_m.O ⊃ R.O^γ THEN
6.              CONTINUE
7.        END IF
8.        WHILE i ≤ m − 1 DO
9.              IF u_i ⊖ u_{i+1} not holds THEN
10.                   BREAK
11.             ELSE
12.                   i++;
13.             END IF
14.       END WHILE
15.       IF i = m THEN
16.             f_s(R).put(SEQ)
17.       END IF
18. END FOR
19. f_s^o(R) = f_s(R).get(0)
```

```
20. FOR i = 1 to f_s(R).size() - 1 DO
21.     IF ℓ(f_s(R).get(i - 1)) ⩾ ℓ(f_s(R).get(i)) THEN
22.         f_s^o(R) = f_s(R).get(i)
23.     END IF
24. END FOR
25. RETURN f_s^o(R)
```

---

The service matchmaking algorithm $SERVICEMATCH$ is illustrated below. While doing matchmaking between a service and a service request, it first checks whether there exists a single functional unit to fulfill the request. If more than one unit satisfies the request, it returns the unit with the largest matching degree to the request. If no unit alone can fulfill the request, it invokes $MATCHSEQUENCE$ to get an optimal matching sequence for the request. If $MATCHSEQUENCE$ returns null, no service can fulfill it.

```
Algorithm: SERVICEMATCH
Input: A service S = (η, σ, ρ, π, δ, ζ) and a functional unit service
request R(I^γ, O^γ)
Output: IF ∃U ∈ δ and U⊥R return U; otherwise return f_s^o(R)
```

---

```
1.  LET f_u be an empty functional unit
2.  FOR each i = 1 to |δ| DO
3.      IF U_i⊥R AND (f_u is empty OR ω(f_u⊥R) ⩽ ω(U_i⊥R)) THEN
4.          f_u = U_i
5.      END IF
6.  IF f_u is not empty THEN
7.      RETURN f_u
8.  ELSE
9.      RETURN MATCHSEQUENCE(S, R)
10. END IF
```

---

### 6.3.3 Performance Evaluation

In order to show the advantages of our service matchmaking algorithm, we have performed a series of experiments in DartFlow. We select the key-word based method of UDDI and one representative semantic-based method proposed by Paolucci (Paolucci M, Kawamura T, Payne TR, Sycara K, 2002) as reference.

We evaluate the performance of our service discovery method by using two well-recognized metrics, namely the service recall rate and precision rate. The recall rate is the proportion of relevant services that are retrieved. The precision rate is the proportion of retrieved services that are accurately matched. In order to prepare the test set for the discovery experiments, we developed a tool based on the IBM XML Generator that enables one to generate random XML files based on schemas. With this tool we generate 200 services in 6 different categories. The name of category and the number of services of each category are shown in the top two rows of Table 6.1. We carry out a serial of service discoveries on each group. We run our experiments on an IBM x260 server with a 2.0 GHz Intel Xeon MP processor and 1 GB of RAM, running over a RedHat Linux operating system.

In total, six group experiments (PhA, TA, PA, SA, PG and TM) are carried

**Table 6.1.** Recall rate and precision comparison

| Service Category Name | Pharmacology Analysis (PhA) | Toxicology Analysis (TA) | Pathology Analysis (PA) | Symptomatology Analysis (SA) | Prescription Generation (PG) | TCM Mining (TM) |
|---|---|---|---|---|---|---|
| Service Number | 42 | 30 | 24 | 15 | 52 | 37 |
| Key-based Method | 51(7) | 35(4) | 31(4) | 14(2) | 64(8) | 45(6) |
| Semantic-based Method | 35(25) | 26(18) | 20(14) | 13(9) | 44(31) | 31(22) |
| Our Method | 44(36) | 32(26) | 26(21) | 16(13) | 58(47) | 40(32) |

out. Each group contains three queries in the test service set for retrieving a category of service using the key-based, semantic-based and our proposed methods, respectively. The experimental results are illustrated in the third to the fifth rows of Table 6.1. The number out of a pair of brackets denotes the total number of services retrieved by the method in an experiment and the number in a pair of brackets denotes the number of correct services in the total number. For example, in the SA group experiment, we get 14, 13 and 16 services in total from the 200 services using the key-based, semantic-based and our method, respectively. However, only 2, 9, and 13 services of each total number of services belong to the SA category.

Table 6.2 shows the recall rate and precision calculated from Table 6.1.

**Table 6.2.** Recall rate and precision comparison

| (%) | | Retrive PhA | Retrive TA | Retrive PA | Retrive SA | Retrive PG | Retrive TM | Average |
|---|---|---|---|---|---|---|---|---|
| Key-based Method | Recall Rate | 16.7 | 13.3 | 16.7 | 13.3 | 15.3 | 16.2 | 15.5 |
| | Precision | 13.7 | 11.4 | 12.9 | 14.3 | 12.5 | 13.3 | 12.9 |
| Semantic-based Method | Recall Rate | 59.5 | 60.0 | 58.3 | 60.0 | 59.6 | 59.4 | 59.5 |
| | Precision | 71.4 | 69.2 | 70.0 | 69.2 | 70.5 | 70.9 | 70.4 |
| Our Method | Recall Rate | 78.6 | 80.0 | 83.3 | 80.0 | 84.6 | 81.1 | 81.5 |
| | Precision | 81.8 | 81.3 | 80.8 | 81.3 | 81.0 | 80.0 | 81.1 |

The average recall rates for these methods are 15.5%, 59.5% and 81.5%, respectively. The average precisions are 12.9%, 70.4% and 81.1%, respectively. It shows that the semantic-based method gets a better recall rate and precision than the key-based method and our method gets better results than the semantic-based method. Compared with the semantic-based method, our proposed method gains 22% and 10.7% improvements in recall rate and precision, respectively. This is due to the fact that more than 50% of services registered in DartFlow have more than one functional unit and more than 30% services have declared their interface dependencies. Compared with the other two methods, our method can utilize the functional unit relations and interface dependencies within services to improve the performance of matchmaking algorithms.

## 6.4 Service Composition in DartFlow

At present there exist a lot of service composition systems and tools based on the workflow technology. They all regard a service composition as a service-oriented workflow, including a set of atomic services, together with the control and data flow among the services. However, most of them require processes to be predefined and services to be statically-bound. Thus, process designers take up too much time and effort in grasping and compiling complex business processes in advance. In our practice when using workflow technology to compose services we are confronted with many cases in which processes cannot be defined completely in advance but determined according to their execution information. Even though we sketch out all the processes after considering all possible execution paths, the processes are too complicated to recognize and to manage. Moreover, the predefined processes and statically-bound services are difficult to evolve conveniently on account of frequent changes arising from enterprise goals, domain/business/user rules, government policies and the dynamic Internet environment. How to improve the flexibility of service composition to alleviate the designers' burden is the issue to be tackled in this study.

One possible promising solution comes from the AI community which regards the service composition problem as an AI planning problem and proposes various AI panning methods to realize automatic service composition. Although AI planning methods can generate service compositions automatically according to users' input/output requirements, they do not take the necessary domain/business/user rules into consideration and have no way to ensure the generated service compositions are in line with the intrinsic core processes of businesses. In fact, on one hand service compositions are affected by many rules such as domain policies, business constraints and user requirement. On the other hand, each business process of a service composition has its own fixed core logics needed to be complied with. Furthermore, in general, most business processes need human beings rather than services to accomplish some activities. Thus it is not suitable for a whole business process to be generated based on automatic service composition by AI planning methods.

In DartFlow, we propose a service composition framework based on a flexible workflow method to enable a part of a process to be created by automatic service composition (Deng S, Li Y, Xia H, et al, 2006).

### 6.4.1 Service Composition Framework

In general, utilizing the workflow technology to compose services undergoes two phases: the service composition modeling phase and the execution phase. At the modeling phase designers build processes according to business logics in a drag-and-drop way within a graphical-style workspace. Each node of the processes is bound to an outer service, while in the execution phase an execution engine is used to interpret and execute the service compositions by invoking services step by step. However, all the current workflow-based service compositions need processes to be predefined. Thus they are not suitable in many cases such as in the aforementioned scenario. In DartFlow, we propose an enhanced service composition framework shown in Fig. 6.6 for service composition based on a flexible workflow method, which utilizes the "black-box" mechanism to deal with those service compositions which can not be predefined completely.

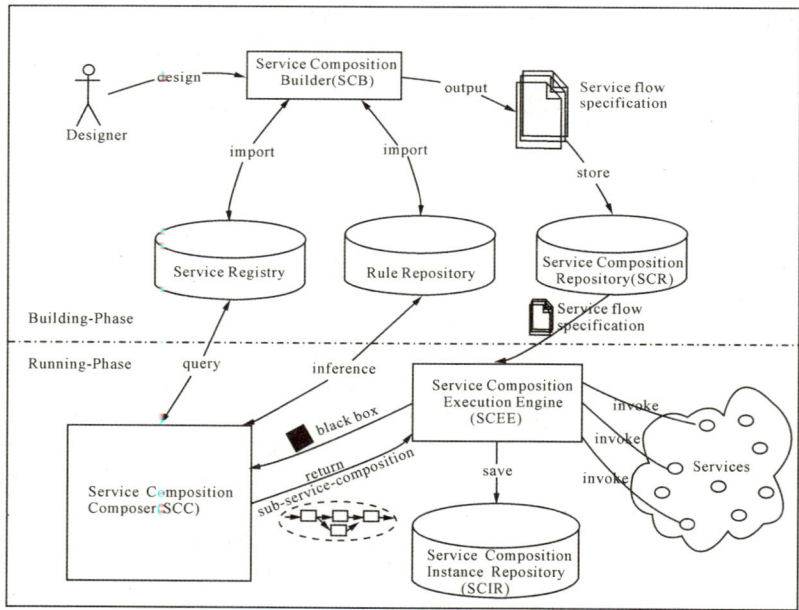

**Fig. 6.6.** Service composition framework

The framework supports both modeling and executing service compositions. It consists of the following main components:
- **Service Composition Builder (SCB):** This component provides an integrated development environment for users to design processes in line with business logics. It enables designers to define the fixed parts of processes in advance and encapsulate the dynamic, uncertain and variable

parts into black-boxes. Each black-box is described using rules selected from RR. For example, designers can encapsulate the advanced analysis step of the aforementioned case into a black-box named advanced analysis black-box with TCM-domain rules and hospital policies from RR to describe the black-box.

- **Service Repository (SR):** This component is responsible for maintaining component services and provides the interfaces for users to advertise and query services.
- **Rule Repository (RR):** This component maintains the domain rules, business rules and user rules. They are used to define black-boxes at the modeling phase and guide how to compose services automatically at the execution phase. For example, one rule may be selected for the advanced analysis black-box in our scenario to indicate that the pharmacology analysis must be selected for a diabetic. The classification and specification of the rules in RR are given in the next section.
- **Service Composition Repository (SCR):** This component is used to maintain service composition specifications and it provides interfaces for SCB to save and load specifications. To avoid starting from scratch, designers can build new compositions based on an existing specification loaded from SCR.
- **Service Composition Execution Engine (SCEE):** It is responsible for interpreting service composition specifications, creating service composition instances, invoking outer services as well as transmitting data among services. When a composition instance runs to one step, SCEE will examine the step first. If the step is a black-box, SCEE transfers it to SCC and waits until SCC returns a sub-service-composition. Otherwise SCEE invokes the service bounded to the step.
- **Service Composition Composer (SCC):** This component generates a service composition automatically according to the rules associated with the black-box. The details on how SCC works are presented in (Deng S, Li Y, Xia H, et al, 2006).
- **Service Composition Instance Repository (SCIR):** It is used to save the information about service composition instances including related data and status.

The target of the framework is to enable services to be composed without a completely-predefined process. The black-box mechanism of the framework enables those uncertain and dynamic factors in service compositions to be determined according to the execution information and predefined rules at the running-phase. Thus it enhances the flexibility for service compositions to a great extent.

**Definition 6.15.** *An abstract service is a 4-tuple:* $\psi = (\mu, \sigma, \gamma, \zeta)$, *where:* $\mu$ *is the name;* $\sigma$ *is the functional description;* $\gamma = \{i_1, i_2, \ldots, i_m\}$ *is the set of the inputs;* $\zeta = \{o_1, o_2, \ldots, o_n\}$ *is the set of the outputs.*

An abstract service represents a functional step rather than a concrete service in a service composition, which is equivalent to the activity concept in a workflow. An abstract service will be bound to a concrete service dynamically in the running-phase.

**Definition 6.16.** *A concrete service is an 8-tuple:* $\chi = (\eta, \tau, o, \omega, \upsilon, \rho, \varepsilon, \varphi)$ *where:* $\eta$ *is the name;* $\tau$ *is the functional description;* $o$ *is the information of the service provider such as the provider name, affiliation;* $\omega = \{i_1, i_2, \ldots, i_m\}$ *is the set of the inputs;* $\upsilon = \{o_1, o_2, \ldots, o_n\}$ *is the set of the outputs;* $\rho$ *is the service precondition;* $\varepsilon$ *is the service effort;* $\varphi$ *is the information about access point and invoking method.*

A concrete service is really an existing physical service provided by an outer organization and must be registered into SR as Fig. 6.6 shows.

**Definition 6.17.** *A bind-relation is a function mapping an abstract service to a concrete service,* $\lambda : A = \{\psi_1, \psi_2, \ldots, \psi_m\} \to C = \{\chi_1, \chi_2, \ldots, \chi_n\}.$

For example, $\lambda(\psi) = \chi$ means the concrete service $\chi$ is bound to the abstract service $\psi$.

**Definition 6.18.** *A black-box in a service composition is a 3-tuple:* $\mho = (\lambda, A, R)$ *where:* $\lambda$ *is the name;* $A = \{\psi_1, \psi_2, \ldots, \psi_m\}$ *is the set of abstract services;* $R = \{r_1, r_2, \ldots, r_n\}$ *is the set of rules and each of them is with the general format:* $r = (t, Ar, e)$ *where: t is the rule type; Ar is the set of abstract services referred by the rule; e is the expression of the rule.*

Note that the set $A$ can be empty at the modeling-phase but will be filled with abstract services in the running-phase. Moreover, users can insert newly-defined rules into $R$ in the running-phase.

### 6.4.2 Rules Types and Definitions

A black-box can be regarded as a container for the uncertain, dynamic and variable parts of service compositions. It must be associated with some rules which will instruct it to select atomic services and compose them into a sub-service-composition at the running-phase. Rules can not only be imported from the RR at the building-phase, but also be added at the running-phase. In general, rules can be classified into three large categories: Domain rules are defined by domain experts according to domain knowledge. In the TCM clinical diagnosis, for example, the pulse analysis service must be selected for a patient with edema. For another example, the pharmacology analysis service must precede the toxicology analysis service if both of them are selected. Business rules are defined by organizations according to their business behavior. For example, a city-level TCM hospital may define a rule stating that the pharmacology analysis service provided by the province-level TCM hospital is preferred to others. User rules are defined by users who participate in the running-phase.

## 6.4 Service Composition in DartFlow

Table 6.3. Rule classification

| Rule Classification | Rule Sub-category | Rule Name |
|---|---|---|
| Domain Rule | Abstract Service Selection Rule (ASSR) | Choice Rule |
| | | Exclusion Rule |
| | | Condition Rule |
| | | Determination Rule |
| | Abstract Service Composition Rule (ASCR) | Sequence Rule |
| | | Adjacency Rule |
| | | Data Dependency Rule |
| Business Rule | Concrete Service Binding Rule (CSBR) | Preference Rule |
| | | Set Confine Rule |
| | | Correlation Rule |
| User Rule | User QoS Rule (UQR) | User QoS Rule (UQR) |
| | | Global QoS Rule |

- **Abstract Service Selection Rule (ASSR)**

ASSR defines how to select abstract services into black-boxes. At present, we only consider the following four rules in the TCM diagnosis scenario in this category.

**Definition 6.19 (Choice Rule).** *Given a set of abstract services $A = \{\psi_1, \psi_2, \cdots, \psi_m\}$, a choice rule, denoted by $\psi_1 \oplus \psi_2 \oplus \cdots \oplus \psi_n$, defines that at least one abstract service $\psi_i \in A(1 \leqslant i \leqslant n)$ must be selected.*

**Definition 6.20 (Exclusion Rule).** *Given $A$ as in the above definition, an exclusion rule, denoted by $\psi_1 \otimes \psi_2 \otimes \cdots \otimes \psi_n$, defines that at most one abstract service $\psi_i \in A(1 \leqslant i \leqslant n)$ is selected.*

**Definition 6.21 (Condition Rule).** *Given two abstract services $\psi_1$ and $\psi_2$, an exclusion rule, denoted by $\psi_1 \triangleright \psi_2$, defines that if $\psi_1$ is selected, $\psi_2$ must be selected.*

**Definition 6.22 (Determination Rule).** *Given an abstract service $\psi$, a determination rule has two forms. If it is denoted by $\odot \psi$, it defines that $\psi$ must be selected; if it is denoted by $\Theta \psi$, it defines that $\psi$ cannot be selected.*

- **Abstract Service Composition Rule (ASCR)**

ASCR defines how to combine abstract services together into sub-service-compositions for black-boxes. It will influence the structures of sub-service-compositions.

**Definition 6.23 (Sequence Rule).** *Given two abstract services $\psi_1$ and $\psi_2$, a sequence rule (denoted by $\psi_1 \rightarrow \psi_2$) defines that $\psi_1$ must be executed before $\psi_2$, but need not be adjacent to $\psi_2$.*

**Definition 6.24 (Adjacency Rule).** *Given $\psi_1$ and $\psi_2$ as in the above definition, an adjacent sequence rule (denoted by $\psi_1 \mapsto \psi_2$) defines that $\psi_1$ must be adjacent to $\psi_2$ and be executed before $\psi_2$.*

**Definition 6.25 (Data Dependency Rule).** *For two abstract services $\psi_1$ and $\psi_2$, a data dependency rule (denoted by $\psi_1 \xrightarrow{D} \psi_2$) defines that all or part of the inputs of $\psi_2$ come from the outputs of $\psi_1$. In fact, the rule $\psi_1 \xrightarrow{D} \psi_2$ implies that the rule $\psi_1 \to \psi_2$ holds.*

Note that we do not consider the parallel rule, which defines two abstract services executed in parallel. This is due to the fact that if there are no composition rules between two abstract services, they can be composed in parallel as default. Thus it is not necessary to define the parallel relationship among abstract services precisely.

- **Concrete Service Binding Rule (CSBR)**

CSBR is used to instruct the selection of a proper concrete service from candidates for abstract services mainly to meet the business needs of organizations. For example, a TCM hospital may establish a series of rules to instruct doctors and patients to select advanced analysis services. Now we consider the following rules in this category.

**Definition 6.26 (Preference Rule).** *Given an abstract service $\psi$ and a concrete service $\chi$, a preference rule (denoted by $\psi \leftarrow \chi$) means the equation $\lambda(\psi) = \chi$ holds, which says $\chi$ is the preferred selection for $\psi$.*

**Definition 6.27 (Set Confine Rule).** *Given an abstract service $\psi$ and a set of concrete services $C = \{\chi_1, \chi_2, \cdots, \chi_n\}$, a set confine rule (denoted by $\chi \prec C$) enables $\exists \chi \in C, \lambda(\psi) = \chi$, which says the service bound to $\psi$ must be selected from $C$.*

**Definition 6.28 (Correlation Rule).** *Given two abstract services ($\psi_1$ and $\psi_2$) and two concrete services ($\chi_1$ and $\chi_2$), a correlation rule (denoted by $\lambda(\psi_1) = \chi_1 \Rightarrow \lambda(\psi_2) = \chi_2$), defines that if $\psi_1$ is bound to $\chi_1$, $\psi_2$ must be bound to $\chi_2$.*

- **User QoS Rule (UQR)**

Binding concrete services to abstract ones means we must consider not only the above business rules but also user rules. At present, we consider the response time and the cost of a service and use the following formula to calculate QoS.

$$QoS(\chi) = T(\chi) \times w + C(\chi) \times (1-w), \text{where } 0 \leqslant w \leqslant 1$$

In this formula, $T(\chi)$ and $C(\chi)$ represent the response time and the cost of consuming the service $\chi$, respectively, and $w$ represent the weight. Note that the parameter $w$ is given by users such as Mary in our scenario. If Mary cares only about the cost, she can assign 0 to $w$. User QoS rule can be divided into the local and global QoS rules as follows.

**Definition 6.29 (Local QoS Rule).** *Given an abstract service $\psi$ and two numerical values ($l$ and $r$, where $l \leqslant r$), a local QoS rule (denoted by $l \leqslant QoS(\lambda(\psi)) \leqslant b$), defines the expected QoS value for $\psi$ ranges from $l$ to $b$.*

**Definition 6.30 (Global QoS Rule).** *Given a black-box $\mho = (\lambda, A, R)$ and the same two values ($l$ and $r$) as above, a global QoS rule (denoted by $l \leqslant QoS(\mho) \leqslant b$), defines the expected QoS value for the whole black-box $\mho$ ranges from $l$ to $b$.*

In general the domain rules and business rules are predefined and stored in the component RR in the framework, whereas the user rules are given by participants at the running-phase.

### 6.4.3 Automatic Service Composition Based on Rules

In the framework, SCC accepts a black-box from SCEE and returns a sub-service composition as the substitute for the black-box. SCC composes services according to the rules associated with a black-box in the following three steps.

**Step 1. Verify Abstract Service Selection Rules**

The target of this step is to verify whether the selection of abstract services by participants is in line with the predefined abstract service selection rules in the black-box. As our scenario shows, Doctor Rose will assess and select the kinds of ATA that Mary would need. All the doctor needs to do is just to drag-and-drop the target ATA into the advanced analysis black-box for Mary. Because the selection is a manual action, the result of the selection is error prone. Thus it is necessary to verify the selection before composing the selected abstract services.

**Step 2. Compose Abstract Services**

Abstract services are composed into a sub-service-composition based on rules associated with the black-box. The definition of sub-service-composition is given below.

**Definition 6.31 (Sub-service-composition).** *A sub-service-composition is a directed acyclic graph, denoted by a 4-tuple: $G = (N, A, C, E)$ where*

*(1) $N = \{start, end\}$ is the set of control node containing two elements start and end, which represent the starting node and end node in the graph, respectively.*

*(2) $A = \{\psi_1, \psi_2, \cdots, \psi_n\}$ is the set of abstract services and each of them is a node in $G$.*

*(3) $C = \{\chi_1, \chi_2, \cdots, \chi_n\}$ is the set of concrete services and satisfies the following relation: $\forall \psi \in A, \exists \chi \in C, \lambda(\psi) = \chi$.*

*(4)* $E \subseteq N \times A \cup A \times N \cup A \times A$ *is the set of directed edges and each edge connects an ordered pair of vertices* $<v, w>$ *where* $v \neq w$, *v is the tail of the edge and w is the head of the edge.*

In order to make the composition achieve the best concurrency, one principle needed to be kept in mind when composing abstract services is that if there are no composition rules defined between two abstract services, they can be composed in parallel as default.

**Step 3. Bind Concrete Services**

After the above two steps, an abstract sub-service-composition is generated for a black-box. This step is for binding a concrete service for each abstract service of the abstract sub-service-composition and for generating the final concrete sub-service-composition for the black-box.

## 6.5 Service Flow Verification in DartFlow

Service flow verification is an important issue which concerns whether the service flow can be executed correctly and can achieve predefined business goals. Compared to the issue of workflow there are two main topics in service flow: to check whether the logic of the flow is correct and to check whether the dynamic interaction between services in the flow is valid. The first topic is a traditional one in the area of workflow and many mature methods can be utilized to resolve it. However, the second is the new topic and has attracted many researchers' attention at present.

As agreed by many researchers, a Web service should include not only the static properties, such as interfaces, message numbers and types, but also the dynamic behavior. It is essential to check the static compatibility including the syntax and semantic compatibility, but a more challenging problem is to check the dynamic compatibility of the service behavior. In DartFlow we propose a method based on $\pi$-calculus for this topic (Deng S, Wu Z, Zhou M, et al, 2006).

### 6.5.1 Overview of $\pi$-Calculus

$\pi$-calculus is proposed by Robin Milner to describe and analyze a concurrent mobile system. A service flow is actually a concurrent system composed of several distributed and autonomous services, where services interact with others by sending and receiving messages. Hence it is intuitive to adopt $\pi$-calculus to model the service behavior and the interaction within service choreographies. Another reason for its use is that it has a series of algebraic theories, such as bi-simulation and congruence, and a number of related tools provided by many researchers to help analyze service behavior and interaction. To introduce the $\pi$-calculus in detail is beyond the scope of this book.

We only illustrate some of its necessary parts, to be used later. Further details can be found in (Milner R, Milner-Gulland R, 1999).

There are two core concepts in $\pi$-calculus: processes and names. A $\pi$-calculus process is an entity which communicates with other processes by the use of names. A name is a collective term for existing concepts like channels, pointers, and identifiers. Each name has a scope and can be unbound (global) or bound to a specific process. The scope of a bound name can be dynamically expanded or reduced during the lifetime of the system by communicating names between processes.

**Syntax:** The $\pi$-calculus consists of an infinite set of names ranged over $a, b, \cdots, z$, which function as all communication channels, variables and data values. A $\pi$-calculus process can be defined as one of the following forms:

(1) 0 The Nil-process: An empty process, which performs no action.
(2) $\bar{a}<x>.P$ Output prefix: The process sends out $x$ over the channel $a$ and then behaves like $P$.
(3) $a<x>.P$ Input prefix: The process waits to read a value from the channel $a$. After receiving the value $u$, the process continues as $P$ but with the newly received name $u$ replacing $x$, denoted by $P\{u/x\}$.
(4) $\tau P$ Silent prefix: The process can evolve to $P$ without any actions.
(5) $P + Q$ Sum: The process can enact either $P$ or $Q$.
(6) $P|Q$ Parallel Composition: The process represents the combined behavior of $P$ and $Q$ running in parallel. $P$ and $Q$ can act independently, and may also communicate if one performs an output and the other an input along the same port.
(7) $(va)P$ Restriction: The process behaves like $P$ but the name $a$ is local, meaning that the name cannot be used for communication with other processes.
(8) $if\ x=y\ then\ P$ Match: The process behaves as $P$ if $x$ and $y$ have the same name, and otherwise it does nothing.

**Operational Semantics:** It is used to describe the possible evolution of a process; more precisely, it defines a transition relation $P \xrightarrow{\alpha} P'$ meaning intuitively that $P$ can evolve to $P'$ in one step through action $\alpha$ (where $\alpha$ is the emission of a message, the reception of a message or a $\tau$ action). This relation is defined by the set of rules below, which give a precise meaning to each operator.

(1) $PREFIX: \dfrac{-}{\alpha P \xrightarrow{\alpha} P}\ \alpha \in \{\tau, x<y>, \bar{x}<y>\}$
(2) $SUM: \dfrac{P \xrightarrow{\alpha} P'}{P+Q \xrightarrow{\alpha} P'}$
(3) $PAR: \dfrac{P \xrightarrow{\alpha} P'}{P|Q \xrightarrow{\alpha} P'|Q}, bn(\alpha) \cap fn(Q) = \phi$
(4) $COM: \dfrac{P \xrightarrow{a<x>} P'\ \ Q \xrightarrow{a<u>} Q'}{P|Q \xrightarrow{\tau} P'\{u/x\}|Q'}$

For instance, the $PREFIX$ rule states that $\alpha P$ can always evolve to $P$ by performing $\alpha$, and the $COM$ rule states that $P$ can evolve to $P'$ by receiving a message from the channel $a$ while $Q$ can evolve to $Q'$ by sending a message from the same channel, and $P|Q$ evolve to $P'\{u/x\}|Q'$ after an inner synchronization action (denoted by $\tau$). A process involving a choice can evolve following one of the processes of the choice.

**Structure Congruence:** it is used to identify the processes that obviously represent the same thing.

(1) $P|0 \equiv P$
(2) $P|Q \equiv Q\ P$
(3) $P|(Q|R) \equiv (P|Q)|R$
(4) $P + 0 \equiv P$
(5) $P + Q \equiv Q + P$
(6) $P + (Q + R) \equiv (P + Q) + R$

### 6.5.2 Modeling Service Behavior Using $\pi$-Calculus

The service behavior refers to the dynamic properties of a service including the state transitions and its supported actions and message exchange sequences. Consider the following example. Note that here we are only concerned with the behavior of the service while ignoring other syntax and semantic aspects.

Fig. 6.7 illustrates a vendor service that interacts with other services through five operations Op1-5. Op1, Op4 and Op5 are one-way-type operations which get input messages named purchase order (PO), cash pay (CP) and bank transfer pay (BTP), respectively. The incoming message of PO triggers the service to start. Op2 and Op3 are the notification-type operations, each of which sends out a message named delivery (DEL) and refusal (REF), respectively. The logic of the service is described as follows: it expects to receive a PO message at the initial state. On a PO message coming, it sends out the delivery if the stock is enough; otherwise it sends back a refusal message and ends the service. In the former case it waits for receiving either a cash payment or bank transfer pay message after sending out the delivery. After that the service terminates.

The behavior of the service in Fig. 6.7 includes two aspects. From the outside it refers to the actions of receiving messages and sending messages through operations. From the inside it refers to the state transitions. Using the $\pi$-calculus to model the behavior of a service, we can define the whole service as a $\pi$-calculus process, in which the operations of the service are channels used to communicate with other processes. In WSDL (Web Service Definition Language), there are four types of operation, i.e., one-way, request-response, solicit-response and notification, as shown in Table 6.4. We use the $\pi$-calculus to model each of them.

According to the above table, we can model the vendor service as the following $\pi$-calculus process which uses the Channels Op1-5 to communicate with other processes.

## 6.5 Service Flow Verification in DartFlow

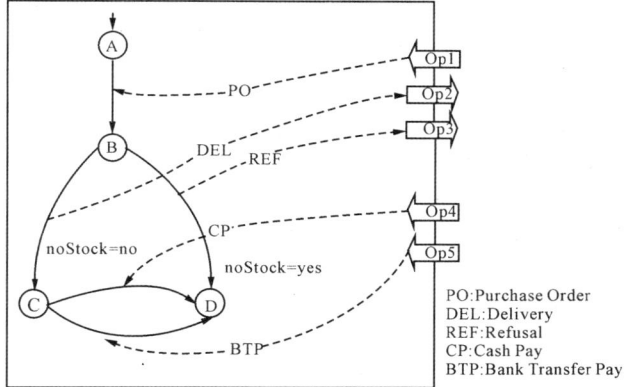

**Fig. 6.7.** A vendor service

**Table 6.4.** Model service operation with $\pi$-calculus

| Service Operation Type | Operation Example | $\pi$-calculus Process Expression |
|---|---|---|
| one-way | `<operation name = "a">`<br>`<input message = "m"/>`<br>`</operation>` | $a<m>$ |
| request-response | `<operation name = "a">`<br>`<input message = "m"/>`<br>`<ouput message = "n"/>`<br>`</operation>` | $a<m>.\bar{a}<n>$ |
| solicit-response | `<operation name = "a">`<br>`<input message = "m"/>`<br>`<ouput message = "n"/>`<br>`</operation>` | $\bar{a}<m>.a<n>$ |
| notification | `<operation name = "a">`<br>`<input message = "m"/>`<br>`</operation>` | $\bar{a}<m>$ |

$$P_V = Op1<PO>.(\overline{Op2}<DEL>.(Op4<CP> + Op5<BTP>) + \overline{Op3}<REF>) \quad (6.1)$$

After modeling services as $\pi$-calculus processes, we can model the interaction between services as the combination of processes. Fig. 6.8 illustrates a scenario where one customer service interacts with the vendor service.

The client service sends out a purchasing order and waits for a delivery or refusal message from the vendor service. If a refusal message comes, the client service ends; otherwise, it sends out a cash pay message to the vendor service and comes to an end. The customer service can be modeled as the following $\pi$- calculus process.

$$P_C = \overline{Op1}<PO>.(Op2<DEL>.\overline{Op4}<CP> + Op3<REF>) \quad (6.2)$$

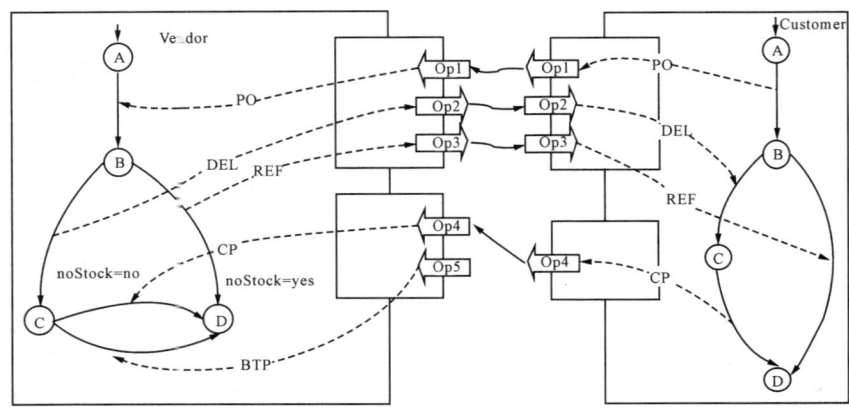

**Fig. 6.8.** Interaction between a vendor service and a customer service

The interaction between the two services can be modeled as the following combination of the π-calculus processes (1) and (2), which means that the interaction between them is the result of the communication carried out between the two processes.

$$P_{Interaction(Vendor,Customer)}$$
$$=P_V|P_C$$
$$=Op1<PO>.(\overline{Op2}<DEL>.(Op4<CP>+Op5<BTP>)+\overline{Op3}<REF>)$$
$$|\overline{Op1}<PO>.(Op2<DEL>.\overline{Op4}<CP>+Op3<REF>)$$

(6.3)

### 6.5.3 Verification of Service Compatibility

Considering the aforementioned scenario, the customer service is completely compatible with the vendor service. There are two different message exchange sequences between them and each of the sequences can eventually lead to an end of the communication. In the first case, after receiving a purchase order from the customer service, the vendor service emits a refusal message due to the shortage of stock and the sequence ends. The customer receives the refusal message and also terminates the sequence. This interaction leads to a business failure. In the second case, after receiving a purchase order, the vendor service sends a delivery message to the customer because there is enough stock and waits for a payment message before continuing. On receiving the delivery message, the customer service sends a cash-pay message, which will be accepted by the vendor service. After that the communication terminates and leads to a successful business. Both of the two message exchange sequences indicate that each service has the ability to accept all the messages

## 6.5 Service Flow Verification in DartFlow

emitted by the other and the communication between them can always terminate. Thus the vendor service and the customer service are completely compatible with each other.

When we say two services are compatible, it means that there is at least one message exchange sequence between the two services, with which the communication of the two services can eventually come to an end. After modeling vendor and customer services as π-calculus processes, the compatibility verification can be carried out formally and automatically. It is intuitive that to check whether the two services are compatible with each other we only need to check whether the π-calculus process (3) can evolve to the Nil-process after finite actions. According to the operational semantics of the π-calculus process, we obtain two possible transitions of the process (3). Note that we label each transition step with the message transferred between the two processes.

$P_{Interaction(Vendor, Customer)}$
$= P_V | P_C$
$= Op1<PO>.(\overline{Op2}<DEL>.(Op4<CP> + Op5<BTP>) + \overline{Op3}<REF>)$
$| \overline{Op1}<PO>.(Op2<DEL>.\overline{Op4}<CP> + Op3<REF>)$
$\xrightarrow{PO} (\overline{Op2}<DEL>.(Op4<CP> + Op5<BTP>) + \overline{Op3}<REF>)$
$\quad (Op2<DEL>.\overline{Op4}<CP> + Op3<REF>)$
$\xrightarrow{REF} 0|0 = 0$

(6.4)

$P_{Interaction(Vendor, Customer)}$
$= P_V | P_C$
$= Op1<PO>.(\overline{Op2}<DEL>.(Op4<CP> + Op5<BTP>) + \overline{Op3}<REF>)$
$| \overline{Op1}<PO>.(Op2<DEL>.\overline{Op4}<CP> + Op3<REF>)$
$\xrightarrow{PO} (\overline{Op2}<DEL>.(Op4<CP> + Op5<BTP>) + \overline{Op3}<REF>)$
$\quad (Op2<DEL>.\overline{Op4}<CP> + Op3<REF>)$
$\xrightarrow{DEL} Op4<CP> + Op5<BTP>$
$\quad \overline{Op4}<CP>$
$\xrightarrow{CP} 0|0 = 0$

(6.5)

The transition sequence (4) is in accordance with the first message exchange sequence (PO.REF) mentioned above, while sequence (5) is in accordance with the second one (PO.DEL.CP). Since each transition sequence of the parallel composition terminates at a Nil-process, it indicates that both two processes can come to an end after some message receiving and sending actions. Thus the two services are compatible with each other. Consider another scenario shown in Fig. 6.9 where a new customer service interacts with the aforementioned vendor service. The new customer service sends a purchase order and then waits for a delivery from the vendor service. On receiving a delivery it sends a cash pay message or a bank transfer pay message. The behavior of the new customer service is modeled as the following $\pi$-calculus process (6).

$$P_{NC} = \overline{Op1}<PO>.Op2<DEL>.(\overline{Op4}<CP> + \overline{Op5}<BTP>) \quad (6.6)$$

In fact, the new customer service is not always compatible with the vendor service. This depends on whether the stock of the vendor service is enough to satisfy the purchase order emitted from the new customer. If the stock is not enough, the vendor sends out a refusal message to the customer. However, the customer service can only accept a delivery message at that time and it is incapable of accepting the refusal message. Thus the interaction between the two services becomes deadlocked in this case. But if the stock is enough, the interaction between the two services can terminate normally. This indicates that the two services are partially compatible. For this scenario we also check whether the parallel composition of the two $\pi$-calculus processes (1) and (6) can reach the Nil-process after finite communicating actions.

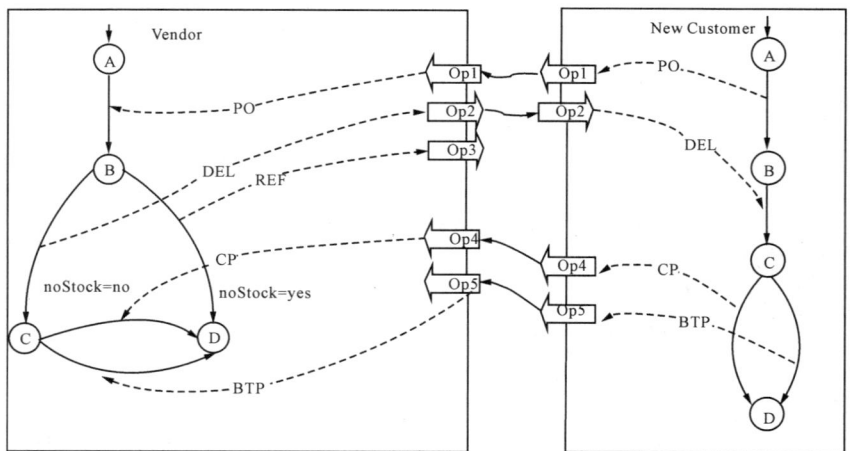

**Fig. 6.9.** Interaction between a vendor service and a new customer service

As the transition sequence (7) shows, the parallel composition can come to an end with two different message exchange sequences (PO.DEL.CP and PO.DEL.BTP). But sequence (8) brings the communication of the two services to a deadlock. This scenario shows that if two services are partially compatible, there is always at least one transition sequence with which the communication between the two services can terminate. From the analysis of the two scenarios above, we reach the following conclusion: in order to check whether two services are compatible we only need to check whether the combination process can evolve to the Nil-process.

$$\begin{aligned}
&P_{Interaction(Vendor,NewCustomer)} \\
&= P_V | P_{NC} \\
&= Op1\text{<}PO\text{>}.(\overline{Op2}\text{<}DEL\text{>}.(Op4\text{<}CP\text{>} + Op5\text{<}BTP\text{>}) + \overline{Op3}\text{<}REF\text{>}) \\
&\quad |\overline{Op1}\text{<}PO\text{>}.Op2\text{<}DEL\text{>}.(\overline{Op4}\text{<}CP\text{>} + Op5\text{<}BTP\text{>}) \\
&\xrightarrow{PO} (\overline{Op2}\text{<}DEL\text{>}.(Op4\text{<}CP\text{>} + Op5\text{<}BTP\text{>}) + \overline{Op3}\text{<}REF\text{>}) \\
&\quad |(Op2\text{<}DEL\text{>}.\overline{Op4}\text{<}CP\text{>} + Op5\text{<}BTP\text{>}) \\
&\xrightarrow{DEL} Op4\text{<}CP\text{>} + Op5\text{<}BTP\text{>})|\overline{Op4}\text{<}CP\text{>} + \overline{Op5}\text{<}BTP\text{>}) \\
&\xrightarrow{CP \ or \ BTP} 0|0 = 0
\end{aligned}$$
(6.7)

$$\begin{aligned}
&P_{Interaction(Vendor,NewCustomer)} \\
&= P_V | P_{NC} \\
&= Op1\text{<}PO\text{>}.(\overline{Op2}\text{<}DEL\text{>}.(Op4\text{<}CP\text{>} + Op5\text{<}BTP\text{>}) + \overline{Op3}\text{<}REF\text{>}) \\
&\quad |\overline{Op1}\text{<}PO\text{>}.Op2\text{<}DEL\text{>}.(\overline{Op4}\text{<}CP\text{>} + \overline{Op5}\text{<}BTP\text{>}) \\
&\xrightarrow{PO} (\overline{Op2}\text{<}DEL\text{>}.(Op4\text{<}CP\text{>} + Op5\text{<}BTP\text{>}) + \overline{Op3}\text{<}REF\text{>}) \\
&\quad |(Op2\text{<}DEL\text{>}.\overline{Op4}\text{<}CP\text{>} + \overline{Op5}\text{<}BTP\text{>}) \\
&\xrightarrow{REF}
\end{aligned}$$
(6.8)

## 6.6 Summary and Conclusion

Service flow management is the most important issue concerning cooperation in the semantic grid environment. In this chapter we introduce the background to the service flow and also review the related work of service flow management. After that preliminary technologies such as workflow and Web service are introduced in brief. Then we introduce three methods proposed in our prototype system DartFlow to deal with service discovery, service composition and service flow verification, respectively.

# References

Benatallah B, Hacid MS, Leger A, Rey C (2005) On Automating Web services Discovery. International Journal on Very Large Data Bases,14(1): 84-96

Brogi A, Corfini A, Popescu R (2005) Composition-oriented Service Discovery. Proceeding of International Conference on Software Composition, 15-30

Bultan T, Fu X, Hull R, Su J (2003) Conversation Specification: A New Approach to Design and Analysis of E-service Composition. Proceeding of World Wide Web Conference, 403-410

Deng S, Li Y, Xia H, et al (2006) Exploring the Flexible Workflow Technology to Automate Service Composition. Proceeding of Asian Semantic Web Conference, 444-458

Deng S, Wu J, Li Y, Wu Z (2006) Service Matchmaking Based on Semantics and Interface Dependencies. Proceeding of International Conference on Web-Age Information Management, 240-251

Deng S, Wu Z, Zhou M, et al (2006) Modeling Service Compatibility with Pi-calculus for Choreography. Proceeding of International Conference on Conceptual Modeling, 26-39

Dustdar S, Schreiner W (2005) A Survey on Web Services Composition. International Journal of Web and Grid Services, 1(1):1-30

Foster H, Uchitel S, Magee J, Kramer J (2004) Compatibility Verification for Web Service Choreography. Proceeding of IEEE International Conference on Web Services,738-741

Klein M, Bernstein A (2004) Toward High-Precision Service Retrieval. Proceeding of IEEE Internet Computing,8(11):30-36

Martens A (2005) Simulation and Equivalence between BPEL Process Models. Proceedings of the Design, Analysis, and Simulation of Distributed Systems Symposium, 34-45

Milner R, Milner-Gulland R (1999) Communicating and Mobile Systems: the Pi-calculus. Cambridge University Press

Paolucci M, Kawamura T, Payne TR, Sycara K (2002) Semantic Matching of Web Services Capabilities. Proceeding of International Semantic Web Conference, 333-347

Papazoglou MP, Georgakopoulos D (2003) Service-Oriented Computing. Communications of the ACM, 46(10):25-28

Rao J, Su X (2004) A Survey of Automated Web Service Composition Methods. Proceeding of Semantic Web Services and Web Process Composition, 43-54

Workflow Management Coalition (1995) The Workflow Reference Model. Wfmc-TC-1031

# 7

# Data Mining and Knowledge Discovery in the Semantic Grid

**Abstract:** Data mining and knowledge discovery focus on the extraction of useful patterns from data. Different from data mining using traditional systems, the Semantic Grid provides a new computational environment, and also a new architecture for data mining. The dynamic extension of algorithms, the transparent integration of data, and the further refinement of knowledge, are the main characteristics of knowledge discovery using such architecture. As high-level services of the Semantic Grid, data mining and knowledge discovery greatly enhance the effectiveness of the Semantic Grid. As a real-world example, a case study of drug community discovery utilizing the TCM Semantic Grid is also illustrated in this chapter.

## 7.1 Introduction

In the late 1980s the area of knowledge discovery and data mining came into being as a multi-disciplinary field with database technology, artificial intelligence, machine learning, statistics, etc. Born with the purpose of fighting with rich data but a poor knowledge situation, this area has been undergoing dramatic development in the last decades.

The term Knowledge Discovery in Database (KDD), was initially coined in the first international conference on knowledge discovery in Detroit, USA in August, 1989, aiming to emphasize that the final output of data-driven discovery is "knowledge" (Fan J, Li D, 1998). In 1992 KDD was defined as a non-trivial extraction of implicit, previously unknown, and potentially useful information from data by William J. Frawley, Gregory Piatetsky-Shapiro and Christopher J. Matheus (Frawley WJ, Piatetsky-Shapiro G, Matheus CJ, 1992). In 1996 a more accurate definition of KDD was used by Usama Fayyad, Gregory Piatetsky-Shapiro and Padhraic Smyth, referring to the non-trivial process of identifying valid, novel, potentially useful and ultimately understandable patterns in data (Fayyad U, Piatetsky-Shapiro G, Smyth P, 1996). This definition is widely accepted by both academia and industry.

The term Data Mining (DM) first appeared in the ACM Annual Conference 1995. Usama Fayyad regarded data mining as one step in the KDD process that consists of applying data analysis and discovery algorithms that, under acceptable computational efficiency limitation, produce a particular enumeration of patterns (or models) over the data (Fayyad U, Piatetsky-Shapiro G, Smyth P, 1996). However, many people treat data mining as a synonym of knowledge discovery, and often use them interchangeably or without distinction. Thus, in most cases, people take a broad view of data mining functionality: data mining is the process of discovering interesting knowledge from a large amount of data stored either in databases, data warehouses, or other information repositories (Han J, Kamber M, 2000). Typical data mining techniques include concept description, association rule mining, classification, prediction, clustering analysis, stream data mining, etc.

The data mining task in the early days was carried out on a single computer, due to small data volume and low computational demand. The wide application of large-scale databases and data warehouses in the following decades, however, creates a new demand for the computational efficiency and running environment of data mining. In order to reduce the time cost for computational-intensive tasks, data mining systems based on parallelized architecture are emerging. Meanwhile, data mining systems based on distributed architecture are coming into being due to the ever-increasing usage of distributed databases in the real world. Such parallelized/distributed data mining systems partly solve the problem of discovery efficiency of large data and the geographical distribution of data.

After entering the 21st century, the ever-increasing information explosion creates a more complicated computational environment with ultra-large-scale, heterogeneous, and highly-dynamic data. Such characteristics pose new problems and challenges for knowledge discovery and data mining. As a solution the Semantic Grid provides a new technology in the new computational environment and also a new architecture for data mining. The dynamic extension of algorithms, the transparent integration of data, and the circular refinement of knowledge, are characteristics of knowledge discovery using such architecture.

The rest of this chapter is organized as follows. An overview of the development history of KDD system architecture evolving from single-computer-based systems to Grid-based systems is provided in Section 7.2. Section 7.3 follows with a discussion of knowledge discovery in the Semantic Grid from three aspects: the virtual organization, the architecture and components, and the characteristics of knowledge discovery in the Semantic Grid. Moreover, the experiments on traditional Chinese medicine (TCM) with an attempt to evaluate the practicality and effectiveness of the approach is reported. In particular, an application case of knowledge discovery in the Semantic Grid: drug community discovery utilizing the TCM Semantic Grid, is introduced.

## 7.2 Development of KDD System Architecture

The architecture of the KDD system undergoes continual development, from being single-computer-based in early days, to grid-based now. Due to small data and low computational demand, the data mining task in the early days could be carried out on a single computer. The wide application of large-scale databases and data warehouses in the following decades, however, created a new demand for the computational efficiency and running environment of data mining. In order to reduce the time cost for the computational-intensive task, data mining systems based on parallelized architecture began to emerge. Meanwhile, data mining systems based on distributed architecture came into being due to the ever-increasing usage of distributed databases in the real world. With the daunting information explosion in the 21st century, the development of grid technology provides new computational environment and system architecture for the data mining community.

### 7.2.1 Single-computer-based Architecture

Matheus, et al, proposed a component-based architecture for the KDD system in 1993 (Matheus CJ, Chan PK, Piatetsky-Shapiro G, 1993), which is a typical single-computer-based architecture (shown in Fig. 7.1).

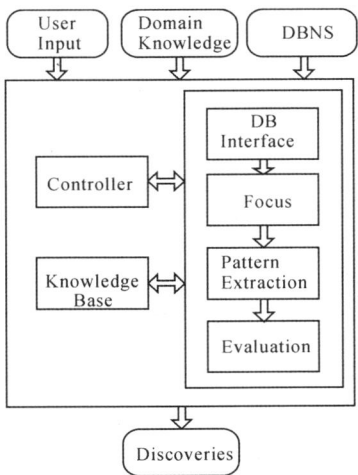

**Fig. 7.1.** Six-component-based architecture

The system is composed of six components:

- **Controller** controls the invocation and parameterization of other components.

160     7 Data Mining and Knowledge Discovery in the Semantic Grid

- **DB Interface** generates and processes database queries.
- **Knowledge Base** is the repository of domain specific information.
- **Focus** determines what portions of the data to analyze.
- **Pattern Extraction** is a collection of pattern-extraction algorithms.
- **Evaluation** evaluates the interestingness and utility of extracted patterns.

Matheus, et al, regarded such a six-component-model as an idealized KDD system (Matheus CJ, Chan PK, Piatetsky-Shapiro G, 1993). They used this model to compare three KDD systems (Matheus CJ, Chan PK, Piatetsky-Shapiro G, 1993). Coverstory is a commercial system developed by Information Resources, Inc. and MIT, and all of the six components of the architecture are exhibited in Coverstory (Schmitz JD, Armstrong GD, Little J, 1990). EXPLORA in 1991 had five of the six components discussed above, except for the DBMS interface (Hoschka P, Klosgen W, 1991). Also developed in 1991, Knowledge Discovery Workbench put the components of controller and evaluation outside the system and let the user handle them (Piatetsky-Shapiro G, Matheus CJ, 1991). We can see from these cases that KDD systems in early days basically accorded with this architecture, and differed in the degree of emphasis on each component.

The data mining tasks in early days emphasized the algorithms themselves, and always with small data volume and low computational demand. Thus it was enough for them to be carried out on a single computer. The KDD systems developed since then, inherited the characteristics of this architecture, more or less.

### 7.2.2 Parallelized Architecture

The ever-increasing data volume involved in knowledge discovery creates a new demand for the computational efficiency of data mining. To solve this problem it is natural to evolve into parallelized system architecture.

In 1994, Marcel Holsheimer and Martin L. Kersten proposed a parallelized architecture for the KDD system (Holsheimer M, Kersten ML, 1994). This architecture includes two levels: the front-end consists of a data mining tool that provides a graphical user interface to formulate and direct the mining activities; all data handling is performed by the back-end, a parallel DBMS server (Monet). In 1997, H.Kargupta, et al. developed an agent-based parallelized/distributed data mining system PADMA (Kargupta H, Park BH, Hershberger D, Johnson E, 1999). The system consists of three parts: data mining agent, agent coordinator and GUI. Each agent maintains its data mining subsystem and works in parallel with the help of coordinators. In the same year McLaren, et al. developed the DAFS system, which introduces parallel processing into the whole KDD process, especially the preprocessing stage (McLaren I, Babb E, Bocca J, 1997). In 1999 Felicity George and Arno Knobbe provided a set of data mining primitives in a parallel data mining architecture (George F, Knobbe A, 1999).

## 7.2.3 Distributed Architecture

The data resources in knowledge discovery are always on a large scale and in many cases are geographically distributed. To solve this problem people began to utilize distributed architecture in KDD systems.

In 1997, Stolfo, et al, designed an agent-based distributed data mining system JAM (Stolfo SJ, Prodromidis AL, Tselepis S, et al, 1997). Based on the idea of meta-learning, each data-node in JAM includes a local database, a learning agent, a meta-learning agent, a configuration module and a GUI. A distributed data mining task is carried out with coordination among nodes. Besides JAM, the afore-mentioned system PADMA (Kargupta H, Park BH, Hershberger D, Johnson E, 1999) is also an agent-based parallelized/distributed data mining system. Each agent maintains its data mining subsystem, and finishes the distributed task with coordinators.

In 1998, Kargupta et al, proposed the concept of collective data mining (CDM) (Kargupta H, Park BH, Hershberger D, Johnson E, 1999). In CDM, the system generates models in local nodes and each local node transmits its model to centre node as a process of integration. In addition, Kensington is a distributed KDD system based on EJB technique (Chattratichat J, Darlington J, Guo Y, et al, 1999). Papyrus is a distributed KDD system which can carry out KDD experiments on three levels: data, task and model (Bailey SM, Grossman RL, Sivakumar H, Turinsky AL, 1999). PaDDMAS is a distributed system similar to Kensington, which provides further support for third-party tools with XML interface (Rana O, Walker D, Li M, Lynden S, Ward M, 2000). In 2002, Ashrafi, et al. presented a distributed architecture consisting of a communication subsystem, database subsystem, data mining subsystem, and analysis subsystem (Ashrafi MZ, Taniar D, Smith KA, 2002).

## 7.2.4 Grid-based Architecture

After entering the 21st century, the information explosion generates a huge amount of data stemming from various applications (military information, government decisions, business analysis, medical research, biological experiments, scientific simulation, etc.) and various devices (satellite, telescope, microscope, sensor, etc.). The data volume in many fields has reached TBs, and even PBs. However, it is difficult to extract useful knowledge from the ever-increasing data. There are several reasons behind this. First, large-scale data are always geographically distributed and dynamically evolved, which means more and more computational resources are needed in order to extract useful knowledge from them. Second, since these data usually come from different organizations, their data format, storage form and access interface are also different. Thus, some unifiedly-defined access interface should be provided in order to use multiple data resources. Confronted with these characteristics, traditional data mining architecture is not enough to handle

162    7 Data Mining and Knowledge Discovery in the Semantic Grid

the problems. As a popular technology emerging from the 1990s, the Grid technology provides a solution for these complicated demands.

There are three main advantages of Grid-based architecture:

- The Grid can provide enough computational ability. Knowledge discovery of large-scale data requires intensive computational resources. The computational Grid can automatically distribute computational tasks to computational nodes, thus enabling efficient, transparent, and distributed knowledge discovery.
- The Grid can provide a transparent data access interface. Data from different organizations usually has different data formats and access interfaces. The Data Grid provides a schema of transparent integration and unified encapsulation of distributed and heterogeneous data. Thus the users do not need to know the specific access interface and source for each section of data.
- The Grid can provide support for dynamically-changed resources. The characteristic of self-organization in the Grid enables a dynamic yet easy entry/exit for any kind of data/computational resources.

In recent years one development trend of Grid technology has been the integration of semantic techniques and knowledge discovery. Mario Cannataro and Domenico Talia proposed the concept of the Next-Generation Grid in 2003, and knowledge discovery and knowledge management are regarded as basic requirements in the Next-Generation Grid (Cannataro M, Talia D, 2003). In 2004 they further proposed three main services which must be provided in the Next-Generation Grid: knowledge management and ontology-based service, knowledge discovery service, and the service of dynamic resource discovery and adaptation (Cannataro M, Talia D, 2004). In the real world the development of knowledge discovery and data mining applications based on the Grid environment has indeed advanced quickly and become a research focus in recent years. Typical projects in this area include Discovery Net, Knowledge Grid and DataminingGrid.

- **Discovery Net**

Discovery Net is a £2.08 million EPSRC-funded project to build the world's first e-Science platform for scientific discovery from the data generated by a wide variety of high throughput devices at Imperial College London (Discovery Net Homepage, 2001). Discovery Net is a multi-disciplinary project serving application scientists from various fields including biology, combinatorial chemistry, renewable energy and geology.

Discovery Net provides a service-oriented computing model for knowledge discovery, allowing users to connect to and use data analysis software as well as data sources that are made available online by third parties. In particular, Discovery Net defines the standards, architecture and tools that: 1) Allow scientists to plan, manage, share and execute complex knowledge discovery

## 7.2 Development of KDD System Architecture

and data analysis procedures available as remote services. 2) Allow service providers to publish and make available data mining and data analysis software components as services to be used in knowledge discovery procedures. 3) Allow data owners to provide interfaces and access to scientific databases, data stores, sensors and experimental results as services so that they can be integrated in knowledge discovery processes.

Discovery Net is based on an open architecture re-using standard protocols and standard infrastructures such as the OGSA and the Globus Toolkit. It also defines its own protocol for workflows, Discovery Process Markup Language (DPML), which allows definitions of data analysis tasks to be executed on distributed resources. Using Discovery Net architecture it is easy to build and deploy a variety of fully distributed data intensive applications. V. Curcin et al. proposed the concept of Knowledge Discovery Service and further divided Knowledge Discovery Service into two types: computational service and data service (Curcin V, Ghanem M, Guo Y, et al, 2002). As a grid-based architecture, Discovery Net provides open standards for specifying: 1) Knowledge Discovery Adapters. 2) Knowledge Discovery Services look-up and registration. 3) Integrated Scientific Database Access. 4) Knowledge Discovery Process Management. 5) Knowledge Discovery Process Deployment.

As a knowledge discovery platform in a grid environment, Discovery Net is utilized in various applications. In 2003 Anthony Rowe et al. applied Discovery Net to discovery in bioinformatics (Rowe A, Guo Y, Kalaitzopoulos D, et al, 2003). In the same year, R.A. Heckemann et al. used Discovery Net in information extraction in medical imagery (Heckemann RA, Hartkens T, Leung K, et al, 2003). In 2004 Discovery Net was used by M. Ghanem et al. to analyze Air Pollution Data (Ghanem M, Guo Y, Hassard J, Osmond M, et al, 2004).

- **Knowledge Grid**

Knowledge Grid is a project of the University of Calabria and the Institute of High Performance Computing and Networking under the supervision of the Italian National Research Council (Knowledge Grid Homepage, 2000). Knowledge Grid is designed on top of computational Grid mechanisms provided by Grid environments such as Globus Toolkit. The Knowledge Grid uses basic Grid services such as communication, authentication, information, and resource management to build more specific PDKD tools and services. The Knowledge Grid services are organized into two layers: Core K-Grid Layer, which is built on top of generic Grid services, and High-level K-Grid Layer, which is implemented over the core layer.

The concept of PDKD (Parallel and Distributed Knowledge Discovery) was first put forward by Mario Cannataro in 2000 (Cannataro M, 2000), which refers to knowledge discovery in a distributed, large-scale and heterogeneous data environment. To perform PDKD, Mario Cannataro utilized a Grid-based cluster to conduct distributed mining, and provided specific knowledge discovery Grid service for data mining tasks (Cannataro M, 2000). In 2000 Mario Cannataro further proposed a Grid-based architecture for Knowledge Grid (Cannataro M, Congiusta A, Talia D, Trunfio P, 2002). In this architecture the Knowledge Grid services are organized in two hierarchic levels: the Core K-Grid Layer, and the High-level K-Grid Layer. The Core K-Grid Layer refers to services directly implemented on the top of generic grid services, including basic services for the definition, composition and execution of a distributed knowledge discovery computation over the Grid. The High-level K-Grid Layer services are used to compose, validate, and execute a parallel and distributed knowledge discovery computation. Moreover, the layer offers services to store and analyze the discovered knowledge. In 2002 Mario Cannataro, et al, implemented a prototype Java system named VEGA (Visual Environment for Grid Applications) (Cannataro M, Talia D, Trunfio P, 2002). VEGA provides a set of facilities supporting the design and execution of Knowledge Discovery applications over Computational Grids running the Globus Toolkit Grid environment. VEGA is integrated within the Knowledge Grid to allow user to access its features and services through an intuitive and easy graphical user interface.

- **DataminingGrid**

The Data Mining Tools and Services for Grid Computing Environments (DataminingGrid) is a grid project funded by the European Commission since September 2004 (DataminingGrid Homepage, 2004). Currently there exists no coherent framework for developing and deploying data mining applications on the Grid. The DataminingGrid project addresses this gap by developing generic and sector-independent data-mining tools and services for the Grid. To demonstrate the developed technology, the project implemented a range of demonstrator applications in e-Science and e-business. The DataMiningGrid Consortium comprises five partners from four countries, including The University of Ulster, Fraunhofer Institute for Autonomous Intelligent Systems, DaimlerChrysler AG, Israel Institute of Technology and the University of Ljubljana.

The main objectives of the DataminingGrid project are: 1) to develop grid interfaces that allow data mining tools and data sources to interoperate within distributed grid computing environments; 2) to develop grid-based text mining and ontology-learning services and interfaces for knowledge discovery in texts and ontology learning; 3) to align and integrate these technologies with emerging grid standards and infrastructures. In order to address a wide range of requirements arising from the need to mine data in distributed computing environments, the DataminingGrid project also developed a test bed consisting of various demonstrator applications, such as mining in biology and medicine, the automotive industry, computer logs, etc. In March 2007, DataminingGrid Tools and Services Version 1.0 beta was released under Apache License V2.0.

### 7.2.5 A Summary of the Development of KDD System Architecture

In the past decade the KDD system architecture has undergone continuous development and improvement. From the perspective of modules, Jiawei Han gives a clear description in his classical book (Han J, Kamber M, 2000): The architecture of a typical data mining system has the following major components: 1) database, data warehouse, or other information repository; 2) database or data warehouse server; 3) knowledge base; 4) data mining engine; 5) pattern evaluation module; 6) graphical user interface. This architecture is similar to the one with six-components in early days. Thus traditional KDD systems basically have these modules in Han's architecture.

With the increasing amount of data volume single-computer-based architecture is not enough. Thus parallelized/distributed architecture for the KDD system was put forward and gained attention. Such parallelized/dis- tributed data mining systems partly solved the problem of discovery efficiency in large volumes of data and the geographical distribution of data.

After entering the 21st century, the challenging information explosion creates a more complicated computational environment with ultra-large-scale, heterogeneous, and highly-dynamic data. Such characteristics pose new problems and challenges for knowledge discovery and data mining. As a solution the Grid-based architecture is proposed for handling these problems in KDD systems.

## 7.3 Knowledge Discovery Based on the Semantic Grid

The introduction of Grid technology provides a new solution to knowledge discovery in an ultra-large-scale, heterogeneous, and highly-dynamic computational environment. However, currently the description and expression of data in the Web are still rough. The data semantics and internal logic are not explicitly expressed, in other words hard-coded in programs. These characteristics have become huge obstacles for the effective integration, processing and analysis of data today. The Semantic Grid, derived from the Semantic Web and Grid technology, provides a new solution to this problem. In this section we will discuss knowledge discovery in the semantic grid from three perspectives: the virtual organization, the architecture and components, and the characteristics of knowledge discovery in the semantic grid.

### 7.3.1 Virtual Organizations of Knowledge Discovery in the Semantic Grid

Ian Foster indicated that the real and specific problem that underlies the Grid concept is coordinated resource sharing and problem solving in dynamic, multi-institutional virtual organizations. Similarly, knowledge discovery in the Semantic Grid is also conducted in an environment with dynamic virtual organizations. Basically, in the context of knowledge discovery in the Semantic Grid the virtual organization should at least include the following roles:

- **KDD Algorithm Provider**

  Various types of KDD algorithms are provided as a form of KDD algorithm services, such as frequent itemset mining, association rule mining, classification, clustering, outlier detection, trend analysis, etc. The responsibility of an algorithm provider is to provide all kinds of information related to the knowledge discovery service for the whole virtual organization. The information that the algorithm provider should provide for sharing in the virtual organization includes: 1) The access interface of the algorithm, including the type, address, port information of the algorithm service. 2) The access parameters of the algorithm service, including the input/output, parameter descriptions of the algorithm service. 3) The access privilege information of the algorithm service.

- **Data Provider**

  The responsibility of the data provider is to provide data resources and the semantic definitions of these resources for the whole virtual organization. The information that the data provider should provide for sharing in the virtual organization includes: 1) The physical access interface of data, such as the type, address, port information of databases or data service. 2) The access privilege information of data, including the privilege mapping between users in databases/data services and roles in the virtual organization. 3) The mapping relationship between the structure of data and the unified ontology in the virtual organization, that is, the semantic registration information.

- **Knowledge Discovery User**

  By means of the unified ontology in a virtual organization, a knowledge discovery user could use accessible data and algorithms to carry out the task of knowledge discovery based on his requirements and privileges. First, knowledge discovery users could access the required data services and do some data cleaning and transformation. Second, knowledge discovery users could select required algorithms from the directory of algorithm services and modify the parameters of the algorithm services. Third, knowledge discovery users could evaluate the results obtained from the knowledge discovery experiments from the application view.

- **Application Expert**

  The application expert in a virtual organization can be someone who is authoritative on the topics in this virtual organization. The responsibility of the application expert is to specify a unified ontology across the whole virtual organization. This ontology is like a thesaurus acknowledged by each member in this virtual organization. All types of data sharing are formed based on this ontology. Members in the virtual organization could also be involved in the proposition and discussion of ontology and the

application experts make a final decision based on the discussion. Considering the unified requirement for the ontology in the virtual organization, the number of application experts in the virtual organization should be small.
- **Manager of Virtual Organization**
  A KDD virtual organization should have at least one manager. The responsibility of the manager is to provide different levels of resource accessibility and role privilege for different members in the virtual organization. Due to the dynamic characteristics of the virtual organization, the manager does not have absolute power. The members of the virtual organization have full autonomy.

### 7.3.2 Architecture and Components of Knowledge Discovery in the Semantic Grid

To support semantic knowledge discovery in an ultra-large-scale, heterogeneous, and highly-dynamic environment, a well-designed architecture is needed. We propose an architecture of knowledge discovery in the Semantic Grid in Fig. 7.2.

From the perspective of components, the architecture could be divided into three parts: knowledge discovery control component, data service component and algorithm service component. They will be introduced as follows:

**Knowledge Discovery Control Component** is in charge of the control of the objective, the data and the algorithm of knowledge discovery. This component includes three sub-components: data control sub-component, algorithm control sub-component and objective control sub-component.

- **Data Control Sub-component** is in charge of the interaction with the data service component, and the selection/control of data. This sub-component includes two parts: the data selection service and the data preprocessing service. The data selection service fetches the current directory of data services from the data service component, and lets the KDD user make a selection in this directory. When data is fetched by the data service component, the data preprocessing service is in charge of the preprocessing tasks (cleaning, transformation, etc.) according to users' requirements.
- **Algorithm Control Sub-component** is in charge of the interaction with the algorithm service component, and the selection/control of the algorithm. This sub-component includes two parts: the algorithm selection service and the process control service. The algorithm selection service fetches the current directory of algorithm services from the algorithm service component, and lets the KDD user make a selection in this directory. When two or more algorithms are needed in a complicated KDD task, process control service takes charge of the configuration and control of the running process, according to users' requirements.

168    7 Data Mining and Knowledge Discovery in the Semantic Grid

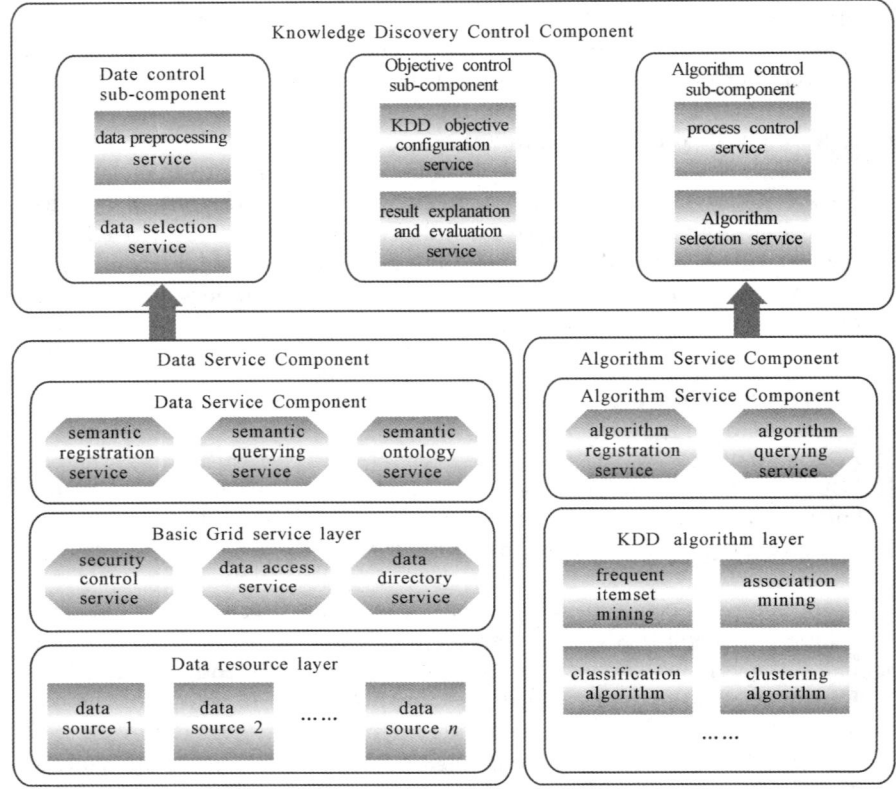

**Fig. 7.2.** Architecture of knowledge discovery based on Semantic Grid

- **Objective Control Sub-component** is in charge of the configuration of the KDD objective and the management of the results. This sub-component includes two parts: the KDD objective configuration service, and the result explanation and evaluation service. The KDD objective configuration service provides candidate KDD general objectives (association rule mining, classification analysis, etc.), and lets the KDD users make a selection. When the objective is determined by the user, the KDD objective configuration service calls the algorithm selection service, fetches the current directory of algorithm services, and recommends the most appropriate algorithm services according to the KDD objective. When one algorithm service is selected, the KDD objective configuration service will let the user specify a result threshold according to the type of the algorithm service. The result explanation and evaluation service is in charge of the explanation and evaluation of the results from the KDD algorithm. If the threshold is not fulfilled an error will be returned.

**Data Service Component** provides available data services for upper-layer applications by semantic integration of heterogeneous data. This component includes three layers: data resource layer, basic Grid service layer, and semantic service layer.

- **Data Resource Layer** includes various types of data resources from data providers. These resources may be from different organizations and normally are heterogeneous.
- **Basic Grid Service Layer** includes data access service, data directory service, and security control service. The data access service is in charge of the control of data resources' access interfaces, including the type, address, port info of the data service. The data directory service is in charge of the management of dynamic publication, join-in, quit and query of data resources. The security control service is in charge of the issues related to security.
- **Semantic Service Layer** includes semantic registration service, semantic query service, and ontology service. The semantic registration service maintains the mapping relationships between data models and ontology. This mapping is crucial for the integration of heterogeneous data. The semantic query service is the interface to data users, which can be used to execute the semantic query constructed based on ontology by users and return the query results. Ontology is the semantic representation of data models, and is usually defined by application experts. The data providers use the ontology and the data model to do mapping, and data users rely on the ontology to do queries. The ontology service provides support for all operations related to ontology, including the definition, publication, maintenance, query and update of ontology.

**Algorithm Service Component** is in charge of the transformation from various types of KDD algorithms to accessible algorithm services. This component includes two layers: algorithm service layer, and KDD algorithm layer.

- **Algorithm Service Layer** includes various types of KDD algorithms provided by algorithm providers.
- **KDD Algorithm Layer** includes algorithm registration service and algorithm query service. The algorithm registration service transforms the KDD algorithm into an accessible Grid service for KDD users. The query of current available algorithms is carried out by the algorithm query service.

### 7.3.3 Characteristics of Knowledge Discovery in the Semantic Grid

From the discussion of architecture and components of knowledge discovery in the Semantic Grid above, some characteristics of knowledge discovery based on the Semantic Grid could be summarized as below:

170     7 Data Mining and Knowledge Discovery in the Semantic Grid

- **Dynamic extension of algorithm**
  In the context of the Semantic Grid, the knowledge discovery algorithm is provided as a service. For various types of data mining algorithms (frequent itemset mining, association rule mining, classification, clustering, outlier detection, trend analysis, etc.), they are encapsulated as accessible and flexible algorithm services. Basically this characteristic is inherited from the Grid technology.

  By the mechanism of service registration, service query, etc., the knowledge discovery algorithm becomes dynamic, open, and extensible. First, by the means of service registration, any new knowledge discovery algorithm could be added easily at any time. Second, by the means of service query, knowledge discovery users can find related algorithms according to their needs, and make a further selection. Moreover, in the context of the Semantic Grid some semantic techniques could be applied to describe the data mining algorithms. For example, we could use the extended version of PMML (PMML, 2000) to semantically describe algorithms, which means the algorithms can be more easily discovered.

- **Transparent Integration of Data**
  To conduct a large-scale knowledge discovery task, usually we need to combine heterogeneous data resources from multiple organizations. The semantic technology provides a proper solution for constructing a unified data model among heterogeneous databases. As a middle model of heterogeneous databases, the semantic view can be used to express the relationship between data and ensure a better connection between multiple databases.

  However it is not enough to provide only semantic mapping. For end users an easy-use accessing mechanism of unified data model should be provided, which is the function of semantic query. The semantic query turns the query of the unified data model into related queries in multiple data resources, and integrates the querying results for users. By the mechanism of semantic query, the users of data resources do not need to know the specific model of each data resource.

  By such semantic encapsulation the various types of data resources become a kind of semantic-based, dynamic and extensible data service. In the context of the Semantic Grid, the access of data also becomes a service. We can add any new data by service registration. Although the data in the Semantic Grid is always distributed and heterogeneous, the users could easily access the data without knowing where the data comes from.

- **Iterative Refinement of Knowledge**
  From the perspective of knowledge discovery itself, data mining is a process in which knowledge gains are refined iteratively. In other words, the rough model and knowledge derived from data could provide experience for the next round of knowledge discovery, which also means that the

knowledge is refined round by round. From the perspective of the data mining process model (e.g. CRISP-DM, that is, CRoss-Industry Standard Process for Data Mining (Chapman P, Clinton J, Kerber R, et al, 2000)), data mining is viewed as a circular and iterative process.

In the context of the Semantic Grid, the circular and iterative characteristic of data mining is more obvious. It should be noticed that the construction of ontology is a process with continuing update, and it is difficult for application experts to set up perfect ontology at the very beginning. The heterogeneous data semantically integrated based on such ontology, is used as the data source of knowledge discovery. Thus the result of such knowledge discovery is sometimes problematic. Note that the outputs of knowledge discovery are pieces of knowledge containing semantics themselves. Thus we could gain a deeper understanding of the semantic ontology based on the experience learned in the previous round of knowledge discovery, and such experience could help us to correct the errors existing in current semantic ontology. In the next round of knowledge discovery the data is integrated based on updated semantic ontology, which could more or less improve the reliability of knowledge discovery. Furthermore, if we treat the instances, properties, and their inter-relationships in ontology as the objective of knowledge discovery, knowledge discovery actually becomes semantic mining. The semantics mined in this process could provide useful support for the next round of knowledge discovery and other related applications. In this process the raw knowledge derived from data and a model based on raw ontology could provide experience for the next round of knowledge discovery and be used as a reference for the correction and update of semantic ontology.

## 7.4 Drug Community Discovery Utilizing TCM Semantic Grid

We have described the basic concepts of knowledge discovery in the Semantic Grid. The Semantic Grid could be a feasible technical framework for building an e-Science environment that provides a variety of knowledge discovery services. In this section we propose a particular methodology called Semantic Graph Mining (SGM), for building agents that discover knowledge based on the Semantic Grid. Fig. 7.3 shows the relationships between SGM and other factors in an e-Science environment: (1) Ontology Engineering provides a variety of ontologies for SGM, and SGM can in turn improve the quality of Ontology Engineering through Ontology Matching and Ontology Visualization; (2) Semantic Query and Search provides data availability for SGM and SGM can in turn improve the quality of Semantic Query and Search through Resource Importance and Semantic Association; (3) Academic Virtual Organization enhances the collaboration between domain experts and also provides data resources for data analysis through SGM; (4) SGM can use the data on the semantic web in the Biomedical domain to discover interesting patterns from complex biomedical networks. Here we first present an overview of our approach of semantic graph mining and then discuss a TCM use case for interpreting TCM Formulae for drug discovery and safety analysis.

**Fig. 7.3.** The roles of semantic graph mining in a semantic e-Science environment

### 7.4.1 Semantic Graph Mining Methodology

The Semantic Web can be modeled as a directed graph that represents a statement with (1) a node for the subject, (2) a node for the object, and (3) an arc for the predicate, directed from the subject node to the object node. The merging of two semantic graphs is essentially the union of the two underlying sets of statements. Within a multiple semantic graph a member graph can obtain a URI as its name for its provenance to be traced. This model gives an elegant solution connecting data from different sources and domains (shown in Fig. 7.4) and makes it possible to integrate medical domain knowledge into the knowledge discovery process, which is beneficial in the following cases:

- *Semantic Graph Resource Importance* aims at determining the importance of resources in a given problem-solving context, and is adopted in a variety of biomedical applications, including retrieving semantically related patents from biomedical patent databases, and mining disease-causal genes from a biological network of multiple relationships. Here domain knowledge and/or personal preference can be used to assign various types of weights to resources and statements.
- *Semantic Associations* are complex relationships between resource entities. Semantic association discovery and ranking have many potential applications in the biomedical domain. Graph algorithms are useful for the computation of Semantic Associations on a memory-resident graph representation of the RDF model within realistic time and resource constraints. The implementation is essentially derivative of the importance of Semantic Web resources.

## 7.4 Drug Community Discovery Utilizing TCM Semantic Grid    173

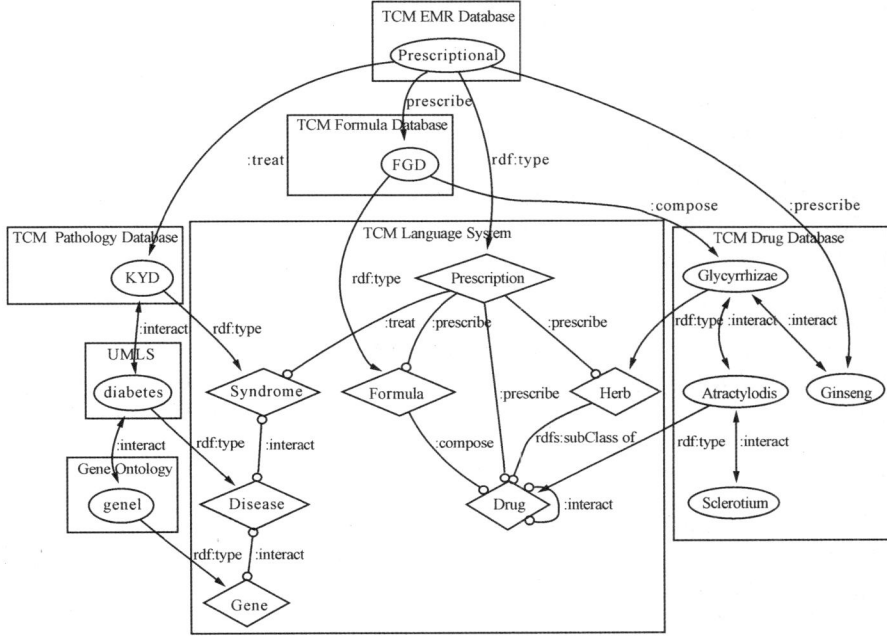

**Fig. 7.4.** A semantic graph connects data from different sources and domains

- *Frequent Semantic Subgraph Discovery.* Frequent patterns are itemsets, subsequences, or substructures that appear in a data set with a frequency no less than a user-specified threshold. We first take the approach of generating semantic annotations for frequent patterns in a medical semantic graph. In the context of a medical semantic graph, discovery of semantic associations and other machine reasoning methods are useful for the generation of semantic annotations for frequent patterns.
- *Deducing rules from discovered patterns.* In the semantic graph concept hierarchies of the resources are available, and users are interested in generating rules that span different levels of the concept hierarchies. In many applications association rules will only be interesting if they represent nontrivial correlations between all constituent items. We take the approach of evaluating generalized association rules based on medical semantic graphs. As we have mentioned above, one of the unique features of medical semantic graphs is that it is composed of attributable statements. The belief of a rule must be calculated based on the trust of authors that make the related statements from which the rule is derived.

## 7.4.2 Use Case: TCM Formulae Interpretation and Herb-Drug Interaction Analysis

The pharmaceutics domain involves a complex network of drug interactions. Besides phenomenal social interactions between caregivers and patients, there can also be ubiquitous interactions between drugs that are less discernable and apt to be overlooked. However, drug interactions are important phenomena in pharmaceutics, which can be real salvations if well controlled and managed, yet can have devastating results if misidentified or overlooked.

A drug community stands for a significant pattern of drug interactions within a problem-solving context, which can be a recommended medical formula, a frequent prescription of drugs specified by a physician, or a set of drugs that a patient frequently consumes. Drug interaction analysis frequently involves identification, differentiation, interpretation, and correlative analysis of drug communities. In order to map a comprehensive network of drug interactions revealing drug communities, explicit knowledge should be integrated from a plurality of heterogeneous databases in the healthcare and life science domain. The following use case is focused on TCM Herbal Formulae, generic patterns of herb community structure defined in TCM pharmaceutics classics.

TCM practitioners have developed an elaborate system of formulae composition, with the essential principle that a formula should embody a proper herb companionship involving social relationships among its participating herbs. The relationships within herb companionship are hierarchical in nature, between a single dominant component, the king herb, and a set of subordinate components such as minister herbs, assistant herbs, and carrier herbs. Four-Gentleman Decoction (FGD) is an ancient herbal formula documented in the Song Dynasty (960–1279), whose actions are to fortify the spleen and to nurture the $qi$ (the vital substance of the human body in TCM). The Four Gentlemen refers to: (1) Ginseng (the king herb, FGD-K) that nurtures the $qi$; (2) Atractylodis (the minister herb, FGD-M) that strengthens the spleen and dries dampness; (3) Sclerotium poria cocos (the assistant herb, FGD-A) that assists king and minister herbs in strengthening the spleen; and (4) Glycyrrhizae uralensis (the carrier herb, FGD-C) that warms and harmonizes the stomach. This TCM approach to drug companionship has been developed for a long time, with its mechanism and effectiveness beyond comprehension.

We apply the Semantic Grid to drug community discovery and interaction analysis, with an approach based on the resources importance and semantic association that takes the following steps:

Step 1. Consolidate a knowledge repository through ontology-based integration of disparate databases, including EHRs, literature databases, and domain knowledge bases.

Step 2. Examine the effectiveness of drug communities discovery through mechanisms including frequent pattern, graph-based search and clustering.

## 7.4 Drug Community Discovery Utilizing TCM Semantic Grid

Step 3. Describe semantic associations for interpreting discovered communities.

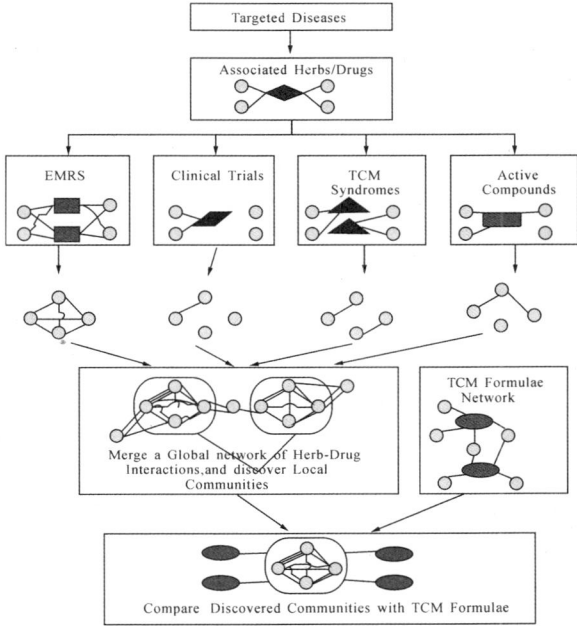

**Fig. 7.5.** A global network modeling approach for analyzing herb-drug interactions and interpreting TCM formulae system

We describe the rationalization of our approach through a TCM use case (shown in Fig. 7.5) to map a global network of herb-drug interactions revealing drug community structure. We first collect all interactions within a drug population and then insert an edge between two drugs that have direct interactions and weight the edge with the frequency of interactions. We choose a threshold to filter out casual relationships and preserve strong relationships. Based on the resulting network we discern communities by first deleting a certain number of centrality nodes, and then deleting a certain number of centrality edges. We first delete nodes with closeness centrality exceeding a predefined threshold, because these nodes are seen as not exclusively belonging to any local community and eliminating these nodes can help to reveal the local communities. We then delete the edge with the maximum betweenness centrality recursively until the population is separated, because these edges are seen as connecting local communities, and therefore eliminating these edges can also help to reveal the local communities. The process of discovering a community, together with the interactions within the community, can serve as semantic annotations to interpret the community. The clustering results will be compared with the TCM formulae system and evaluated by domain experts

## 7.5 Summary and Conclusion

This chapter first gives a brief introduction to data mining and knowledge discovery. Then an overview of the development history of KDD system architecture is provided, from being single-computer-based systems to Grid-based systems. The ever-increasing information explosion in the 21st century has created a more complicated computational environment with ultra-large-scale, heterogeneous, and highly-dynamic data. Such characteristics put forward new problems and challenges for knowledge discovery and data mining. As a solution the Semantic Grid provides a new technology in the new computational environment, and also a new architecture for data mining.

In summary, the relationship between knowledge discovery and the Semantic Grid is as follows: (1) the Semantic Grid provides the capability of dynamic extension for knowledge discovery algorithms. (2) the Semantic Grid provides transparent integration of heterogeneous data for knowledge discovery. (3) Knowledge discovery provides support of semantic mining for the Semantic Gird.

We have also introduced an application case of data mining in the Semantic Grid, that is, drug community discovery utilizing the TCM Semantic Grid. Thanks to knowledge discovery and the Semantic Grid, the discovery of true diamonds from data-mountains can be expected.

## References

Ashrafi MZ, Taniar D, Smith KA (2002) A data mining architecture for distributed environments. In: Innovative Internet Computing Systems, Second International Workshop (IICS 2002). Germany: Springer LNCS 2346: 27-38

Bailey SM, Grossman RL, Sivakumar H, Turinsky AL (1999) Papyrus: a system for data mining over local and wide area clusters and super-clusters. In: Proceedings of the 1999 ACM/IEEE Conference on Supercomputing. Portland, Oregon, USA: ACM Press 63-63

Cannataro M (2000) Clusters and grids for distributed and parallel knowledge discovery. In: High Performance Computing and Networking: 8th International Conference (HPCN Europe 2000). Heidelberg: Springer LNCS 1823: 708-716

Cannataro M, Congiusta A, Talia D, Trunfio P (2002) A data mining Toolset for Distributed High-Performance Platforms. In: Proc. 3rd Int. Conference Data Mining 2002. Bologna, Italy: WIT Press 41-50

Cannataro M, Talia D (2003) Towards the next-generation grid: a pervasive environment for knowledge-based computing. In: Proc. 4th IEEE Int. Conf. on Information Technology: Coding and Computing (ITCC2003). Las Vegas: IEEE Press 437-441

## 7.5 Summary and Conclusion

Cannataro M, Talia D (2004) Semantics and knowledge grids: building the next-generation grid. Intelligent Systems 19(1): 56-63

Cannataro M, Talia D, Trunfio P (2002) Distributed data mining on the grid. Future Generation Computer Systems 18(8): 1101-1112

Chapman P, Clinton J, Kerber R, et al (2000) CRISP 1.0 process and user guide. Available at http://www.crisp-dm.org/

Chattratichat J, Darlington J, Guo Y, et al (1999) An architecture for distributed enterprise data mining. In: Proceedings of the 7th International Conference on High-Performance Computing and Networking. Amsterdam: Spinger LNCS 1593: 573-582

Curcin V, Ghanem M, Guo Y, et al (2002) Discovery Net: towards a grid of knowledge discovery. In: The Eighth ACM SIGKDD International Conference on Knowledge Discovery and Data Mining (KDD 2002) 658-663

DataminingGrid Homepage, http://www.datamininggrid.org/

Discovery Net Project Homepage, http://www.discovery-on-the.net/

Fan J, Li D (1998) An overview of data mining and knowledge discovery. Journal of Computer Science and Technology 13(4):348-368

Fayyad U, Piatetsky-Shapiro G, Smyth P (1996) From data mining to knowledge discovery in databases. AI Magazine 17(3):37-54

Frawley WJ, Piatetsky-Shapiro G, Matheus CJ (1992) Knowledge discovery in databases: an overview. AI Magazine 13(3):57-70

George F, Knobbe A (1999) A parallel data mining architecture for massive data sets, http://citeseer.ist.psu.edu/article/george99parallel.html

Ghanem M, Guo Y, Hassard J, Osmond M, et al (2004) Grid-based data analysis of air pollution data. In: Fourth International Workshop on Environmental Applications of Machine Learning, Available at: http://www-ai.ijs.si/SasoDzeroski/ECEMEAML04/accepted_papers.html

Han J, Kamber M (2000) Data mining: concepts and techniques. Morgan Kaufmann Publishers, 7-9

Heckemann RA, Hartkens T, Leung K, et al (2003) Information Extraction from Medical Images (IXI): Developing an e-Science Application Based on the Globus Toolkit. In: 2nd UK e-Science All-hands Conference. Nottingham, UK 775-779

Holsheimer M, Kersten ML (1994) Architectural Support for Data Mining. KDD Workshop: 217-228

Hoschka P, Klosgen W (1991) A support system for interpreting statistical data. Knowledge Discovery in Databases: 325-346

Kargupta H, Hamzaoglu I, Stafford B (1997) Scalable, distributed data mining using an agent based architecture. In: Proceedings of the 3rd International Conference on Knowledge Discovery and Data Mining (KDD 97). Newport Beach, CA: AAAI Press, 211-214

Kargupta H, Park BH, Hershberger D, Johnson E (1999) Collective data mining: A new perspective toward distributed data mining. In Advances in distributed data mining, AAAI/MIT Press, 133-184

Knowledge Grid Lab Homepage, http://dns2.icar.cnr.it/kgrid

Matheus CJ, Chan PK, Piatetsky-Shapiro G (1993) Systems for knowledge discovery in databases. IEEE Transactions on Knowledge and Data Engineering 5(6):903-913

McLaren I, Babb E, Bocca J (1997) DAFS: supporting the knowledge discovery process. In: Proc. 1st Int. Conf. Practical Applications of Knowledge Discovery and Data Mining. Practical Application Company Ltd. 179-190

Piatetsky-Shapiro G, Matheus CJ (1991) Knowledge discovery workbench: an exploratory environment for discovery in business databases. In: Workshop Notes from the Ninth National Conference on Artificial Intelligence: Knowledge Discovery in Databases. Menlo Park, CA: AAAI Press 11-24

PMML, http://www.dmg.org/pmml-v3-0.html

Rana O, Walker D, Li M, Lynden S, Ward M (2000) PaDDMAS: parallel and distributed data mining application suit. In: Proceedings of the Fourteenth International Parallel and Distributed Processing Symposium. Cancun, Mexico: IEEE Press 387-392

Rowe A, Guo Y, Kalaitzopoulos D, et al (2003) The discovery net system for high throughput bioinformatics. Bioinformatics 19(Suppl. 1): 225-231

Schmitz JD, Armstrong GD, Little J (1990) CoverStory - automated news finding in marketing. DSS Transactions 46-54

Stolfo SJ, Prodromidis AL, Tselepis S, et al (1997) Jam: java agents for metalearning over distributed databases. In: Proceedings of the 3rd International Conference on Knowledge Discovery and Data Mining (KDD 97). Newport Beach, CA: AAAI Press 74-81

# 8
# DartGrid: A Semantic Grid Implementation

**Abstract:** The Semantic Grid combines many technologies coming from the Grids, the Web Service and the Semantic Web. Organic integration of these technologies that are actually complementary with each other can result in competent implementation for both Grid and Semantic Web applications. This chapter presents a semantic grid implementation, called DartGrid, which constitutes several components that are intended to support data integration and service management in Grids.

## 8.1 Introduction

DartGrid[1] is a semantic grid framework developed by the CCNT Lab of Zhejiang University. It is intended to provide a generic semantic infrastructure and a collection of toolkits for information sharing and collaborative problem solving in a network-based interconnection environment. It leverages upon technologies from both the Semantic web and the Grid. Basically it consists of a data management component, a service flow management component, and some other plugging components such as those for knowledge discovery.

The first proof of the concept of DartGrid was finished during late 2003. It was originally designed to provide a generic semantic infrastructure in support of the development of database grid application where a huge amount of data resources may be distributedly located and heterogeneously co-exist. The very first prototype system was developed upon Globus Toolkit 3.0, and made use of RDF as the ontology description language. Generally the prototype system implemented several key semantic services including an ontology service for exposing domain ontologies, a semantic registration service for maintaining mediation and mapping information, a data semantics service for publishing the schema information for specific databases. A set of

---

[1] DartGrid: http://ccnt.zju.edu.cn/projects/dartgrid

tools were also developed for the purpose of facilitating all the data management tasks, including a semantic browser for graphically browsing ontology and constructing semantic queries, semantic registration tool for defining the mapping from legacy relational databases to RDF ontologies.

The initial prototype has very limited functions. DartGrid II was then released in early 2005. The new version included a service flow management component and a completely re-engineered data integration component. In this new version the function of semantic-based service matching and process mediation were particularly enhanced and the data management component also has a great improvement in performance with a newly designed query rewriting algorithm and user-friendliness with several re-developed components including a browser-based semantic query interactive user interface and keyword-based semantic search engine that provides semantic-based search across database boundaries. In addition, the data component was firstly deployed at the China Academy of Traditional Chinese Medicine (CATCM) for integrating and managing the ever-increasing number of databases stemming from the traditional Chinese medicine community.

As the development of DartGrid keeps going, new components are added. For example, we are developing the knowledge discovery component based on the integration capability of underlying grid components. On the one hand high-level distributed data mining requires resolving the semantic heterogeneity obstructing and undermining the possibility of cross-database mining. On the other hand the semantically integrated data offers the possibility of doing structured multi-relational knowledge discovery and semantic link mining across database boundaries. That means the semantic grid approach could enable logic-based integrative knowledge discovery from a possible unbound of structured data repositories as never before. Chapter 7 offers more introduction on this issue.

In this chapter we emphasize the two basic components that have been fully implemented in DartGrid. They are the data management component DartDB and the service management component DartFlow.

## 8.2 DartDB–A Semantic Data Integration Toolkit

### 8.2.1 Overview

In many e-Science applications such as life science, climate modeling, high-energy physics, etc., advanced instruments and procedures for systematic digit observations, simulations, and experiments generate a wealth of highly diverse, widely distributed, autonomously managed data resources. The data produced and the knowledge derived from it will lose value in the future if the mechanisms for sharing, integration, cataloging, searching, viewing, and retrieving are not quickly improved. Faced with such an impending data crisis, one promising solution is to describe the data semantics explicitly and formally so that the data can be easily combined, reused, integrated for different applications, middlewares, sensors, instruments and even various pervasive devices. The explicitly represented data semantics even makes the data more readable and meaningful to humans which will greatly facilitate data sharing between different scientists working for different research institutes.

In this section the database grid component (DartDB) of DartGrid is presented. DartDB is built upon several techniques from both the Semantic Web and the Grid research areas and is intended to offer a generic semantic infrastructure for building database grid applications. Generally speaking, DartDB is a set of semantically enabled tools and grid services such as a semantic browser, a semantic mapping tool, an ontology service, a semantic query service, a semantic registration service, which support the development, management and deployment of database grid applications.

Within a database grid application built upon DartGrid,

- database providers are organized as an ontology-based virtual organization (VO),
- by uniformly defined domain semantics, such as domain ontologies, the database can be semantically registered and seamlessly integrated to provide a uniform semantic query service,
- we raise the level of interaction with the database grid system to a domain-cognizant model in which query requests are specified in the terminology and controlled vocabularies of the domains, which enables the users to publish, discover, query databases in a more intuitive way.

### 8.2.2 System Features

Technically speaking, the following five features distinguish DartDB from other similar semantic data integration tools, as can be seen in the following sections.

- **View-based Mapping from Relational Data to Semantic Web Ontologies**. In DartDB, an ontology acts as a semantic mediator for showing up the semantic gaps among heterogenous databases. Relational database schemata are mapped to classes or properties, and related by semantic relationship defined in the ontology. To be more specific, the mappings are defined as semantic views, that is each relational table is defined as a view of this shared ontology. Chapter 5 elaborates on this issue in much more detail.
- **Reasoning-enabled Query Rewriting**. A view-based query rewriting algorithm is implemented for rewriting a SPARQL query into a set of SQL queries. This algorithm extends earlier relational and XML techniques for rewriting queries using views, with consideration of the features of web ontology languages. In addition this algorithm is also enriched by

additional inference capabilities on predicates such as **subClassOf** and **subPropertyOf**.
- **Visualized Semantic Mapping Tool.** Defining mappings has proven to be a labor-intensive and error-prone task. In our system a new database can be added to the system by using a visualized mapping tool, avoiding manually editing and defining complex mappings. It provides many functionalities easy to use, such as drag-and-drop mapping, mapping visualization, data source annotation and so on, to facilitate the user in this task.
- **Ontology-based Dynamic Query Interface.** A form-based query interface is offered to help end-users construct semantic queries over shared ontologies. It is automatically generated at runtime according to property definitions of classes, and can be used to construct SPARQL query, which is the standardized RDF query language from W3C.
- **Semantic Search Interface.** The system also provides a Google-like search interface that is capable of making a complete full-text search over all databases. Users can semantically navigate in the search results, and explore an extendable set of databases based on the semantic relationships defined in the semantic layer. Meanwhile the search system can generate a suggested list of concepts which are ranked based on their relevance to the keywords. Thereafter users can explore the semantic query interface of those concepts and specify a semantic query of them to get more accurate and appropriate information.

### 8.2.3 System Architecture

Basically, DartDB deploys the service-oriented architecture (SOA). As depicted in Fig. 8.1, the system kernel consists of four major components: the ontology service, the semantic registration service, the semantic query service, the semantic search service, serving with different roles in the architecture.

- **Ontology Service** is used to expose the RDF/OWL ontology for open inquiry, query, and ontology maintenance.
- **Semantic Registration Service** is the container for the mapping information for relational-2-RDF/OWL mappings for which a visualized semantic mapping tool is provided to alleviate the burden of the mapping tasks as introduced in the next section.
- **Semantic Query Service** is the component for query rewriting. Firstly it retrieves relevant views from the semantic registration service. Next it translates the input SPARQL query into SQL queries using the rewriting approach introduced in previous sections and dispatches the SQL queries to specific databases. Finally the results of SQL queries will be merged and transformed back to RDF/OWL format.
- **Semantic Search Service** supports full-text search over all databases. The search results are also mapped to the ontology and transformed into

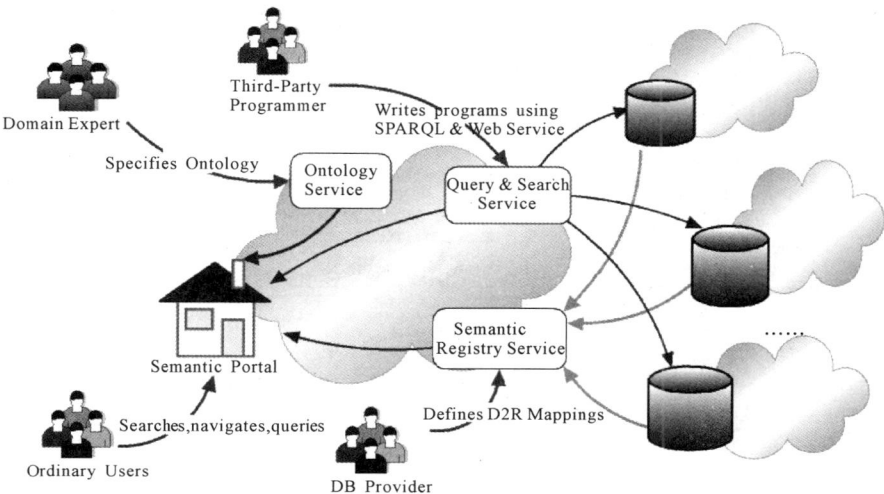

**Fig. 8.1.** Architecture of the system kernel

RDF/OWL format. Additionally the results are statistically calculated to yield a concepts ranking, enabling users to get more appropriate and accurate results.

### 8.2.4 Mapping from Relational Data to Semantic Web Ontology

The informal approach taken for the selection of names and values within relational databases makes the data only understandable for specific applications. The mapping from relational data to the Semantic Web layer makes the semantics of the data more formal, explicit, and prepared for sharing and reusing by other applications. However, because of the inherent model difference between the relational data model and the Semantic Web languages, mapping is always a complicated task and can be time-consuming and error-prone. We have therefore developed a visualized mapping tool to simplify the work as much as possible, as Fig. 8.2 displays. The tool generates mapping rules that are used when a SPARQL query is rewritten into a set of SQL queries.

Specifically, the tool has the following features.

- **Drag-and-drop mapping operation.** The tool supports creating the mapping views in a drag-and-drop way. Users can import relational schemata from different data sources into the DBRes panel, and import the ontology in RDF/OWL syntax into the OntoSchem panel. Typically, users drag tables or columns from DBRes panel, and drag classes or properties from OntoSchem panel, then drop them into the mapping panel to establish the mappings.

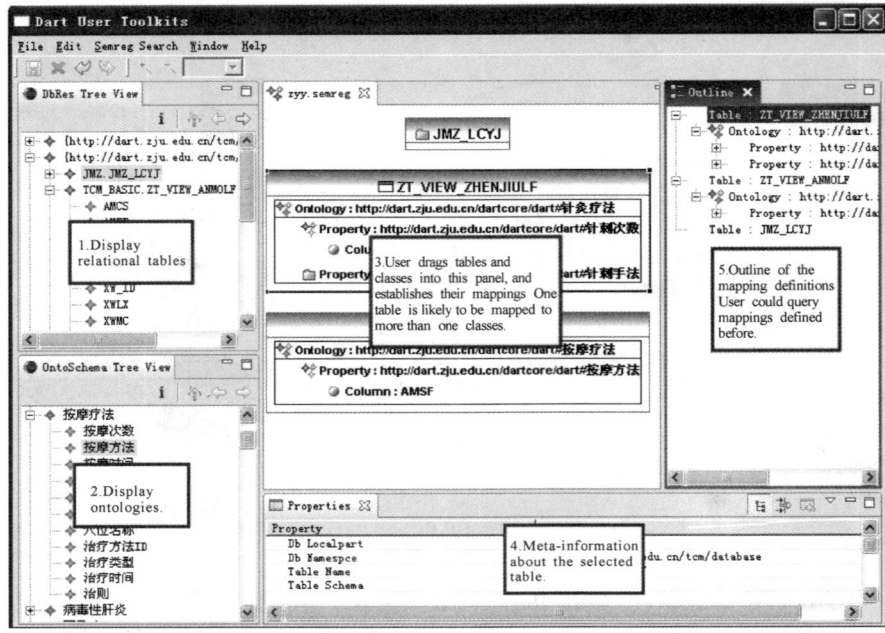

**Fig. 8.2.** A tool for mapping from relational data to semantic web ontology

- **Mapping visualization.** The mapping panel graphically displays the elements of the mappings views, facilitating the database integrator to visualize, search and manipulate the view specifications more easily.
- **Mapping inference.** After the initial mappings are set up, the tool is able to automatically infer further knowledge about the mapping. For example, it can infer "foreign key" relationships among relational tables based on the semantic relation defined at the ontological level.

### 8.2.5 Semantic Browser and Query Tool

We have also developed a semantic-based query and search portal to assist in user interaction with the system. Basically this system consists of two components. The search component enables users to perform full-text searching through all of the integrated data sources using keywords that are similar to common Internet search engines, while the query component supplies us with a means for handling more complex semantic queries posed by the semantic web ontology.

The ontology plays an important role in the mediation of the query, search and navigation. First it serves as a logic layer for users in constructing semantic queries. The form-based query interface is automatically generated based on the ontological structure. The constructed semantic query will then be translated into SQL queries based on the mapping rules generated by the mapping tool. Second it enables semantic navigation across database boundaries during query and search. Third it also serves as a control vocabulary to facilitate a search by making semantic suggestions such as synonyms and related concepts.

The semantic browser and query tool are intended to facilitate users in browsing ontologies and posing SPARQL queries for the ontologies. Basically, the tool includes the following technical features.

- Ontology-based dynamic query interface. The query form is automatically generated based on RDF/OWL ontological structures. This feature guarantees the extensibility of the query system: When ontology is extended or updated, the interface can dynamically adapt to the updated ontology.
- Semantic navigation. The user can navigate across database boundaries as long as the semantic relations between the databases are defined.

Fig. 8.3 illustrates a typical working scenario: starting from the ontology view panel on the left, the user browses the ontology tree and selects one class. A query input dialog, which is generated automatically based on the property definitions of the selected class, is displayed in the middle. Next, the users can select the properties of interest and input the query constraint in the text boxes (e.g., the name of disease). Accordingly a SPARQL query is constructed and submitted to the semantic query service. Users sometimes may want to define queries spanning several classes. In the lower-middle part of Fig. 8.3, a list of classes semantically related to a currently selected class is displayed. By following the links the users are led to the query form for these classes and able to select more properties of related classes and input new query constraints. The SPARQL query statement is submitted to the system and converted into a set of SQL queries according to the mapping information between database schemata and the ontology. The SQL queries are then dispatched to specific databases that return all satisfactory records. Since the direct query result from databases does not expose any semantics, the system converts the result into a data stream in RDF format so that the semantics of the result is fully represented.

### 8.2.6 Semantic Search Engine

Besides the query interface, a semantic-based search engine called Dart-Search, is developed for full-text search over all databases. Users can perform a search on the integrated databases using keywords in a similar way to common Internet search engines. However, a search here is different from a Google-like search in that the search process is performed based on the semantic relations in the ontology and we call it a semantic search, which is searching for data objects rather than Web pages. Semantics is presented in three aspects in DartSearch:

186    8 DartGrid: A Semantic Grid Implementation

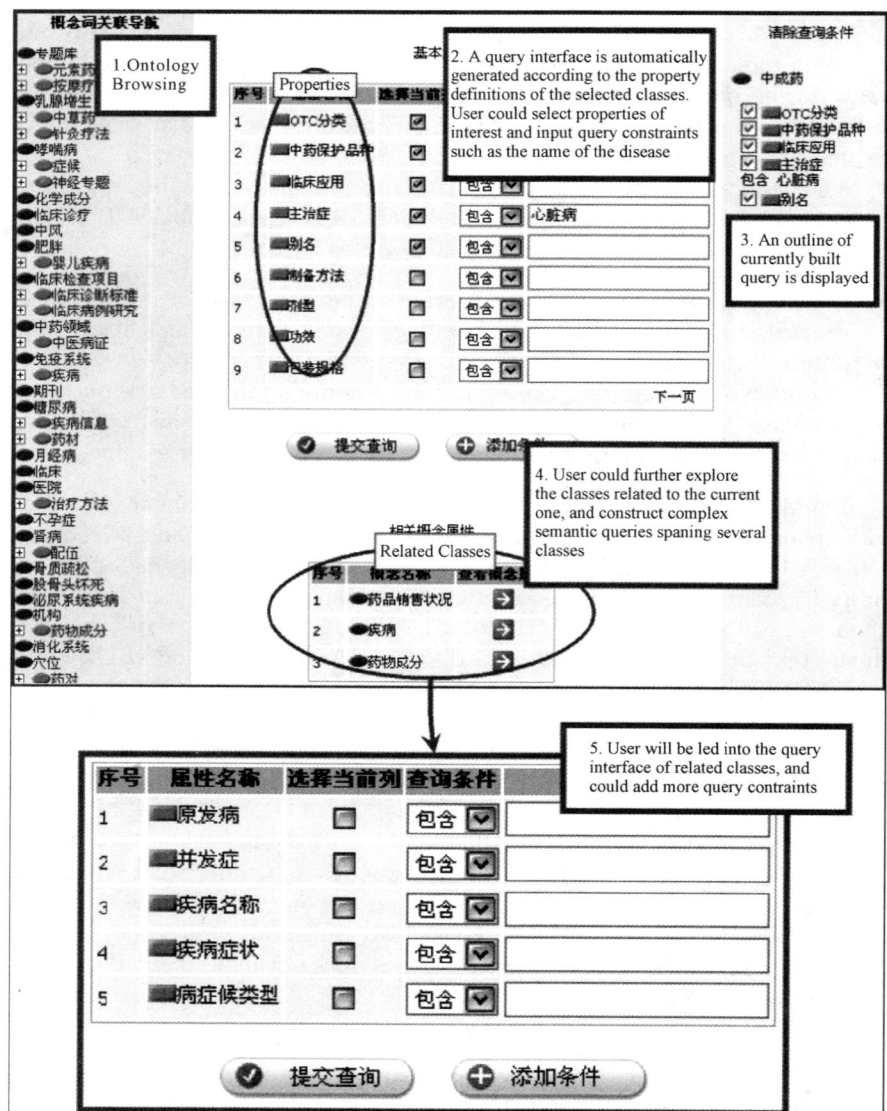

**Fig. 8.3.** Semantic query builder

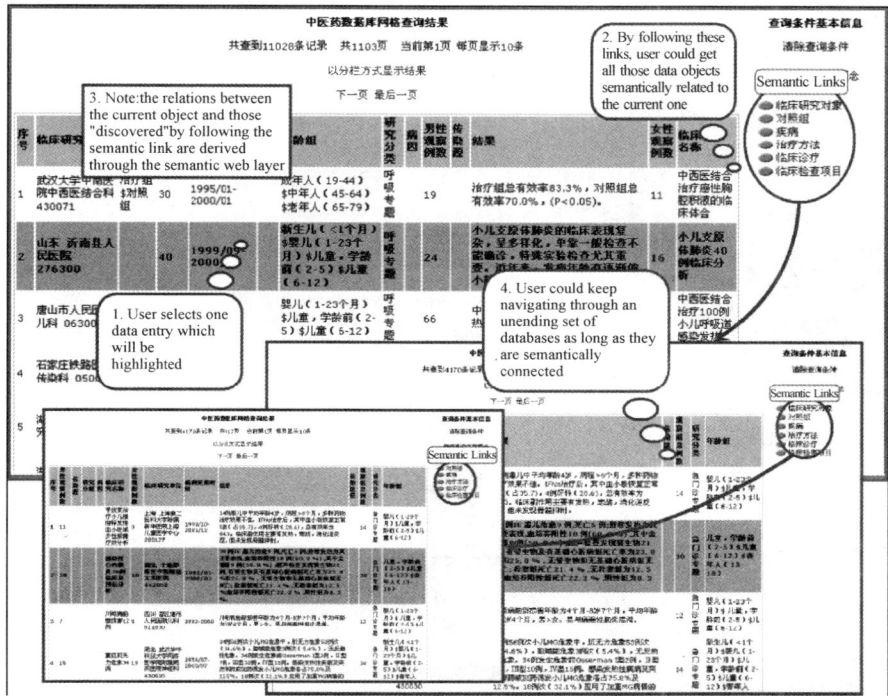

**Fig. 8.4.** Semantic navigation across databases based on ontologies

- Semantic navigation. Users can navigate through the searched data objects by following the semantic relations defined in the ontology. For example, the result of a semantic search request is shown in Fig. 8.5. Each data object in the list is a piece of information from databases that have been mapped to some ontology classes. At the bottom of each object there are some semantic links to the classes semantically related to the mapped classes. By following those links users could get all of the data objects semantically related to the current object.
- Intuitive search with concept ranking. One key feature of the system is to take advantage of the ontology to mediate the structured query and unstructured search. Fig. 8.5 depicts a typical scenario of combined search and query. If a keyword search is trigged, the system firstly performs a full text search over all candidate data sources. Simultaneously, the system performs a search of the RDF ontology, and returns a set of RDF classes ranked in a descending order according to their matching degrees to the input keyword based upon a certain calculation mechanism. These classes are linked to their corresponding semantic query interface so that users could further specify a semantic query to refine the search result and retrieve more accurate and appropriate information.

188    8 DartGrid: A Semantic Grid Implementation

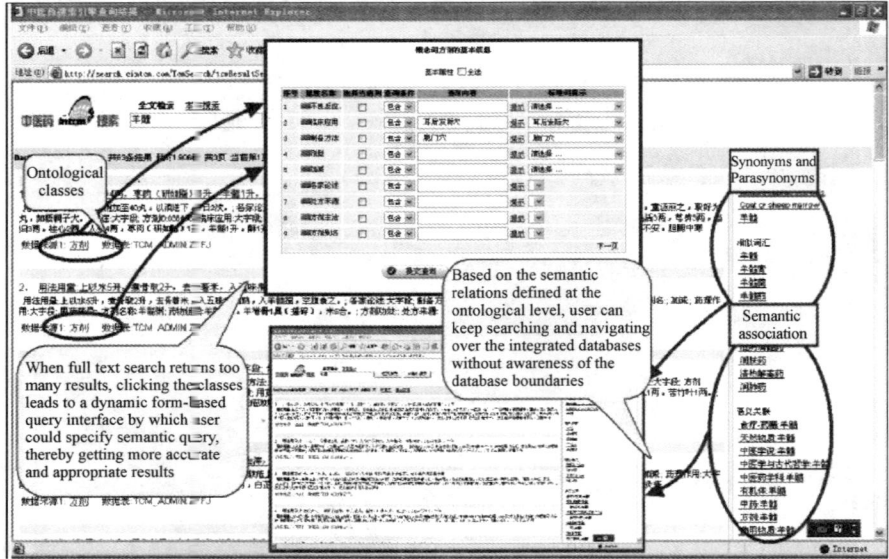

**Fig. 8.5.** Semantic search engine

## 8.3 DartFlow–A Service Flow Management Prototype

### 8.3.1 Overview

As a part of the DartGrid, DartFlow provides all-round service management functions including service registration and annotation, service matchmaking and discovery, service flow building and verification, service flow execution and monitoring. The objective of DartFlow is to provide an infrastructure for users in VOs to realize service reuse and sharing, cooperation and process management. In this section we give an introduction to its architecture, functions and characteristics.

### 8.3.2 System Architecture

The architecture of DartFlow is shown as below, which is divided into two parts: DartFlow IDE and DartFlow Server.

- DartFlow IDE is an integrated development environment for DartFlow users including service providers, service consumers and service flow designers. As shown in Fig. 8.7, it contains four main perspectives: service registration/annotation perspective, service flow design perspective, service flow simulation/debug perspective and service flow execu-

## 8.3 DartFlow–A Service Flow Management Prototype

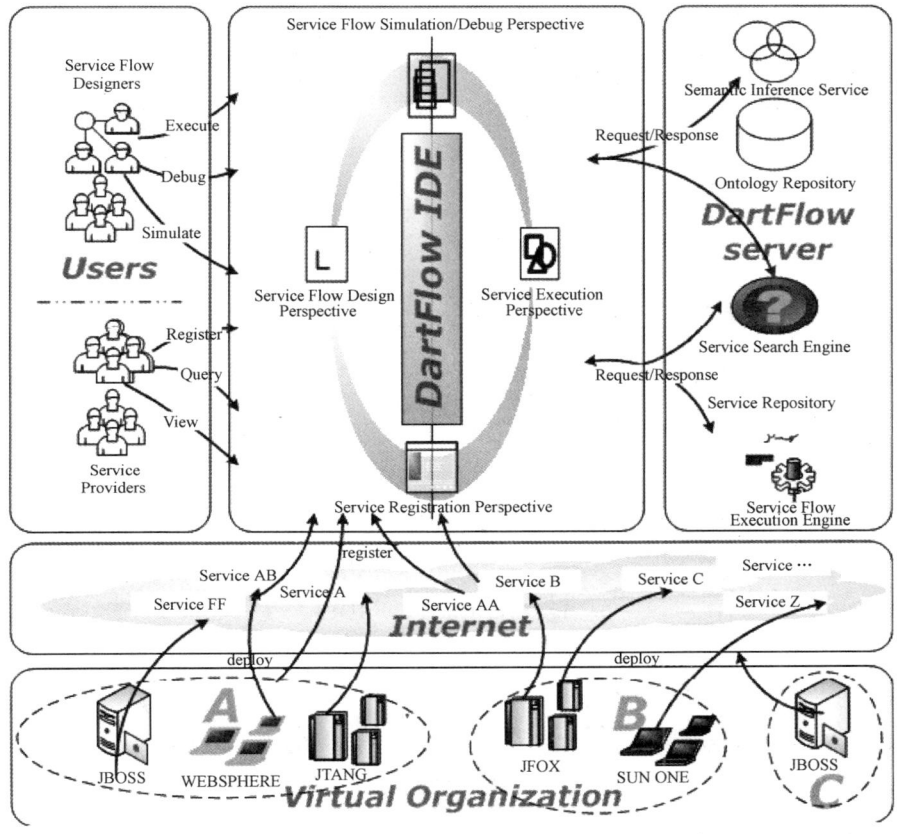

**Fig. 8.6.** Architecture of DartFlow

tion/monitor perspective. Through these four perspectives users can register, annotate, query, invoke, compose and execute services.

- DartFlow Server provides the core services, interfaces and components of DartFlow. It includes the ontology repository, semantic inference service, service search engine, service repository and service flow execution engine. The ontology repository is used to store domain ontologies and to provide interfaces to query and retrieve concepts and terms. Semantic inference service supports inference on ontology concept to discover their relations. The service search engine provides interfaces for DartFlow IDE to invoke query services. Service repository stores the registered information of services. The service flow execution engine is responsible for interpreting service flow specification, generating and executing service flow instances.

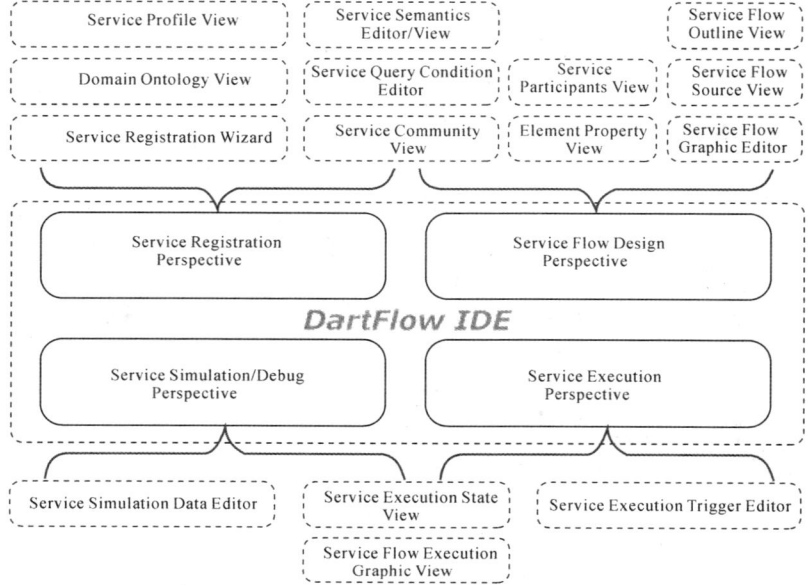

**Fig. 8.7.** DartFlow IDE

### 8.3.3 Main Functions

As mentioned before, the life cycle of a service flow, the same as that of workflow, includes two phases: building-time phase and run-time phase. In order to facilitate users in a VO to manage a service flow during its life cycle, DartFlow provides the following main functions for users.

#### 8.3.3.1 Service Registration and Annotation

In DartFlow a service provider must publish his/her service through the service registration/annotation perspective of DartFlow IDE in order to realize the reuse of the service by other users. DartFlow IDE provides a wizard for service providers to advertise service information such as service description, classification and the provider's information. It also helps users to annotate the service with semantics. When service providers want to register their services they only need to provide the URL of WSDL or URL of the service. The IDE will parse the WSDL and then display the contained elements in a graphic view. After that service providers can annotate inputs/outputs with ontology concepts. At present we have developed the registration and annotation perspective of the IDE as shown in Fig. 8.8. At the right top it is the graphical illustration of ontology concepts. At the right bottom it is the graphical illustration of a service to be registered. A user can assign a concept to the input/output element of a service. After a service is annotated with

8.3 DartFlow–A Service Flow Management Prototype    191

semantics the registration information will be formatted into an XML file. A snapshot of the semantic information contained in an XML file is shown as below. Notice that the operation name, input and output are all annotated with ontology concepts.

```
............
<Operation Name=GetWeatherOntoClass=GIS:Weather>
    <Inputs>
        <Input OntoClass=GIS:City/>
        <Input OntoClass=GIS:Date/>
    <Inputs>
    <Outputs>
        <Output OntoClass=GIS:Weather/>
    <Outputs>
............
```

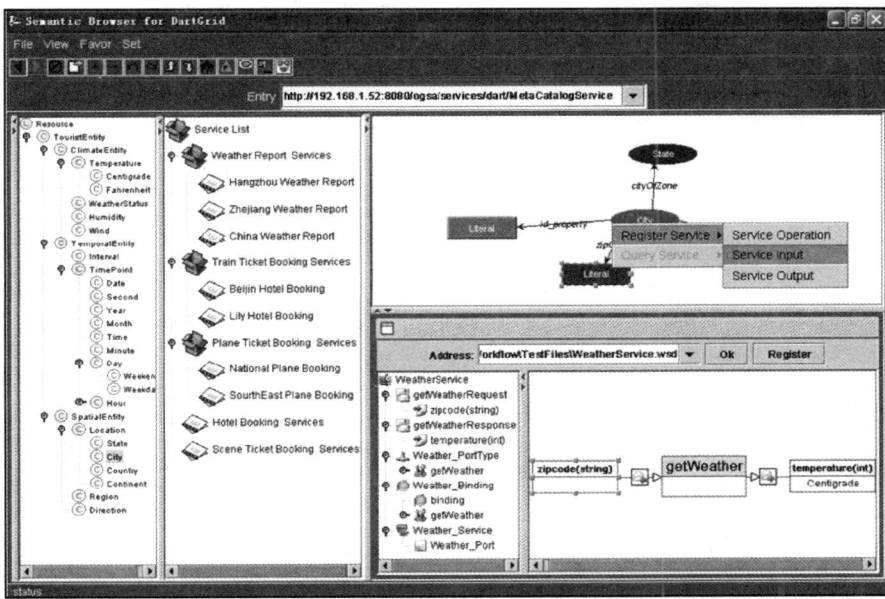

**Fig. 8.8.** Service registration and annotation in DartFlow

### 8.3.3.2 Service Classification and Clustering

In order to help users to find a target service quickly, DartFlow IDE provides a service classification and clustering perspective for users. This perspective illustrates the service community by the function classification of services. At

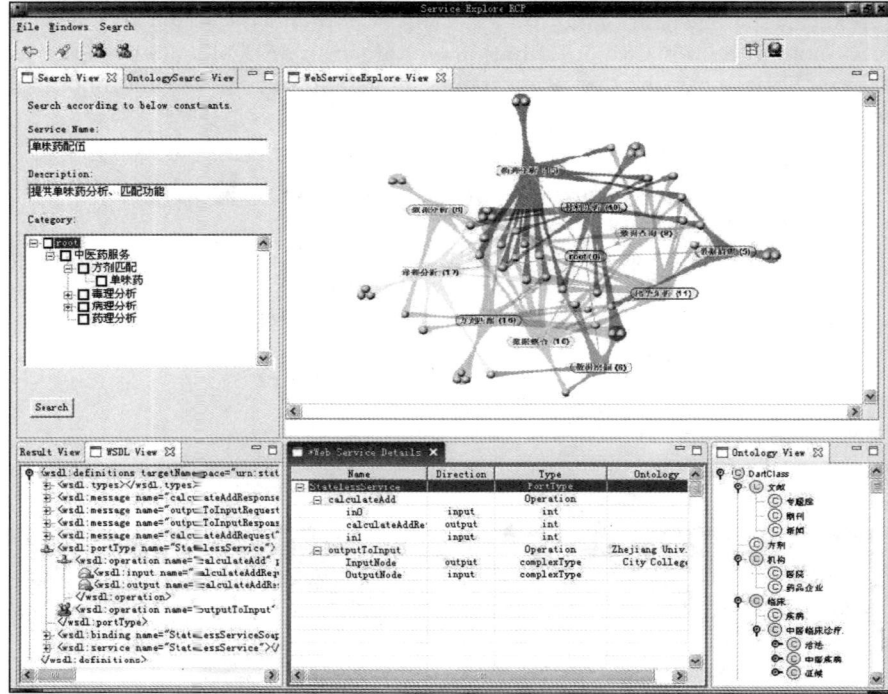

**Fig. 8.9.** Service classification and navigation in DartFlow

present this perspective uses Aduna Cluster Map[2] to show the classification graph as shown in Fig. 8.9. Each node represents a service and each group represents a cluster of services with the same functions. Notice that if a node belongs to more than one group it means that the service has more than one function. With this perspective a user can browse services according to function categories he or she chooses. It can help a user to find his/her target service quickly.

### 8.3.3.3 Semantic-based Service Discovery

Although a user can discover services manually through browsing services according to function categories, it is very time-consuming, especially when the number of services is large. Therefore DartFlow provides the ability for the user to query services automatically based on a semantic-based service discovery mechanism. When a user wants to query services, he/she constructs a query by designating inputs/outputs ontology concepts for the target service and then submits the query to the DartFlow server. The following query

---

[2]http://www.aduna-software.com/technologies/clustermap/overview.view

example shows that the user wants to retrieve the services with two inputs (City and Date) and one output (Weather). The query is sent to the DartFlow server and the server will parse the query and execute the query based on the semantic matchmaking between services and the query. After that those services that match the query are returned to the DartFlow IDE and illustrated for users.

```
<ServiceRequest OntologySpace=
       http://Middleware.zju.edu.cn/shuiguang/GISOnto>
. . . . . . . . . . . .
    <Inputs>
       <Input OntoClass=GIS:City/>
       <Input OntoClass=GIS:Date/>
    </Inputs>
    <Outputs>
       <Output OntoClass=GIS:Weather/>
    </Outputs>
. . . . . . . . . . . .
</ServiceRequest>
```

#### 8.3.3.4 Service Flow Design and Deploy

In order to help a user build his/her business process in a convenient and efficient way, DartFlow provides a service flow design and deploys a perspective for a user to build processes through the drag-and-drop method. At present we have implemented the perspective using Eclipse GEF. As shown in Fig. 8.10, each node of the center view represents a step in the business process. A user can select a service and bind one of its operations to the step to accomplish the business goal of this step. After the user has drawn up the whole service flow he can invoke the verification function through the menu to verify the service flow. And also, he/she can simulate the service flow before deploying it. During the simulation a user can debug it step by step through the execution of the process to monitor the process data, invoked service and the process status. After the verification and simulation the user can deploy the service flow process into the DartFlow Server.

#### 8.3.3.5 Service Flow Execution and Monitor

In order to realize the business goal of a service flow, a service flow must be put into execution. In DartFlow a user can select a service flow and submit it to the DartFlow Server to execute it. During the execution a user can monitor the status of execution, the data, and the invoked services through the DartFlow IDE. At present the execution engine in the DartFlow Server is implemented by using JAVA 1.5 and makes use of WSIF (Web Service Invocation Framework) to invoke services.

194   8 DartGrid: A Semantic Grid Implementation

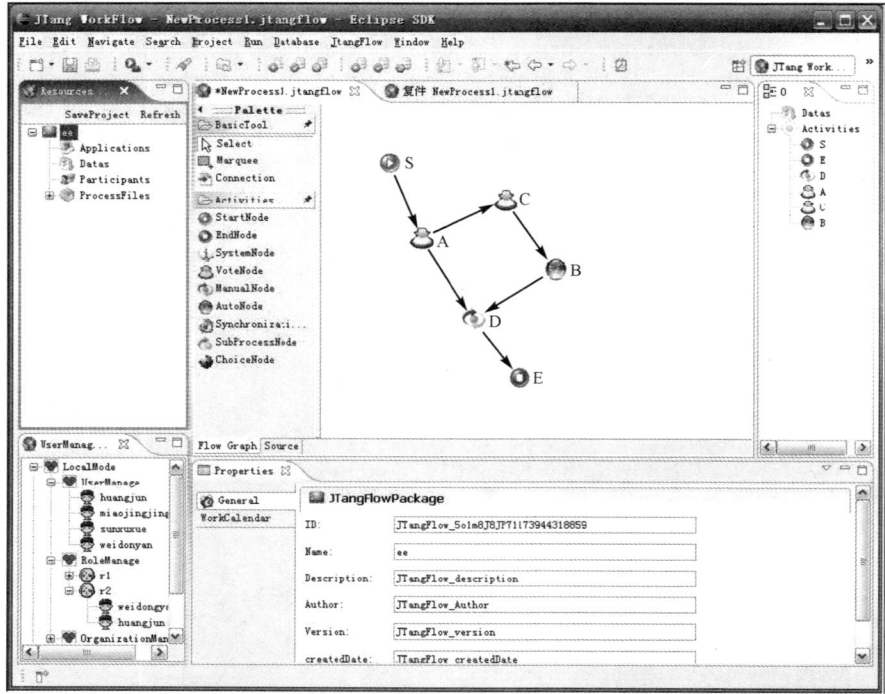

**Fig. 8.10.** Service flow design in DartFlow

## 8.4 Summary and Conclusion

In this chapter, the implementation of a semantic grid platform is introduced in detail. Basically the platform provides a generic infrastructure to support ontology-based information management in a grid setting. The platform consists of two basic components with different purposes and application needs.

We believe for the future Internet-based working environment like the Grid, semantics and ontology will play an indispensable role in reconciling the semantic gaps widely existing in many application areas. We are still working on more advanced components such as the KDD over the Semantic Grid that has been mentioned in Chapter 7. We are also concerned with more advanced features for the search component, such as a facet-based search interface and object ranking mechanism.

# 9
# Semantic Grid Applications for Traditional Chinese Medicine

**Abstract:** In this chapter, we present the utilization of the DartGrid technical framework to build an E-Science Environment for Traditional Chinese Medicine (TCM) domain. The diversification, heterogeneity, and interdisciplinary characteristics of this domain have been properly addressed by the Semantic Grid infrastructure. The services composition and management mechanism based on a work flow engine enables the construction of over 70 TCM scientific databases. The infrastructure supports a cross-organizational collaboration of ontology engineering, resulting into the Unified TCM Language System (UTCMLS), the largest TCM Semantic Web ontology including 5,000 concepts and 20,000 instances. The semantic integration of disparate scientific databases enables information retrieval and knowledge discovery across database boundaries. The platform and underlying methodology are proved effective in use cases such as personalized healthcare with TCM characteristics and TCM drug discovery and safety analysis. This project demonstrates the Semantic Grid's advantages in connecting data across domain and community boundaries to facilitate interdisciplinary and cross-cultural studies.

## 9.1 Background, Status, and Problems of TCM Informatics

Traditional Chinese Medicine (TCM) is essentially an information/knowledge-intensive medical system of fully developed theoretical and practical aspects. TCM takes deep root in traditional Chinese culture and reflects the thoughts of Chinese philosophy and therefore reflects traditional Chinese culture and philosophy. Since the threshold of China's reform and opening-up, medical practitioners both in China and worldwide have deepened their interest in TCM, both as an independently evolved knowledge system of great values in and of itself, and as a reservoir of insights and guidelines for the reform of the Chinese healthcare system. Therefore the reservation and utilization of the

TCM knowledge base have become a critical issues. In this section we first present an overview of the background and status of TCM informatics and then discuss its critical problems, with their causes and possible solutions.

### 9.1.1 Background of TCM Informatics

The knowledge base of TCM is large in scale and is almost beyond comprehension, analysis, and computerization. There are three major reasons for this situation. First, TCM knowledge is commonly available in the form of ancient classics and confidential family records. Second, these documents are disparate among people and organizations across geographical areas. Third, the written records of TCM are mainly in classical Chinese that has become increasingly alienated from modern Chinese during two thousand years of linguistic evolution.

The expansion of TCM practice results in an ongoing accumulation of more and more research documents and clinical data, which dramatizes the innate challenges of TCM knowledge and information management. The unavailability of intelligent resources and supporting evidences inhibits clinical decision-making, drug discovery, and education. Therefore the computerization and formulation of data become a necessity for the effectiveness and durability of TCM.

### 9.1.2 Status of TCM Informatics

We have witnessed the revolutionary impact of the Web and XML on biomedical information interoperability in recent years. Meanwhile biomedical informatics has become an important application area of data mining and knowledge discovery. However, the related studies are mostly concerned with enabling applications in orthodox medicine. We need to analyze the differentiating characteristics of TCM and address its unique requirements.

In developed countries biomedical informatics has been driving the progress of evidence-based medicine. The resources for biomedical researchers mainly take the form of textual databases, such as MEDLINE, EMBASE and NAPRALERT. Service providers integrate biomedical databases and provide uniform access for end users through web portals, such as PubMed, EMBASE.com, and NAPRALERT.org. The successes in orthodox medicine are attributable to the maturity and consistency of its domain model. By contrast the domain model of TCM has such exceptional characteristics as ambiguity, complexity, and diversity, which increase the difficulties of TCM informatics.

The TCM community's emphasis on TCM informatics has grown steadily since the 1980s, which ignited a series of initiatives for digitalizing literatures and clinical data. Meanwhile the Chinese Academy of TCM (CATCM) has established over 70 legacy relational databases and a variety of applications for providing information services. A typical case is the integration of TCM-drug-related literatures on a large scale utilizing a database-federation mechanism, enabling data and text mining methods for drug/formula discovery. However, the further development of the federation of TCM information repositories caused a series of critical problems.

### 9.1.3 Problems of TCM Informatics

The problems plaguing TCM informatics results in a deteriorating situation. The lack of a standardized terminology leads to the unavoidability of flaws in data quality planning and management. The combination of the above two problems leads to a set of negative consequences, including (a) the stalemate of information integration and sharing, (b) the isolation of disparate databases as information islands, and (c) the under-utilization of information resources.

- **Lack of Terminological Standard**

The prolonged evolution of TCM practices intensifies the diversity of terminology among different communities of TCM practitioners. The unstructured nature of TCM data, together with the diversified representations of concepts, makes it difficult for the extraction of semantic information from TCM documentation. The standardization efforts in the TCM domain are still insufficient for the construction of TCM scientific databases, while the application of available standards in the construction of databases was still in its infancy period. The incompleteness and insufficient adoption of TCM terminology standards limit the construction of a TCM conceptual network, which further hindered a variety of high-layer applications such as semantic search, data analysis and data mining. The fusion and updating of current standards into a coherent form is essential for the success of TCM Informatics.

- **Flawed Data Quality Management**

The existence of flaws in data quality management contributes to a major inhibitor of TCM informatics. Most TCM resources are innately unstructured. We need to adopt a knowledge representation system to express TCM knowledge and to make the semantics of information explicit. Ontology learning methods are applicable for (semi-)automatically generating semantic annotations of unstructured documents. We also need to express quality assurance rules in terms of domain language and to embed these rules in all data entrances. The education and training of practitioners are immediate needs to help them comply with guidelines and e-Learning is a suitable way to achieve this. The above three measures, among others, depend on a terminological standard, the lack of which thus becomes a major causality of the concerned QA flaws.

- **Limited Data Integration and Sharing**

The geographical distribution and organizational isolation of databases make data integration and sharing a difficult problem. We initially used the federated-databases mechanism in the development of a TCM scientific data-sharing platform. Despite early successes and contributions, this mechanism is ultimately limited to addressing the TCM data integration and sharing problem, and we need to find an alternative technical approach.

Ontology is useful for data integration and knowledge sharing across organization boundaries, but providing agreed ontological structures to legacy databases can be very time-consuming and labor-intensive. Incremental steps should be taken toward rich semantics of integrated databases, from terminological standardization, to semantic network construction, to ontology engineering, to semantic integration, and finally to information retrieval and knowledge discovery.

- **Under-utilization of TCM Databases**

The major reasons for under-utilization of TCM databases are: (a) the problems with data quality limit the level of applicability; (b) the lack of propagation for constructed databases; (c) the network infrastructure is not established; (d) TCM database heterogeneity makes database integration very hard to achieve.

Improving the data quality, updating the cyber-system and integrating data are three key issues for improving the utilization of TCM databases. Basic query functions prove to be inadequate for the exploitation of TCM data. We need to adopt advanced methods. The ultimate goal of TCM database construction is to discover medical evidence and rules from a massive amount of data, in order to support (a) the development of TCM evidence-based medicine, and (b) the establishment of a TCM quality assurance system. Information retrieval and knowledge discovery are two major enabling techniques toward this goal. We need to embark upon a full solution that considers the above aspects in order to improve the utilization of resources.

- **The Challenges of Collaborative Research on a Global Basis**

The Internet provides an inter-connected information space for collaborative research on a global basis. There is a growing dependency among TCM practitioners on the availability and usability of Web resources. Open collaboration in a global environment requires a higher level of resource allocation and process coordination capabilities, including (a) loosely-coupled activities, services and resources, (b) on-demand integration of information resources and (c) asynchronous and an agile workflow mechanism.

TCM Informatics practitioners came to a gradual realization that the root of the problems plaguing TCM Informatics lies in the dislocation of its IT infrastructure. The mismatch between business goals and IT solutions accumulated during the TCM Informatics process, leading to a crisis point necessitating in a major reformation of the IT infrastructure. The envisioned IT infrastructure should be agile and resilient enough to address the critical problems of information/knowledge representation, management, and sharing, to boost efficiency and productivity of researchers, and to satisfy the specific requirements of the TCM domain. We will describe the proposed infrastructure, the TCM e-Science Semantic Grid, in the next section.

## 9.2 The Architecture of TCM e-Science Semantic Grid

We propose the Semantic Grid as an alternative technical solution to address the problems plaguing TCM Informatics. As described in the previous chapters, the Semantic Grid provides a seamless integration of Grid Computing and the Semantic Web to better address large-scale database integration and service coordination in a virtual organization. Related works show that the Semantic Grid can provide a sound e-Science infrastructure for a knowledge-intensive discipline in general, which implies the suitability of the Semantic Grid for TCM as a classical knowledge-intensive discipline. We will focus on explaining how the Semantic Grid resolves the TCM Informatics issues in particular.

### 9.2.1 Overview

In this section we present an overview of the TCM e-Science environment, which utilizes the Semantic Grid technical framework to establish an agile and resilient infrastructure for better addressing the unique requirements of TCM. We use domain ontologies to integrate TCM database resources and services in a semantic cyberspace and deliver a semantically superior experience including browsing, searching, querying and knowledge discovery to users (Chen HJ, Wang YM, Wu ZH, 2007).

CCNT and CATCM started to apply semantic grid technology to the core of the TCM data sharing platform in 2002 (Chen HJ, Wu ZH, et al., 2007). This approach aims at:

- Providing a standardized representation of TCM knowledge and information;
- Establishing a dynamic and extensible framework for the management and allocation of distributed and heterogeneous resources;
- Providing a coherent query interface through semantic integration of all databases held by CATCM and its affiliated institutions;
- Providing a collection of high-level applications including semantic browsing, semantic searching, OLAP, and data mining;
- Implementing a TCM e-Science environment for collaborative obtaining and filtering, transparent storing, and personalized delivery of TCM information and knowledge.

## 9.2.2 Three Layers of TCM e-Science Environment

TCM e-Science has the architectural pattern of the Semantic Grid. As shown in Fig. 9.1, the architecture contains three separate layers:

- **Resource Layer**

The Resource layer provides a uniform mechanism for management, storage, and accessibility of a plurality of resources in the TCM domain, such as databases, terminological systems, ontologies, and files. It supports the typical remote operations on the contents of resources on the Web and querying the meta-information of databases, and services. *Resource Access Service* supports the typical remote operations on the contents of databases and execution of services. *Information Service* supports inquiring about the meta-information of the database or service resources.

- **Service Layer**

The Service layer works for semantic-based information manipulation and integration. *Process Semantic Service* exports services as OWL-S descriptions. *Database Semantic Service* exports the relational schema of databases as RDF/OWL semantic description. *Ontology Service* exposes the shared TCM ontology and provides basic operations on the ontology. *Semantic Mapping Service* establishes the mappings from local resources to the mediated ontology. *Semantic Query Service* accepts semantic query and then converts it into a set of SQL queries. The service wraps the results of SQL queries by semantics and returns them as triples. *Semantic Search Service* indexes all databases mapped to mediated ontology and accepts semantic-based full-text search.

- **Application Layer**

This layer utilizes the services of DartGrid to satisfy three major TCM requirements, including *Academic VO, Personalized Healthcare*, and *Drug Discovery*. This layer contains four major components, including (a) The TCMLS Engineering Platform and The TCM Data Resources Metadata Directory, (b) The TCM Data Sharing Platform, (c) The TCM Database Construction Platform; and (d) The Distributed Data Mining Platform.

## 9.2.3 Application Platforms in TCM e-Science Environment

Since this chapter mainly describes the TCM application of DartGrid, in the remaining part of this chapter we will focus on the application layer. Let us take a closer look at the four key applications in the TCM e-Science environment:

## 9.2 The Architecture of TCM e-Science Semantic Grid

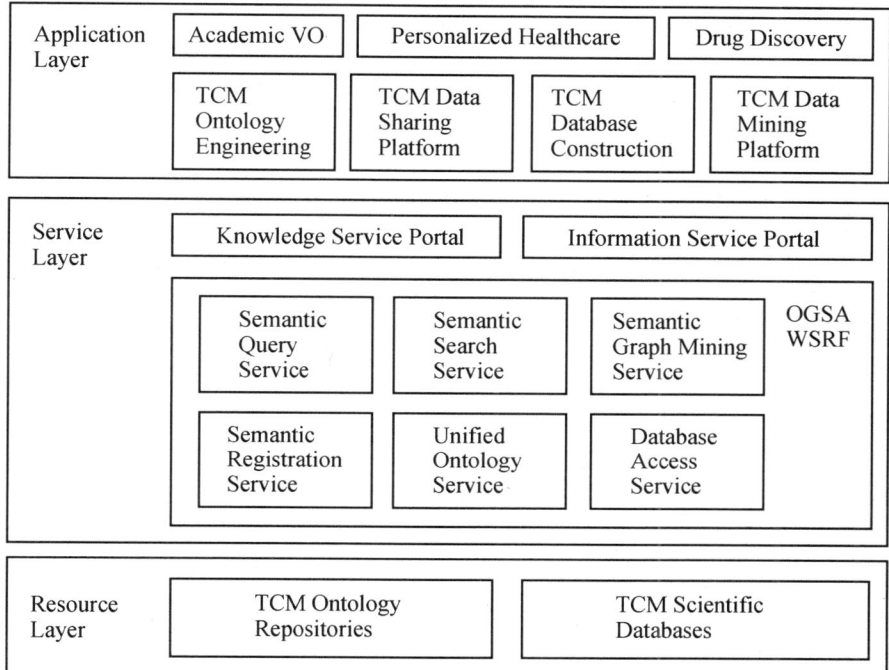

**Fig. 9.1.** The architecture of TCM e-Science environment

- **The TCM Ontology Engineering Platform**
  The TCMLS is an integrated semantic network of concepts and their relationships in the TCM domain. It serves as the foundation of knowledge management for TCM, and provides the means for knowledge discovery from massive clinical data and documents.
- **The TCM Information Sharing Platform**
  The new TCM Data Sharing Platform is essentially a grid environment for databases. This platform achieves the semantic integration of autonomous and heterogeneous database resources and provides a universal data query and information retrieval interface, which supports a class of high-level applications. It utilizes Globus Toolkit 4 to implement grid services and utilizes the semantic web recommendations to express metadata and knowledge.
- **The TCM Database Construction Platform**
  The TCM Database Construction Platform supports collaborative scientific data collection and editing within an academic Virtual Organization (VO). This academic VO physically includes more than ten scientific data centers that are geographically distributed across the country. This platform provides a set of services and resources for the well-coordinated

treatment of this process, including (a) a virtual environment for communication and interaction between TCM experts and scientists, (b) a framework for TCM database modeling, maintenance, and quality assurance, (c) user profile, authentication, and authorization management, and (d) managerial services such as resource planning, task delegation, and activity scheduling.

- **The Distributed Data Mining Platform**
  The Distributed Data Mining Platform adopts Web service technologies to modularize a variety of data mining operations. It takes advantage of the Data Sharing Platform as its data source, and takes advantage of the TCMLS Engineering Platform as its knowledge source. Only when a universal knowledge base is available and all the information is integrated on the semantic level can we fully exploit TCM data for actionable knowledge, namely patterns and rules, to be discovered, managed and used for decision-making.

TCM academic VO serves as the Web Services Portal for the TCM e-Science environment. Let us further explain the relationships between the TCM academic VO and the four backbone platforms as is illustrated in Fig. 9.2. First, academic VO wraps the interfaces of the four platforms and provides TCM experts with a coherent user experience. Second, Ontology Engineering provides knowledge, terminology, and a data modeling service to other platforms. Third, the data sharing platform provides a universal data query and information retrieval interface for all other components. Fourth, the database construction platform is responsible for the construction and maintenance of all databases within the VO. Fifth, the data mining platform takes raw knowledge and data from the VO and expresses actionable knowledge in business rules. In the remaining parts of this section we will further explain the academic VO and the four key components in detail.

We have presented an overview of the architecture and applications of TCM e-Science infrastructure. We will further illustrate how the infrastructure can be implemented with the DartGrid Toolkit and how the infrastructure supports TCM applications in the following sections.

## 9.3 Collaborative TCM Ontology Engineering

TCM Ontology Engineering Project is at the core and foundation of the TCM semantic grid construction, including (a) the research on knowledge representation framework of TCM, and (b) the construction of an Ontology Engineering Platform.

We first rephrase our works on the knowledge representation framework of TCM in Chapter 2:

- The formal representation of TCM Ontology based on descriptive logic.

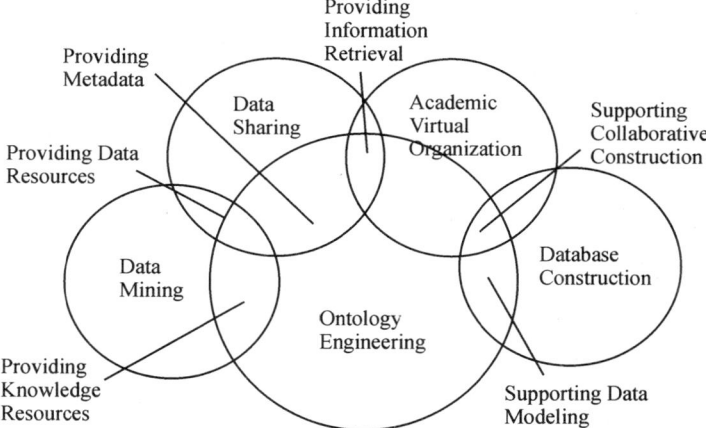

**Fig. 9.2.** The relationships between the academic VO and the four platforms

- The formal representation of TCM rules based on Horn logic and this scheme particularly supports the representation of the rules that guide the combination of drugs in formulas in TCM.
- The formal representation of TCM clinical cases and case inference function embedded in clinical decision-making system.

These works provide a solid theoretical foundation for the construction of a practical platform, which we did in 2005. It mainly took the form of a TCMLS development platform as is illustrated in Fig. 9.3, though the true potential, as is revealed in academic works, is that this platform evolves into a knowledge base encompassing a terminological system, clinical cases, clinical evidences, and actionable/executable rules.

The platform enables cross-organization collaboration through the Internet, and resolves the usability and reliability of large-scale ontology engineering. It enables a well-defined policy-making and compliance auditing system through the representation, exchange and maintenance of ontology, which support multiple and customizable roles. These innovations provide a better assurance of ontology quality.

A comparison between TCMLS and the Protégé project from Stanford University is as follows:

- Our tool utilizes Ajax to present a sound user experience while omitting installation, while Protégé's Swing-based UI is more elaborate in terms of their class and instance editors and their customizable forms.
- With our tool as it is deployed in a grid environment, multiple users are able to collaborate in construction in a distributed fashion. Protégé's support for distributed editing is based on another technical approach that is characterized as peer-to-peer computing.

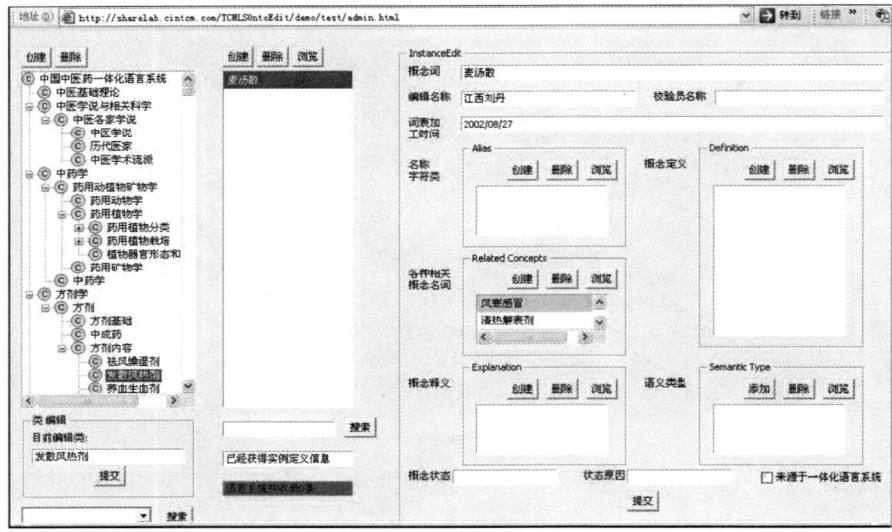

**Fig. 9.3.** The user interface of the TCM ontology engineering tool

- In our implementation the ontology is stored in RDBMS and is published as an OWL file after an automatic transformation. Protégé supports RDFS, OWL and its native format, but it does not support a two-way transformation between relational model and RDF model.

There are more than 20,000 classes and 100,000 instances defined in the TCM ontology and the ontology has become a distributed large-scale knowledge base for the TCM domain. The ontology has become large enough to cover different aspects of the TCM discipline and is used to support semantic e-Science for TCM. The consolidation of a TCM Language System potentially enables a set of applications in the TCM domain, such as semantic integration of disparate databases, ontology learning for information extraction and clinical-case-based knowledge reference and they will become the focus of the remaining part of this chapter.

## 9.4 Creating a Semantic Grid of TCM Databases

Recent advances in TCM informatics have resulted in massive amount of TCM information resources (literature, clinical records, experimental data, etc.). The vast amount of TCM information resources today is distributed among many specialized databases like medical formula database, electronic medical record database, clinical medicine database and so on (Feng Y, Wu ZH, et al., 2006). The TCM information-sharing platform utilizes semantic grid technology to provide data searching and semantic query services based on heterogeneous databases (Chen HJ, Wu ZH, et al., 2006). In this platform, the TCM ontology plays the following roles:

- **Standardized terminology**

Terminology in TCM ontology is used as candidate keywords of semantic query and data searching, for example the alias defined in ontology is used to enhance the accuracy of information retrieval.

- **Retrieval of associated concepts**

The system retrieves from the ontology all the semantic associations involving the input keyword and provides the user with a set of associated concepts. The user can use these associated concepts to extend the query.

- **Mix and match for heterogeneous schemas**

The ontology is used for the mix and match of heterogeneous schemas in order to provide usage transparency of underlying heterogeneity. In the system relational databases remain to provide the service of persistent data storage, while the mapping between the local database schema and the ontology is edited with a graphical tool, as is explained in Chapter 8. A mediated query engine translates the user-specified semantic query into a set of queries against the local schemas and wraps the results in RDF/OWL.

- **Logical interface for semantic query**

The ontology is used to feed a logical interface for semantic query. The user specifies the semantic query in terms of the domain ontology while the system is responsible for the orchestration of the query plan against underlying relational databases.

The user interface of this platform is shown in Fig. 9.4. By entering keywords an end user is able to search over the TCM databases grid. The end user can choose to jump from search page to semantic query page for generating accurate semantic query. Fig. 9.4 illustrates the search results of an unrestricted search with the keyword as the Chinese label of a TCM drug "Da Huang". The results include not only documents that contain the keyword but also all concepts that have certain kinds of semantic associations with the keyword. By following semantic links between concepts the end user is able to navigate through the entire information space of the semantic grid.

Administrators of Healthcare information systems are able to deploy the DartGrid solution in an intuitive way utilizing our class of graphical configuration tools; and end users are able to take advantages of semantic search, navigation and query functions to retrieve the information they need for decision-making in day-to-day operations.

Based on the proposed approach we have built a fundamental e-Science platform for TCM in CATCM and the system currently provides access to

**Fig. 9.4.** The results of a fuzzy searching request

over 50 databases. The result has shown that integrating databases and coordinating services with a large-scale domain ontology is an efficient approach to achieve on-demand e-Science for TCM and other similar application domains, such as life science and biology (Chen HJ, Wu ZH, et al, 2007).

## 9.5 A Semantic Grid Environment for Database Construction

As an ongoing trend among TCM research organizations, methods and processes for database construction and management have been available as services which requires coordination of various TCM services to support collaborative and on-demand scientific activities (Chen HJ, Wu ZH, et al, 2007). In order to address this requirement we utilize the Semantic Grid framework to establish a database construction and management platform.

This platform coordinates the construction of TCM scientific databases across more than ten data centers that are geographically distributed in China. Approximately 200 computers from more than 20 institutions join our Database Construction and Management Semantic Grid. This platform supports accumulation and fusion for data forms such as literature, document, image, and video. This platform contains three components:

- **RDF Generation Component**

This component translates user-input raw data into a RDF model that complies with the domain ontology. The generated RDF model is not stored back to the storage layer (the storage layer is implemented with traditional RDBMS, with database grid or with other forms of persistent media), but in an embedded RDF warehouse.

- **Semantic Assistant Component**

This component contains a compact knowledge base (which could take its simplest form as a terminology dictionary tailored from TCMLS) and provides data-processing-assistance services such as: terminology query, automatic semantic annotating and checking.

- **Storage Layer Adaptive Component**

This component adapts the platform to different forms of storage layer, by automatically transforming between the RDF model and the native data model of the storage layer. For example, in order to load the RDF model into relational tables we first define the relational schema corresponding to the domain ontology, then generate the corresponding SQL queries for data loading and finally execute those SQL queries utilizing data manipulation methods provided by the storage layer.

As shown in Fig. 9.5, the user interface of this platform contains three areas. Ontology browsing area is on the left side as a tree-like view of domain ontology. The domain ontology, expressing domain concepts and their relationships, is adopted in the generation of medical documentation templates. The content editing area is in the center and presents the RDF graph of edited RDF instances. The edited content is in the form of RDF/XML and is stored in an embedded RDF warehouse. The semantic assistant area is on the right side presenting a search form of a compact TCM knowledge-base.

The platform provides a convenient and efficient way for TCM practitioners to collaborate in database construction and management. It offers interfaces to enable users to register, query, compose, and execute services in the semantic layer, which increases the agility and feasibility of the business process.

## 9.6 TCM Knowledge Discovery Platform

The TCM e-Science, utilizing the Semantic Grid technology for sharing and utilizing knowledge/information repositories and services, has the potential of having a great impacts on TCM knowledge discovery and decision-making. In order to realize that potential we initiate a knowledge discovery platform based on the TCM e-Science environment. Since its deployment this platform has been effective in obtaining a series of exciting TCM discoveries, using a series of KDD methods ranging from frequent pattern mining to a

**Fig. 9.5.** The user interface of database construction and management semantic grid

latent structure model. Considerably interesting discoveries are obtained by these methods, such as novel TCM paired drugs, functional community of related genes, the high proportion of toxic plants in the botanical family Ranunculaceae and the association between M-cholinoceptor blocking drug and Solanaceae (Feng Y, Wu ZH, et al., 2006).

However, the underlying methodology of TCM knowledge discovery based on the Semantic Grid is still approaching its coherent and mature form. We present Semantic Graph Mining (Yu T, Jiang XH, Feng Y, 2007), a methodology for computer-aided extraction of actionable rules as an initial effort toward this goal. The methodology logically includes four elements. First, generate semantic annotations of a set of heterogeneous information resources in terms of medical domain ontology. Second, merge a medical semantic graph by means of semantic integration of the annotated information resources. Third, discover and recognize patterns from the medical semantic graph. Fourth, generate and evaluate a set of candidate rules which are organized and indexed for interactive discovery of actionable rules.

As is explained in Chapter 7, the TCM knowledge discovery platform adopts the Semantic Grid architecture. The semantic integration of heterogeneous databases contains a wealth of implicit domain knowledge which is yet rarely discoverable by manual process. Therefore scientists need the assistance of a toolkit of intelligent methods, interactive or not, in order to discover the implicit knowledge. Our method integrates several semantic-based data mining algorithms like the associated and correlated pattern mining to achieve knowledge discovery on distributed databases. Scientists are able to select a knowledge discovery service according to the requirements of the research task and perform knowledge discovery over a selective set of information from distributed databases (Yu T, Jiang XH, Feng Y, 2007).

## 9.7 Summary

We utilize the DartGrid Toolkit to establish a TCM semantic grid platform that integrates resources ranging from knowledge, information, computing power and methods and people. This platform is a successful use case of the DartGrid Toolkit and the major components of this platform include: (1) collaborative ontology engineering of TCM domain; (2) semantic integration of disparate TCM databases; (3) database construction and management of semantic grid; and (4) TCM knowledge discovery application of the semantic grid.

# References

Chen HJ, Wang YM, Wu ZH (2007) Introduction to semantic e-Science in biomedicine. BMC Bioinformatics 8(Suppl 3):S1

Chen HJ, Wu ZH, et al (2006) Towards a semantic web of relational databases: A practical semantic toolkit and an in-use case from traditional Chinese medicine. In ISWC:750-763

Chen HJ, Wu ZH, et al (2007) Towards semantic e-Science for traditional Chinese medicine. BMC Bioinformatics 8(Suppl 3):56

Feng Y, Wu ZH, et al (2006) Knowledge discovery in traditional Chinese medicine: state of the art and perspectives. Artificial Intelligence in Medicine 38(3):219-236

Yu T, Jiang XH, Feng Y (2007) Semantic graph mining for e-Science. In AAAI Workshops: Semantic e-Science (Accepted)

# 10

# Semantic Grid Applications in Intelligent Transportation Systems

**Abstract:** Intelligent Transportation System (ITS) plays an increasingly important role in modern transportation systems. It is typically abundant in all kinds of information sources such as different types of sensors, monitoring video cameras, station information terminals, etc. This chapter introduces an undergoing effort, the goal of which is to build an integrated intelligent transportation information and service system, to facilitate the integration of traffic data resources and inter-operation of existing ITS systems and services. We systematically utilize the Grids, Semantic Web and Web Service technology to implement a distributed infrastructure in support of information resource management and coordinated resource sharing.

## 10.1 Introduction

With the rapid development of modern transportation systems, the demand for fast delivery of goods makes transportation become a major obstacle to economic development for almost all countries and regions (Wang FY, et al, 2003). For instance the Yangtze River Delta, one of the most prosperous regions in China, is experiencing significant transportation problems. The traffic conditions deteriorate rapidly as China's economy increases faster and faster. Recent improvements such as new highways and more lanes on existing roads have alleviated traffic congestion considerably (Wang FY, Tang S, 2004). However, solutions do not keep pace with the growing transportation demand. Intelligent Transportation Systems (ITS) based upon advances in information, Internet, communication, and cybernetics technologies, offer a promising approach to solving many knotty traffic problems. As more and more countries and regions develop and deploy ITS systems and services one prominent issue with respect to those ITS systems is the difficulty of system integration and inter-operability, which calls for a range of standards and protocols that can bridge the gaps between heterogenous subsystems.

Many governments and organizations have devoted significant energy and resources to establish their own national ITS architectures and standards for facilities and protocols. However, those architectures and standards are not able to resolve many important ITS problems, such as integrating heterogeneous data on the semantic level, managing dynamic service flow, cooperating among different domains and storing and sharing massive data among different systems and departments. The Semantic Grid, evolved from many mature industry technologies, is capable of offering a promising alternative approach to addressing these issues (Wu ZH, et al, 2004). In brief, it can be used to support semantic-based traffic data integration, intelligent resource scheduling and sharing, service-oriented ITS resource discovery and management, and global-scale distributed computing that can connect all kinds of resources (Chen HJ, Wu ZH, 2003) within a unified informatics infrastructure. We have made use of many new technologies to build a system called ITS-Grid, a semantic ITS platform to support resource sharing, service flow management, and cross-domain cooperation (Wu ZH, Chen HJ, et al, 2005; Shi W, Wu J, Deng SG, et al, 2006; Shi DC, Yin JW, Li YY, et al, 2007).

In the following we briefly discuss the relationships between our work and other existing researches involved in Grid Service and Ontology, such as the application of Web Services and the Grid into ITS and the construction of a transportation ontology model.

### 10.1.1 ITS System and Grid Computing

SOA (Service-Oriented Architecture) is an advanced technology for the construction of loosely-coupled distributed systems and services. Many ITS implementations have employed SOA as their underlying system architecture. The Grid architecture based on SOA can easily integrate computation resources or storage resources to provide high performance computing and massive data storage spaces for ITS. Web Service, an implementation of SOA, can provide the capability for dynamic business integration of heterogeneous traffic application systems (Tao XF, Jiang CJ, Han YJ, 2005; Li Y, Wu ZH, Deng SG, 2004).

The American Federal Transportation Advisory Group (FTAG) proposed a report (USDOT, 2004) that aims at integrating civilian and commercial transportation into the American defense system's Global Information Grid (GIG) to ensure adequate resources and expertise to maintain and operate the American information infrastructure for transportation.

Chun-Hsin Wu and his colleagues presented the design and implementation of an intelligent transportation web service (ITWS) and publishes more than 20 web services such as basic information services and value-adding services (Wu CS, Su D, Chang J, et al, 2003a).

The ARGOS (Dynamic Composition of Web Services for Goods Movement Analysis and Planning) project is a flexible data query and analysis system based on the web service paradigm. They examined several goods movement planning problems and their effects on spatial urban structure. They designed a unified framework in which all operations are modelled as web services and the scientific workflows as compositions of web services and provided user-friendly tools for manual specification and composition of the web services, as well as automatic composition based on expressive web service descriptions for given application domains (such as transportation planning) (Giuliano G, 2004).

The RWIN (a real-time Road Weather Information Network) project developed a data exchange component that is fundamentally based on the concept of web service for accessing the RWIN repository (Koonar A, Delannoy P, Scarlett B, 2004).

The K-Wf Grid project presented an infrastructure for future transportation workflow creation and management in handling different complex traffic planning and management tasks. The research domain of the project includes workflow management, Grid monitoring and performance analysis, and the Semantic Grid (Wu CS, Wei C, Shu D, Chang M, Ho J, 2003; Wu CS, Su D, Chang J, et al, 2003a; Chang M, Wu C, Ho J, 2002; KwfGrid, 2004).

The ShanghaiGrid project has already developed a handful of softwares and tools called ShanghaiGrid Operation System aiming at the construction of a metropolitan-area Transportation Information Service Grid and has established an open standard for widespread upper-layer transportation applications for both communities and the government. Specifically, the project aims at integrating computational resources and various transportation systems, emphasizing massive transportation data fusion, and large-scale and complex traffic-flow simulation (Li ML, Liu H, Jiang CJ, et al, 2003; Li ML, WU MY, Li Y, et al, 2005a; Li ML, WU MY, Li Y, et al, 2005b).

Agathocles Gourgoulis and his colleagues implemented a transport simulation on a graphical parallel programming environment called P-GRADE. Their implementation takes advantage of parallel computing, which can be accessed as Grid services and even participate in complex Grid workflows (Gourgoulis A, Kacsuk P, Terstyanszky G, Winter S, 2004).

Joey Anda and his colleagues proposed an *ad hoc* networking and computational grid called VGrid that can be formed by leveraging inter-vehicle and vehicle-to-roadside wireless communications. VGrid actively uses pertinent data to perform computations for solving traffic-related problems. The goal is to evolve intelligent transportation engineering from a centralized approach to a distributed approach, in which vehicle computers can cooperate and solve vehicular traffic-flow control problems autonomously (Anda J, Lebrun J, Ghosal J, Zhang D, 2005).

In May 2005, Zhejiang Transportation Bureau, the government agency that oversees public transportation in the Province of Zhejiang in China, enabled more than 100 transportation companies to share ticketing data and computing resources when it engaged IBM Business Consulting Services to connect them via a grid computing infrastructure.

## 10.1.2 ITS System and Ontology

One prominent requirement of ITS systems is to enable organizations to coordinately share resources and seamlessly integrate services among distributed transportation organizations. The realization of these goals relies upon the concrete and sound conclusion of agreements among parties that specify the terms and conditions of coordination for transportation services. Many countries and regions have developed their transportation ontologies based on local transportation aspects, such as transportation architecture, laws and rules.

J. Javier Samper and his colleagues summarized the state of the art in their research on existing vocabularies and traffic ontologies and built a representation schema of road traffic, with a well defined semantics, to enable the development of an integrated architecture of traffic information based on semantic web service technology (Samper JJ, Tomas VR, Martinez JJ, Berg L, 2006).

Marcel Becker and Stephen F. Smith of the Robotics Institute in Carnegie Mellon University proposed an ontology model for multi-modal transportation planning and scheduling. They took the OZONE scheduling ontology as a general basis for formulating scheduling domain models, then extended this core framework to capture the essential characteristics and constraints of multi-modal transportation planning and scheduling through defining a fairly large base of transportation terms (Becker M, Smith SF, 1997).

The report of the REWERSE project gives a comprehensive survey of standardization efforts for geographic information and a description of the Geographic Data Files (GDF) standard that is already a sophisticated ontology for ITS transportation networks. They have also turned the GDF ontology into á formal OWL-based ontology OTS (Ontology for Transportation Systems) (REWERSE, 2005).

Clark P., affiliated to Boeing, designed a transportation ontology expressed in the Knowledge Interchange Format in a layered graph. This ontology uses graph "node" as transportation "place" and graph "arc" as transportation "conduit" and defines above all transporting actions and movements, and constraints on them (Clark P, 2002).

Vrba P. and Hrdonka V. designed a material transportation ontology for material transportation in a factory. This ontology is expressed as a list of XML tags and attributes with their meaning described using natural language in a tabular form (Vrba P, Hrdonka V, 2002).

Zhang, T. defined general concepts and relations for a general transportation description of the Berlin local transportation service within the Agentcities project. This ontology is expressed in DAML. The main classes are "Connection" and "Address", which can be connected via relations "destination" and "source". Based on these main entities, the ontology then describes in greater details the means of transportation in the city, such as buses or taxis (Zhang T, 2003).

Marek Obitko and Vladimr Mark chose the before-mentioned three ontologies and created a way of expressing partial mappings between ontologies and using these mappings for communication between agents (Obitko M, Marik V, 2005).

TeKnowledge created many terms to represent transportation-related information in the CIA World Fact Book (2002). Additional transportation concepts, terms definitions and references were taken from Universal Joint Task List (Version 4), online Glossary of Landform and Geologic Terms, Householders Goods Forwarders Association of America and Congressional Research Service (CRS) reports (TeKnowledge, 2003).

SABINE TIMPF described two ontologies in a way-finding project with multiple transportation modes in an urban area. One mode is developed from the perspective of the traveler, which is derived from the material provided to the traveler, e.g., maps, timetables, station layout and signs; the other is presented from the perspective of the public transportation system. The ontologies in wayfinding were derived from a case study in the city of Hamburg, Germany.

## 10.2 Layered Architecture for ITS-Grid

ITS has a range of functions with different intentions and purposes. A sound layered architecture is pivotal to build a robust Grid-based ITS system. Fig. 10.1 displays a layered architecture for the proposed ITS-Grid. Generally it is composed of five layers including ITS applications, ITS subsystems, advanced ITS services, basic services, and resources. In the following we describe them accordingly.

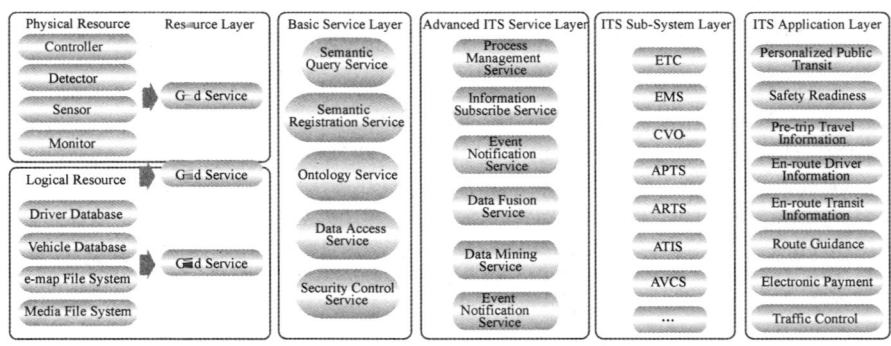

**Fig. 10.1.** ITS-Grid architecture

**High-level Application Layer**: The application layer addresses end users' ITS requirements. This includes route guidance, electronic payment services, personalized public transit and many others as shown in Fig. 10.1. All end-user requests can be fulfilled by ITS subsystems at the lower level, either alone or in cooperation with related subsystems.

**ITS Subsystem Layer**: ITS can be typically categorized into several subsystems. Fig. 10.1 presents seven mostly typical ones: the Advanced Public Transportation System (APTS), the Advanced Rural Transportation System (ARTS), the Advanced Traffic Information System (ATIS), the Advanced Vehicle Control System (AVCS), the Electronic Toll Collection (ETC), the Emergency Medical Service(EMS), and the Commercial Vehicle Operations(CVO). The ITS subsystem layer is based on the advanced ITS layer at the lower level.

**Advanced ITS Layer**: This layer provides many ITS-oriented advanced services such as data mining, data fusion, information subscription, event notification, and dynamic service-flow management. Each service type corresponds to an indispensable functionality for higher ITS subsystems. For example, the data mining service is essential for discovering useful traffic information and traffic rules to make correct control and management decisions.

**Basic Service Layer**: The basic service layer provides secure, transparent and semantic-based data access, sharing, and management on which the upper layers can build advanced application-oriented services. Basic services in this layer improve the reusability of data from lower-layer resources by adding semantics to it through ontology and semantic registration services. This layer implements security and semantic-based data access and query services through the security control, data access, and semantic query services.

**Resource Layer**: This layer provides data resources for upper layers. The resources on this layer are divided into two categories:

- *Physical Resources* include terminal equipment such as sensors, detectors, controllers, and any other facilities installed on roads, freeway, and vehicles. The equipment collects information such as dynamic and real time traffic information, weather information, geographical information and road conditions.
- *Logical Resources* consist of various databases and file systems usually containing static information, such as vehicle database, driver database, and e-map file systems.

## 10.3 ITS Semantic Grid

### 10.3.1 The Development of an ITS Ontology

To develop an ITS Semantic Grid the first step is to develop a high-quality ITS ontology that will be integrated into the ITS-Grid as the information mediator for heterogenous ITS subsystems. Based on Chinese Intelligent Transportation National System Architecture, a two-layer traffic ontology framework was proposed covering those most basic and common traffic concepts and properties.

The upper layer in the framework is the category layer, which is a hierarchical classification container of traffic concepts. These concepts consist of a group of associated traffic elements, which may be some macroscopical concept sets, or basic concepts. However, the category layer itself does not include basic concepts. In addition, the category layer can also be viewed as a standard classification of traffic concepts, which is based on the Chinese Intelligent Transportation System Architecture. Basically the architecture defines eight traffic service domains, six traffic user agents, nine traffic service agents and seven traffic terminals. A detailed description of these components is listed in Table 10.1.

Table 10.1. The main components of Chinese intelligent Transportation System Architecture

| Traffic Service Domains | Traffic User agents | Traffic Service agents | Traffic Terminals |
|---|---|---|---|
| Traffic Management and Planning | Road Users | Traffic Management Centers | Road Users |
| Electronic Payment Service | Road Constructors | Passenger Transportation | Roadway |
| Traveler Information System | Traffic Management Departments | Traffic Information Service Provider | Vehicle |
| Vehicle Safety and Driving Assistance | Operation Managers | Emergency Management | Freight |
| Emergency and Security | Public Security and Safety Departments | Infrastructure Management Departments | Consignor |
| Transportation Operation Management | Related Organizations | Freight Transport Service Providers | Banks |
| Inter-Model Transportation | | Product Equipment Manufacturers | System Operators |
| Automated Highway System | | Product Services Providers | |
| | | Law Enforcement Management | |

The lower layer in the framework is called the Basic Element Layer, which is a mass of self-contained and undivided basic concepts, each of which is governed by one top-level concept. These lowest concepts are translated into nine kinds of atomic ontologies including the Geography, the Vehicle, the

People, the Organization, the Device, the Operation, the Data, the Event and the State. The detailed description of Basic Elements is depicted in Table 10.2.

Table 10.2. The detailed description of Basic Elements

| Basic Element | Description |
| --- | --- |
| *Geography* | Traffic geography information, such as Town, District, Highway, Crossroad, Lane, etc. |
| *Vehicle* | Transit tools, such as Bus, Car, etc. |
| *People* | Travelers and traffic managers, such as Driver, Passenger, Police, etc. |
| *Organization* | Traffic participation organizations, such as Traffic Command Center, Bus Company, etc. |
| *Device* | Traffic control and communication devices, such as Light, Sensors, Software, etc. |
| *Operation* | Action sets operated by agents, such as Drive, Walk, Prohibit, Guide, etc. |
| *Data* | Traffic Data, such as Volume, Occupation, Speed, etc. |
| *Event* | All kinds of discrete and random events, such as Accident, Peccancy, etc. |
| *State* | The historical snapshot or current state of traffic objects, such as Red, Yellow, Green. |

The above-mentioned two-layer ontological framework was developed by using the Protégé ontology tool. Fig. 10.2 shows some aspects of a traffic ontological tree, (a) is the top-level traffic ontological tree, (b) is a part of the complete traffic ontology hierarchical model, and (c) is a case of the lowest-level traffic ontologies and their relations.

### 10.3.2 ITS-Grid Applications

In this section we make a general discussion on some implementation aspects of typical ITS-Grid applications.

#### 10.3.2.1 Multi-domain ITS Cooperation

One typical requirement for ITS-Grid is multi-domain cooperation (MDC). MDC is crucial for many traffic problems such as load balancing, remote traveler support and commercial vehicle administration involving multi-domain cooperation and Grid technologies effectively support it. Furthermore, ITS

218    10 Semantic Grid Applications in Intelligent Transportation Systems

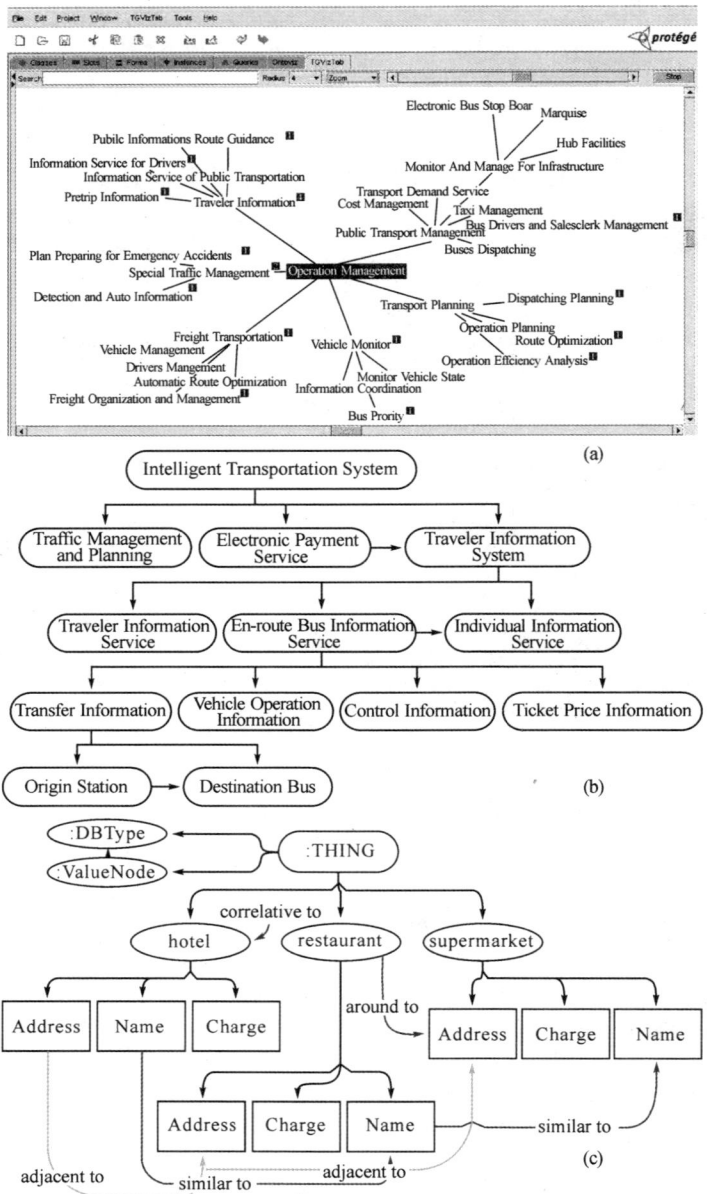

**Fig. 10.2.** Some aspects of traffic ontological tree

command centers provide cross-domain functionalities by composing and executing dynamic service flows from heterogeneous services deployed on Grid nodes worldwide.

## 10.3 ITS Semantic Grid

As Fig. 10.3 shows, for example one grid node might be used to analyze information collected from real-time traffic information subscription services distributed all over the grid. It then needs to negotiate and cooperate with another grid node to balance the whole traffic network load.

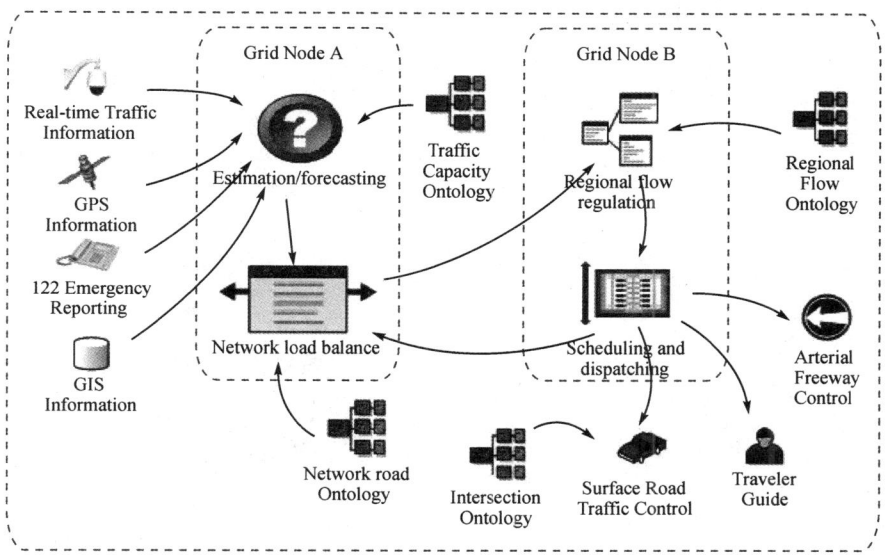

**Fig. 10.3.** Multi-domain cooperation in ITS-Grid

### 10.3.2.2 Semantic-based Traffic Information Integration and Sharing

ITS involves many regions, organizations and domains as well as huge amounts of heterogeneous data either stored in very large databases or produced by real-time traffic detectors. These data resources offer both a gold mine for application development and an obstacle to it. Developing data integration and sharing technologies that can mine the nuggets and overcome the obstacles present a real challenge.

ITS-Grid encapsulates all data sources into grid services with uniform interface and communication protocols. Taking full advantage of semantic and grid technologies, grid services integrate and share data among a broad range of ITS subsystems, departments and organizations. The data integration and sharing are cross-domain and transparent to end users.

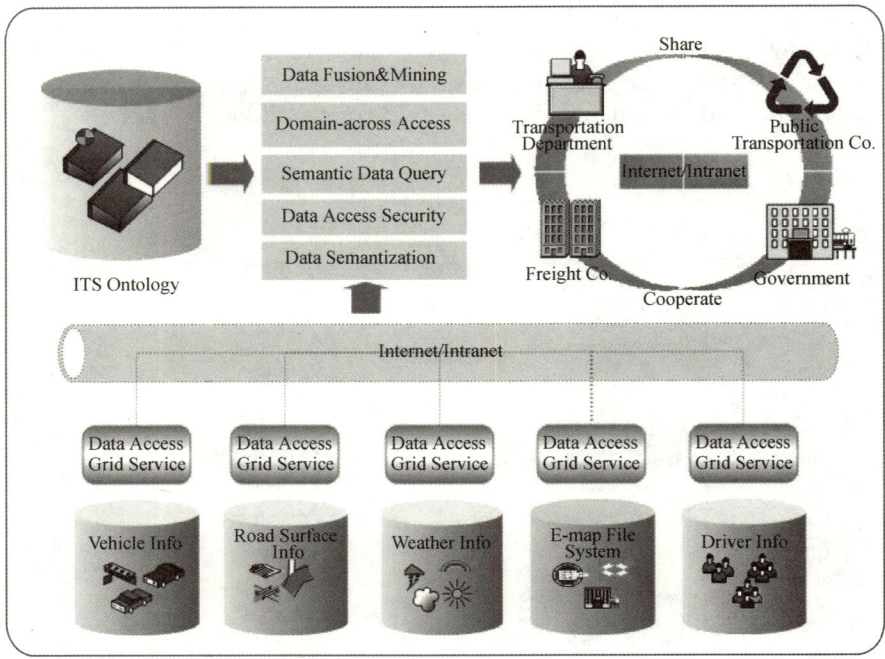

Fig. 10.4. Data sharing and data management in ITS-Grid

### 10.3.2.3 Semantic-based Geographical Information Systems

Some core design principles and characteristic components such as ontology-based data integration and semantic registration can also be applied to integrate heterogeneous geographical data on the semantic level, which will enable users to retrieve more precise geographical data that they are interested in, based on the semantics associated with these data without the need to care about the details of the distributed geographical data sources.

Semantic-based GIS adopts a series of Semantic Web standards such as RDF and OWL to represent the semantics embedded in the geo-spatial information and make geographical data visible to users in an ideal, high-quality format. It can then be used to mediate heterogeneous geospatial database schemas and enables users to interact with the systems at a semantic level (Xu Z, Wu ZH, Chen HJ, 2005).

### 10.3.2.4 Semantic-based Message Middleware for Traffic Sensor Grid

ITS-Grid system typically contains many types of sensors, forming a so-called sensor grid. In a sensor grid, data published by heterogeneous sensors differ greatly in formats and semantics. A semantic-based message publish/subscribe system is used as a general infrastructure for a sensor grid, in which many sensors communicate with each other at a semantic level (Chen HJ, Wu ZH, Xu J, 2003; Shi DC, Yin JW, Li YY, et al, 2007). The architecture is shown in Fig. 10.5 and is divided into three layers, i.e. Physical layer, Fusion layer and Dissemination layer (Chen HJ, Ye ZY, Wu ZH, 2005; Ye ZY, Chen HJ, Wu ZH, 2003).

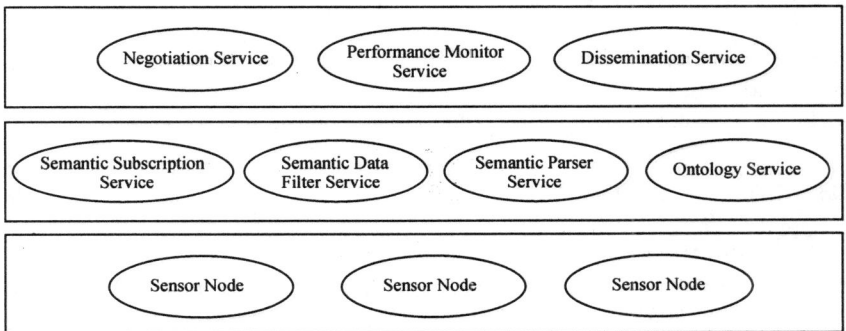

**Fig. 10.5.** The layered architecture of the ITS sensor grid

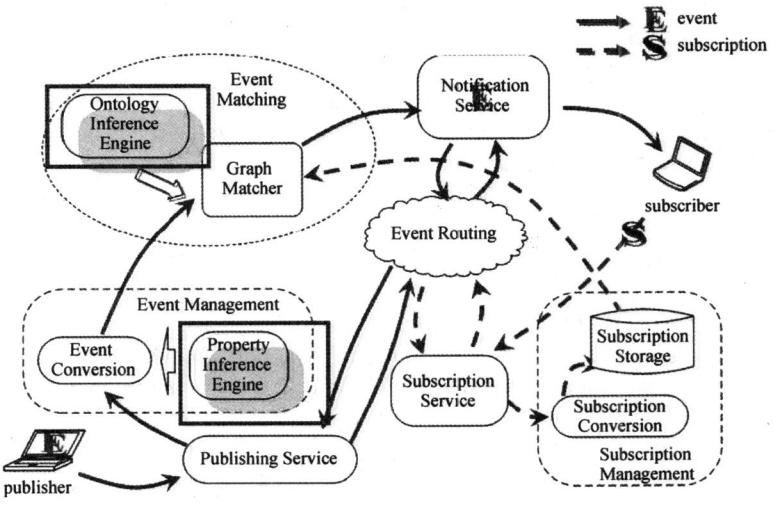

**Fig. 10.6.** The core components of the ITS sensor grid

**Dissemination Layer.** This layer provides intelligent and flexible mechanisms to disseminate data to the subscriber. It includes the Negotiation Service, the Performance Monitor Service and the Dissemination Service.

**Fusion Layer.** This layer offers the capability of fusing data from heterogeneous sensors and filtering data to meet the needs of subscribers. The layer includes the Ontology Service, the Semantic Parser Service, the Semantic Subscription Service and the Semantic Data Filter Service. Services in this layer are designed for querying data based on the global ontology and parsing it into RDF-based data and then filtering data to meet the subscribers' interests.

**Physical Layer.** This layer is composed of sensor nodes deployed in the sensor grid. These sensor nodes collect dynamic and real-time traffic data, weather data, geographical data, road surface data, and so on.

#### 10.3.2.5 Dynamic Traffic Service Flow

By combining several services into a value-added service or otherwise composing a dynamic service flow, ITS-Grid can offer diversified functionalities to meet end users' needs. In addition, service discovery, matchmaking, filtering, monitoring and other management facilities play important roles in service combination and composition. They provide the essential building blocks for an effective dynamic service-flow platform, supporting ITS-Grid's basic service layer.

As Fig. 10.7 displays, dynamic service-flow agents bridge the gap between end users and many services. The figure also shows how ITS-Grid capitalizes on service management facilities and dynamic service-flow agents to fulfill users' requests. First, an end user submits a request to a dynamic service-flow agent, which then asks for the service-flow management module to select and execute the appropriate services to compose a flow. After execution an optimal route is returned to the end user.

## 10.4 Case Study

The Yangtze River Delta region, which consists of Shanghai and parts of Jiangsu and Zhejiang Provinces, is playing an increasingly vital role in China's overall economic growth, particularly at a time of globalization and industrialization. This economic zone, with 2 percent of the national territory and 10 percent of the population, contributes to at least 20 percent of China's total gross domestic product and 30 percent of its foreign trade.

This region has established an intensive transportation infrastructure. For example, the total railroad mileage in Zhejiang Province has grown to 1,500 kilometers and the total highway mileage is more than 3,000 kilometers, including 1,307 kilometers of expressways.

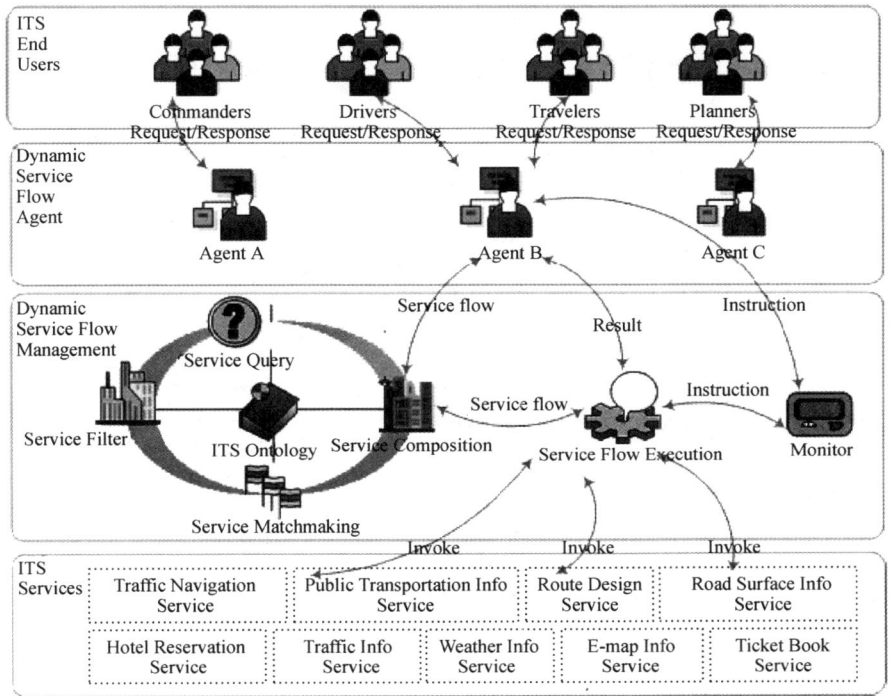

**Fig. 10.7.** Management of dynamic service flow in ITS-Grid

However, the rapidly developing economy and explosive growth in the Chinese automobile industry have generated an urgent need for more convenient, efficient and secure transportation support. The Yangtze River Delta has therefore shifted its focus from building road infrastructure to developing transportation intelligence for a high performance and better service. We have prototyped an ITS-Grid semantic grid platform as part of this effort.

The Yangtze River Delta has selected five metropolises as main nodes to deploy ITS-Grid: Shanghai, Hangzhou, Nanjing, Ningbo, and Wenzhou. We can regard every main node as an ITS management domain that contains several branch nodes, as shown in Fig. 10.8.

For example, the Hangzhou main node dominates the Huzhou, Quzhou, and Jinhua nodes. Every branch node is responsible for managing its own transportation and providing grid services. Branch nodes belonging to the same domain can share information and cooperate with each other through their main node. The ITS-Grid deployment allows the nodes to share data and other ITS information and cooperate easily across a wide range of services and resources.

Regional projects, like that of the Yangtze River Delta, represent test beds for ensuring the integration and inter-operability of different ITS components

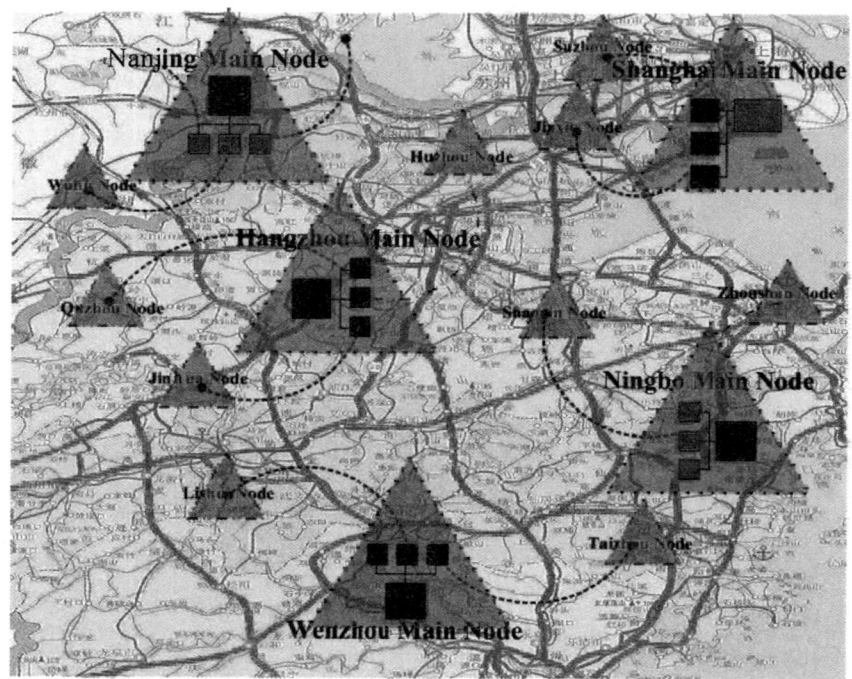

**Fig. 10.8.** ITS-Grid deployment in the Yangtze River Delta

in China's National ITS Architecture. The ITS-Grid semantic grid platform establishes a framework for such projects in an important commercial center of China's booming economy.

## 10.5 Summary and Conclusion

This chapter presents an ontology-based grid service oriented information integration architecture and its implementation for intelligent transportation systems. Our approach has the following characteristics.

- It introduces a novel five-level grid service-oriented framework for an Intelligent Transportation System.
- It develops a two-level traffic ontology model based on Chinese Intelligent Transportation System Architecture.
- It utilizes the above traffic ontology model to integrate and share distributed and heterogeneous traffic information.

Based upon our experience in developing the applications, many technologies of the Semantic Grid such as the ontology and web service will play a more and more important role in future ITS systems.

# References

Anda J, LeBrun J, Ghosal J, Zhang D (2005) Vehicular adhoc networking and computing grid for intelligent traffic control. The 61st IEEE Vehicular Technology Conference. VTC(5):2905-2909

Becker M, Smith SF (1997) An Ontology for Multi-Modal Transportation Planning and Scheduling. Report CMU-RI-TR-98-15, Robotics Institute, Carnegie Mellon University

Chang M, Wu C, Ho J (2002) An Embedded Route Information Gathering Tool for Supporting ITS. Available at: http://www.iis.sinica.edu.tw/~wuch/publications/2002-icos-gpsits.pdf

Chen HJ, Wu ZH (2003) OKSA: An Open Knowledge Service Architecture for Building Large Scale Knowledge System in Semantic Web. Proc. IEEE Int'l Conf. Systems, Man, and Cybernetics, IEEE Press. IEEE SMC 3:4858-4863

Chen HJ, Wu ZH, Xu J (2003) Towards Building Large-Scale Knowledge System in Semantic Web. Knowledge-based Intelligent Information and Engineering Systems, Part 2, LNCS 2774, Springer-Verlag:2773-2774

Chen HJ, Ye ZY, Wu ZH (2005) DartDataFlow: Semantic-based Sensor Grid. EUC:326-334

Clark P (2002) Transportation Ontology. http://www.cs.utexas.edu/users/pclark/kr-web/other/passenger-vehicle/transportation.km

Giuliano G (2004) Dynamic Composition of Web Services for Goods Movement Analysis and Planning. http://www.isi.edu/ argos/

Gourgoulis A, Kacsuk P, Terstyanszky G, Winter S (2004) Creating Scalable Traffic Simulation on Clusters. PDP:60-65

Koonar A, Delannoy P, Scarlett B (2004) A Real-time Road Weather Information Network (RWIN) Spatial Data Management and Information Delivery Architecture. The Proceedings of the Third International Conference on Information Technology and Applications. ITAC 2:501-507

KwfGrid (2004) The Knowledge-based Workflow System for Grid Applications. http://www.kwfgrid.net/

Li ML, Liu H, Jiang CJ, et al (2003) ShanghaiGrid in Action: The First Stage Projects towards Digital City and City Grid. GCC (1):616-623

Li ML, Wu MY, Li Y, et al (2005a) ShanghaiGrid as An Information Service Grid: An Overview. IEEE SCC:351-354

Li ML, Wu MY, Li Y, et al (2005b) ShanghaiGrid: A Grid Prototype for Metropolis Information Services. APWeb:1033-1036

Li Y, Wu ZH, Deng SG (2004) Research on Service-Oriented Software Framework. GCC 3252:27-35

Obitko M, Marik V (2005) Integrating Transportation Ontologies Using Semantic Web Languages:99-110

REWERSE (2005) Ontology of Transportation Networks. Project Document. Reasoning on the Web with Rules and Semantics. Available at: http://rewerse.net/deliverables/m18/a1-d4.pdf

Samper JJ, Tomas VR, Martinez JJ, Berg L (2006) An Ontological Infrastructure for Traveller Information Systems. The 2006 IEEE Intelligent Transportation Systems Conference:1197-1202

Shi DC, Yin JW, Li YY, et al (2007) JTangPS: An RDF-based Publish/Subscribe System. Third International Conference on Semantics, Knowledge and Grid. SKG: 342-345

Shi W, Wu J, Deng SG, et al (2006) ITSGrid: A Novel Integrated Intelligent Transportation Information and Service Platform. The proceeding of the 2006 IEEE International Conference on Service Computing. IEEE SCC:519

Shi W, Wu J, Li Y, Kuang L (2006) Intelligent Transportation Information Sharing and Service Integration in Semantic Grid Environment. The 2006 IEEE/WIC/ACM International Conference on Web Intelligence. WI:174-180

Tao XF, Jiang CJ, Han YJ (2005) Applying SOA to Intelligent Transportation System. IEEE SCC 2:101- 104

TeKowledge (2003) http://reliant.teknowledge.com/DAML/Transportation.owl

US Department of Transportation (2004) Vision 2050 - An Integrated National Transportation System. http://scitech.dot.gov/

Vrba P, Hrdonka V (2002) Material Handling Problem: FIPA Compliant Agent Implementation. Multi-Agent Systems and Applications II. LNCS Vol.2322:268-279

Wang FY, et al (2003) Toward Intelligent Transportation Systems for the 2008 Olympics. IEEE Intelligent Systems. IEEE IS 18(6):8-11

Wang FY, Tang S (2004) Artificial Societies for Integrated and Sustainable Development of Metropolitan Systems. IEEE Intelligent Systems (IEEE IS) 19(4):82-87

Wu CS, Su D, Chang J, et al (2003a) An Advanced Traveler Information System with Emerging Network Technologies. Available at: http://www.iis.sinica.edu.tw/~wuch/publications/2003-itsap-atis.pdf

Wu CS, Su D, Chang J, et al (2003b) The Design and Implementation of Intelligent Transportation Web Services. The Proceedings of IEEE Conference on Electronic Commerce, EC:49-52

Wu CS, Wei C, Su D, Chang M, Ho J (2003) Travel Time Prediction with Support Vector Regression. The Proceedings of IEEE Intelligent Transportation Systems Conference. IEEE ITSC 5:272-281

Wu ZH, Chen HJ, et al (2005) DartGrid II: A Semantic Grid Platform for ITS, IEEE Intelligent Systems, 20(3)

Wu ZH, et al (2004) DartGrid: Semantic-Based Database Grid. Programming, Software Engineering, and Operating Systems, Part 1, LNCS 3036, Springer-Verlag:59-66

Xu Z, Chen HJ, Wu ZH, Mao YX (2006) Saga: Towards a Semantic-based Map Navigator. The 1st International Workshop on Semantic-based Geographical Information Systems 1:156-162

Xu Z, Wu ZH, Chen HJ (2005) Applying Semantic Web Technologies to Geodata Integration and Visualization. In Proceedings of 24th International Conference on Conceptual Modeling, Workshop CoMoGIS:320-329

Ye ZY, Chen HJ, Wu ZH (2003) Dart-Dataflow: Towards Communicating Data Semantics in Sensor Grid, GCC:517-522

Zhang T (2003) Local Transport Ontology. http://www.agentcities.org/EURTD/Ontologies/local-transport.v2.daml

# Index

$\pi$-calculus, 148

ABox, 25
abstract service, 143
advanced ITS layer, 215
agent, 49, 79
ALCQI, 106
algorithm control sub-component, 167
algorithm service component, 169
algorithm service layer, 169
answering queries using views, 107
applicable class mapping rule, 119
application expert, 166
artificial intelligence, 17
assignable relation, 133

basic element layer, 216
basic grid service layer, 169
basic service layer, 215
Bayesian analysis, 80
Bayesian risk, 97
Bayesian sequential analysis, 92
biomedical informatics, 196
black-box, 144
business rules, 144

category layer, 216
CBR, 61
CDPS, 49
CGSP, 3
Chinese intelligent transportation system architecture, 216
class mapping rules, 117
classical Chinese, 196

clinical decision-making, 196
CLIPS, 85
closed trust model, 86
CoAKTinG, 12
collaborative research, 198
CombeChem, 11
computational grid, 2
concept, 4
concept names, 107
concept structure, 41
concrete service, 144
conjunctive queries, 108
constraint mapping, 109
consultant agents, 83
consultant fee, 82
consultant service charge, 82
context dependent, 81
contextual class, 58
controlled vocabularies, 32

D2R server, 105
D2RQ, 104
DAI, 50
DAML+OIL, 29
DartFlow, 188
data analysis, 197
data control sub-component, 167
data grid, 2
data mining, 158, 197
data provider, 166
data quality management, 197
data resource layer, 169
data service component, 169

# 228 Index

database heterogeneity, 198
DataminingGrid, 164
decision, 87
description logic, 23
device grid, 2
direct knowledge, 56
discovery net, 162
dissemination layer, 222
distinguished variables, 108
distributed architecture, 161
distribution, 86
DL-Lite, 106
DO-Agent, 70
domain model, 196
domain rule, 144
DPML, 163
drug community discovery, 171
drug discovery, 196
dynamic memory model, 61
dynamic traffic service flow, 222

e-Learning, 197
electronic medical record, 204
Enterprise Grid Alliance, 4
entity, 42
event, 42
evidence-based medicine, 196
existential variables, 108
expected utility, 86
extraction, 67

final service charge, 82
first-order logic, 17
frame, 20
framework, 34
frequent pattern mining, 207
fully-dependent output, 132
functional unit, 132
fusion layer, 222

Gaussian distribution, 93
GE, 62
Global Grid Forum, 3
global ontology, 55
global-as-view, 107
global-local-as-view, 107
Globus Toolkit, 3
goal, 49
GRDDL, 6

grid, 1
grid computing, 1
grid-based architecture, 161

healthcare system, 195
herb-drug interaction analysis, 174
high-level application layer, 214

immediate decision, 92
incomplete semantics, 115
information interoperability, 196
information management, 196
information retrieval, 198
initiator agent, 84
intelligent transportation system, 210
interface dependency, 133
inverse role, 106
ITS ontology, 215
ITS subsystem layer, 215
ITS-Grid, 211
ITS-Grid architecture, 214

Jena, 7

K-WF grid, 8
KDD algorithm layer, 169
KDD algorithm provider, 166
KDD system architecture, 159
knowledge, 15
knowledge acquisition, 33
knowledge cache, 58
knowledge discovery, 157, 198
knowledge discovery control component, 167
knowledge discovery in database, 157
knowledge discovery user, 166
knowledge grid, 163
knowledge representation, 17, 197
knowledge search, 72
knowledge set, 58

local-as-view, 107
Local-KB, 58
local-ontologies, 55
logic, 17
logical resources, 215

manager of virtual organization, 167
manipulation, 67

MAPS, 50
marginal distribution, 89
MAS, 50
matching sequence, 137
medical evidence, 198
medical rules, 198
multi-domain cooperation, 217
myGrid, 11

Named Graph, 7
nil-process, 149

objective control sub-component, 168
OGSA, 3
OGSI, 3
OLAP, 199
ontology, 17
ontology development, 32
ontology grid, 55
ontology grid node, 56
ontology integration, 37
ontology learning, 197
ontology management, 54
ontology repository, 63
ontology reuse, 61
ontology service, 104, 182
ontology-based dynamic query interface, 182
Open Grid Forum, 4
open trust model, 91
operational cost, 82
operational semantics, 149
operator, 49
opportunity cost, 82
optimal matching sequence, 138
orthodoxy medicine, 196
OWL, 6

parallel composition, 149
parallelized architecture, 160
partially-dependent output, 132
PDKD, 163
physical layer, 222
physical resources, 215
PMML, 170
population quality, 96
posterior density, 92
posterior distribution, 86
precision, 140

preposterior analysis, 91
prior density, 87
prior distribution, 86
prior information, 84
probability theory, 83
problem, 48
problem description, 69
property, 30
Protégé, 203
provider agent, 83
PS-Agent, 70
PSE, 51

quality assurance, 198

Racer, 7
RDF, 6
RDF gateway, 105
reasoning, 18
recall rate, 140
rectification, 89
relation, 19
reliability factor, 87
reputation information, 84
resource layer, 215
resources, 51
Rule Interchange Format, 7

search engine, 16
semantic annotation, 197
semantic graph mining, 171, 208
semantic grid, 8
semantic integration, 198
semantic mining, 10
semantic network, 18, 198
semantic query service, 104, 182
semantic registration service, 104, 182
semantic relationship, 36
semantic search, 197
semantic search service, 182
semantic service layer, 169
semantic structure, 41
semantic system, 36
semantic type, 36
semantic view, 59
semantic web, 4
semantic-based GIS, 220
semantic-based message middleware, 220

## Index

service behavior, 150
service charge, 82
service compatibility, 152
service composition, 129, 141
service composition framework, 142
service composition verification, 130
service discovery, 128
service flow, 126
service flow management, 127
service interaction, 152
service matchmaking, 128, 131
service model, 131
service operation, 151
service request, 136
service-oriented computing, 126
SHIQ, 106
SHIQ data instance, 113
SHIQ-RDM mapping system, 110
SHIQ-RDM view, 110
SHIQ-role, 106
simple role, 106
single-computer-based architecture, 159
skolem function, 114
solution, 49
source ontology, 58
SPARQL, 6
sub-ontology, 58
sub-service-composition, 147
subclasses, 40
SubO, 58
SubO evolution, 56

task, 69
TBox, 24

TCM, 195
TCM informatics, 195
terminology, 32
terminology standard, 197
top-level categories, 40
traditional Chinese medicine, 32, 195
traffic ontological tree, 217
traffic sensor grid, 220
transition sequence, 153
transitivity, 84
traverse, 67
triple group, 118
triple mapping, 119
trust, 80

UMLS, 36
Unicore, 3
URI, 28
user rule, 144
UTCMLS, 17
utilities, 82
utility function, 82

view reasoning rules, 113
virtual organization, 1, 165
Virtuoso, 105
visualized semantic mapping tool, 182

W3C, 6
web portal, 196
workflow, 126
WSRF, 3

XML, 23